Tagore's Mystique of Dance

Tagore's Mystique of Dance

Utpal K. Banerjee

NIYOGI
BOOKS

Published by

NIYOGI BOOKS
D-78, Okhla Industrial Area, Phase-I
New Delhi-110 020, India

Tel: 91-11-26816301, 49327000
Fax: 91-11-26810483, 26813830

email: niyogibooks@gmail.com
www.niyogibooks.com

Editor: Madhuparna Banerjee/Niyogi Books

Design: Write Media

ISBN: 978-81-89738-96-9

Year of Publication: 2011

Printed at: Niyogi Offset Pvt. Ltd., New Delhi, India

Contents

Preface

This book germinated from three observations. First, dance being only a passion with Tagore to be transmuted to his near and dear ones in Santiniketan but not certainly a major preoccupation with him, it never received the due attention. Perhaps, as Tagore himself knew that it was an art form in which he could never be a creative 'professional', he felt more attracted towards it. The abiding interest that he took in the form and the critical acumen he evinced in promoting it in Santiniketan—eventually shaping into full-bodied dance-dramas—seems nowhere to be documented, barring the earnest writings and memoirs of primarily, Santidev Ghosh and Pratima Devi and secondarily, by the bevy of ardent students through whom the art was propagated—only in Bengali. There appears to be no connected account of the genesis, growth and full flowering of this domain of Tagore in English.

Second, there has been not much effort to connect—even in the Bengali narratives on Tagore's dance—with the enormous wealth of illustrations and graphics that exist in Santiniketan's various archives, including Tagore's manuscripts, photographs and paintings related to dance. Especially in the latter genre, the invaluable paintings, drawings and sketches that Tagore put forth in the last decade of his life, do not seem to have been correlated with the music dramas, recitative dramas and dance-dramas that he was creating for the proscenium stage around the same time.

Third, whatever the level of knowledge and reverence is in today's India in general and in Bengal—both West Bengal and Bangladesh—in particular about the Poet, the rest of the world—especially its upcoming generations—still seems to be very largely unaware of Tagore's dance. This last aspect became painfully evident to me when I presented my invited paper on 'Tagore's Dance: Evolution and Cross-Cultural Evolution' for the World Dance Alliance—Global Summit in Brisbane, Australia, in 2008. The very large audience of dancers, choreographers and dance-scholars who gathered there were very agreeably surprised that a colossus who made outstanding contributions in so many genres of literature, philosophy, education, politics, religion and performing and visual arts, was not merely passionately interested in dance but even had brought it as a discipline to Santiniketan far ahead of his time from the rest of India.

Hence the author's research began with a preliminary preview of Tagore's Dance, looking at as many primary or secondary sources of inspiration that Tagore could have had; understanding the visionary steps he had taken to let dance be accepted as a part of education and urban culture and to encourage the consolidation of classical dances that only began in his times; and visiting Santiniketan to probe the archives with enthusiastic support of the concerned persons. To the initially brief research paper and the subsequent collection of material was added the active interest shown by Indian Television (Doordarshan) Archives to produce eventually one or more DVDs on Tagore's dance. This helped the author considerably to consolidate the information and hasten up the book-writing process to complement the audio-visual production of DD Archives on Tagore's Dance.

Structurally, the book is conceived into twelve chapters:

First, 'Wellspring of a Legend', outlines Tagore's multi-faceted persona, in the briefest possible manner, by way of a universal introduction;

Second, 'Tagore's Milieu', captures the little covered ground—how Santiniketan, in its small ways, nurtured Tagore's virtuoso genius;

Third, 'European Fount', explores the craigs and crevices of European culture—British, German and Polish—with which young Tagore was likely to have interacted;

Fourth, 'Era of Free Movement', looks at how Tagore brought in dance at Santiniketan as an Indian pioneer and initiated mood dance;

Fifth, 'Indian Subcontinental Influences', witnesses the emerging and gradual introduction of classical dances in Santiniketan;

Sixth, 'Winds of Asia-Pacific', observes the sojourns of the peripatetic Poet within Asia-Pacific culture of dance and his bringing in what suited the Indian genius;

Seventh, 'First Flowering', looks at the efflorescence of wonderful seasonal odes, with music and dance that would bloom into nascent 'music dramas';

Eighth, 'Final Fruits', enumerates on the final bursting on the scene of exquisite musical dramas and dance-dramas that remain unparalleled in Indian cultural milieu;

Ninth, 'Canons of Choreography', recapitulates the basics of Indian grammar of dance and re-maps Tagore's dance in that light;

Tenth, 'Midas Touch of Music', looks gratefully back at the treasure-trove of Tagore's music and reconnoiters how it has nurtured and nourished Tagore's dance;

Eleventh, 'Panoply of Paintings', unearths from a mature Tagore's painting foray, the dancing figures that are little analysed so far and tries to unravel their mysticism;

Twelfth, 'Tagore's Dance Legacy', invites the country's foremost choreographers and takes stock of how they have been using the dance legacy: even seven decades after the Poet's demise!

The author is aware that his efforts are of a near beginner which need more quests and illumination from the literati and cognoscenti into the subject-area. But in the true spirit of a researcher—who must find out what information already exists, add a little knowledge to it and point out what areas need to be further looked into—the results are submitted here. If this satisfies some curious readership and draws some more to join the quest, his efforts would be amply rewarded.

To note, each chapter has additional documentary material appended to provide extra information for the inquisitive reader. Free translations of Tagore's songs—usually the *sthayee* (the first of the four parts)—are by the author. All quotations related to Tagore or his works are translations from Santidev Ghosh's books in Bengali or the Bengali original cited by Amita Sen. These works are gratefully acknowledged in the Bibliography.

Utpal K. Banerjee

Foreword

In order to dilate upon Tagore's thoughts on dance, one has to state at the outset that Tagore's own writings on this subject are minimal, almost nil. Whatever is available exists strewn among his letters and other essays: hidden among many other dialogues. Although at a late age he transformed his music dramas into dance-dramas and adorned them afresh with scenes and sceneries, yet there is little material of distinction available from his pen on dance structures or about his mindset on dance. It is also worth pondering that many have noticed a similarity between Tagore's wide canvas of colours and paintings and the styles of dance in the space of the proscenium stage. Indeed, when Tagore was strongly entrenched in the role of an artist, he launched his dance plans, albeit indirectly. So, one can easily weave a garland blending Tagore's fine arts with his terpsichorean arts.

Tagore's late-age efflorescence in the realm of paintings was a remarkable event which blossomed in the last ten–twelve years of his life. Painted in a limited period, this large oeuvre (two thousand and five hundred paintings) could be a matter of great credit for any artist of the world. Subject-wise, one can categorise these paintings among portraiture; nature; weird animal motifs, masks; flowers and water-containers; apart from a few dance figures. The latter does not demarcate any specific dance style, but combines lines and forms into a mode of rotational form as their weight, and to which has been added the integrated texture of colours and lines.

If one looks at Tagore's figures engaged in dance, one does discern hints of foreign dances, such as, in the number 00.2387.16. It does not need elaboration that there is a clear stamp of the Western dance style on this painting. Again, the painting of the dancing girl (00.2601.16) in red skirt and holding a red handkerchief is easily identified as a Spanish dancer. Yet the white portion below the painting bears the appellation 'Jodhpur', that is, the red-skirted woman is in reality a Rajasthan danseuse. It is, thus, both difficult and unwise to categorise Tagore's paintings, since this may be highly misleading. All that can be clearly stated is that Tagore's dance psyche has been nourished by classical and folk dances of India as well as abroad, which is reflected in his dancing figures.

If one has to say a few words on the evolution of Tagore's thoughts on dance, one has to retrace his earlier experiences. His first journey to the UK was not a happy one. Although he had seen many things, summarily nothing perhaps left a lasting impression in his mind. Nevertheless, he wrote *Valmiki Pratibha*, a dance-drama, immediately on return. Dances used to be performed earlier at JorasankoThakurbari such as *Vasanta Utsav* and *Manmayee*, but no clear picture is available to us of those events. Hence, it is difficult to surmise about their costumes or dance styles. Though the dances of 'Vanadevis' in *Valmiki Pratibha* were conducted by the women of Thakurbari, the idea was muted only after Tagore's experience of viewing Western operas.

Tagore, during his second visit to the UK, in the 1890s, was decidedly more mature and the routine for the trip was better planned. He himself had acknowledged of having seen more than one opera. Out of this, the experience of witnessing *The Gondolier* (by William Gilbert and Arthur Sullivan, as part of 'the Savoy Operas', opening in London in 1889) at Savoy Theatre was especially worth mentioning:

> It gave an ethereal feeling of being in a fantasy land—in its lighting, music, aesthetics, variety of colours, 'mise en scene', dance, laughter and humour. In an interim part, there were quite a few male and female dancers performing. I thought, for a while, that there has been a shower of flowers from the dancing heavens. It appeared as though a wind of crazy youth is blowing in the world of beautiful people who are turning everything topsy-turvy—with illumination and rainbow-colours, in music and eyes lit with bright smiles, breaking asunder everywhere in a thousand-fold manner... (*Europe Jatrir Diary,* Ed. I, Part II).

Though the above description does not capture a special moment or a specific scene of the opera, yet it is evident that Tagore was captivated with the entire milieu of light, shadow, colour, grace and techniques, which must have influenced his later vision of dance. Even besides the paintings of dance figures, other canvases too carry this operatic flavour. We shall see in a later period how, far from the Western opera, he was more impressed by the dance of the Far East. Fifteen years after the Savoy experience, he was equally moved seeing Japanese dance:

> I saw the Japanese dance one day and felt as if it was a melody of body movements. This melody belongs to the elaboration on *vina* of our land, that is, with glides after

> every note. In the variety of stylised expression, there was no gap among them...The whole body was oscillating at once, showering flowers all around. Pure European dance is like the 'Ardha-Narishwar'—half dance and half gymnastics. In it, there are leaps and jumps, merry-go-rounds, kicking out into the sky. Here in Japan, it is complete dance. In its decorative costume, there is no trace of nudity. Dance in other countries mix the physical beauty with carnal attraction. Not a hint of libido was evident in any body movement here...(*Japan Jatri*)

It was the exposure to Japanese dance that wiped out the charming after-effect of the opera. What loomed large was the lust for body and exposure to nudity compared to which the Japanese dance appeared as 'the music of the body'. One could forcefully join issues with Tagore on the subject, but that would be a different matter. Tagore's dance hereafter more or less flowed through this channel. After another ten years since the *Japan Jatri* (the Sojourner to Japan) came not too dissimilar an experience of viewing Javanese dance as narrated here:

> The two young girls danced with Gamelan music: with wonderful grace. In all their limbs and parts of limbs, there were oscillations of unusual softness, variety and delicacy—what a supple expression it was! In other dances the danseuse is seen to move the body, but here it seemed that the two bodies were as though the spontaneous fountain of a dance! The girls are not allowed to dance after the age of twelve, as if such spontaneity of undulation would stay any longer...(*Java Jatri Patra*).

In other words, if Japanese dance was 'melody of the body', Javanese dance included the swing of rhythm, grace, delicacy, easy outward expression, whereas European dance was half-dance and half-exercise—as Tagore unequivocally would explain.

Whatever dance kinetics have been manifest in Tagore's paintings, their rhythms and forms are much like creeper-plants with blossoms—at times dependent on bent lines and at other times swinging as straight lines. The bends of the dancing body are often diagonally spread on the canvas as if to create a linear geometry. In like manner, the dancing image creates a 'silent tension' within the frames of space and form. Its counterpart would be the creation of physical manifestations of the male and female dancer on stage. This 'silent tension' seems to be the leitmotif of his dance psyche. And attraction of this tension perhaps made him mix much of his youthful poetry and verse into later-life music and dance and create—like the painter Tagore—newer creations of his dance-drama: creating altogether a new chemical solution!

Sushovan Adhikary
Curator, Kala Bhavan, Visva-Bharati

A dramatic scene from Tasher Desh.

Part One

Evolution

The towering genius of Tagore might have derived its vital inspiration from several sources, but what always emerged was an unmistakable creativity of his own. This is evident in Tagore's dance too

Wellspring *of a* Legend

Twin phenomena: Two seminal trends can be discerned simultaneously in the creative span of Rabindranath Tagore (1861–1941)—between the young Rabi of sixteen and the accomplished Titan at eighty—from 1877 to 1940. The first can be drawn from a *Kathopanishad* simile, the evolution of the Supreme Spirit compared to an 'inverted tree', with its roots that draw sap from diverse founts and yet grow skywards with a vertical thrust. The towering genius of Tagore might have derived its vital inspiration from several sources, but what always emerged was an unmistakable creativity of his own. This is evident in Tagore's dance too, where cross-cultural dialogue played a role in the evolving dance idiom. The second is an endearing French idiom, *Je suisl'autre*—'I am the other'. Whenever there was a linear growth of creativity in a particular field, Tagore turned around to be the 'other', always an unexplored facet!

Both these traits continued throughout Tagore's lifespan in tandem. He was not merely among the foremost poets of the late nineteenth and early twentieth centuries, but also a short-story writer, a novelist, a playwright, a composer, a visual artist, an educator, a philosopher, an institution builder, a political thinker, a humanist and a spirited advocate of India's freedom movement, whose visionary insight in all these arenas was of the highest order. He had the innate ability to draw inspiration from different fount-heads and switch energy from one field to another to fuel multitasking.

Chequered Life

The Tagore family, which was steeped in the Adi Brahmo Dharma faith, reared a culture that combined traditional Indian values with Western ideas. Tagore's grandfather, Dwarakanath Tagore, had established a huge financial empire, which sustained the later generations and absolved them substantially of financial worries.

Tagore was born of parents Maharshi Debendranath Tagore (1817–1905) and Sarada Devi (1830–75). He lost his mother when he was very young. Tagore left Kolkata with his father in 1873 to tour India for several months. He visited his father's estate at Santiniketan and then Amritsar, before reaching the Himalayan retreat at Dalhousie, where he read biographies; studied history, astronomy, modern science and Sanskrit; and dipped into the classical poetry of Kalidasa—all of which provided Tagore an enriching experience that sustained him life-long.

Valmiki Pratibha: *Indira Devi as Lakshmi and Tagore as Valmiki.*

Tagore's family wanted him to be a Bar-at-Law. He enrolled at a public school in Brighton in 1878 and studied law at University College, London, but returned to India in 1880 without a degree. He married Mrinalini Devi (1873–1900) in 1883 and had five children, two of whom died before reaching adulthood. In 1889, Tagore began managing his family's vast estates in Silaidaha, a region now in Bangladesh, where he was joined by his wife and children in 1898. While living out of the family's luxurious barge on the Padma River, he travelled across the estate, collecting token rents and blessing villagers. In return, the appreciative villagers held feasts to honour their zamindar!

The *Sadhana* period (1892–95), named after his magazine, proved to be very fertile, during which he penned half the stories of *Galpoguchchha* (Anthology of Stories) that comprised eighty-four stories compiled into three volumes. For a city-bred Tagore without any earlier exposure to villages, these stories captured a vivid picture of Bengal's rural lifestyle.

Leaving Silaidaha in 1901, Tagore moved to Santiniketan, Bengal, to found an Ashram comprising a prayer hall, an experimental school and a library, besides gardens, trees and groves and a residential complex. By now his work was growing increasingly popular in India and abroad alike. In 1913, he won the Nobel Prize in literature, the first in Asia, based on a small body of his translated material, including *Gitanjali* (Song Offering).

The poems were translated to English by the author himself. In 1912, the Irish

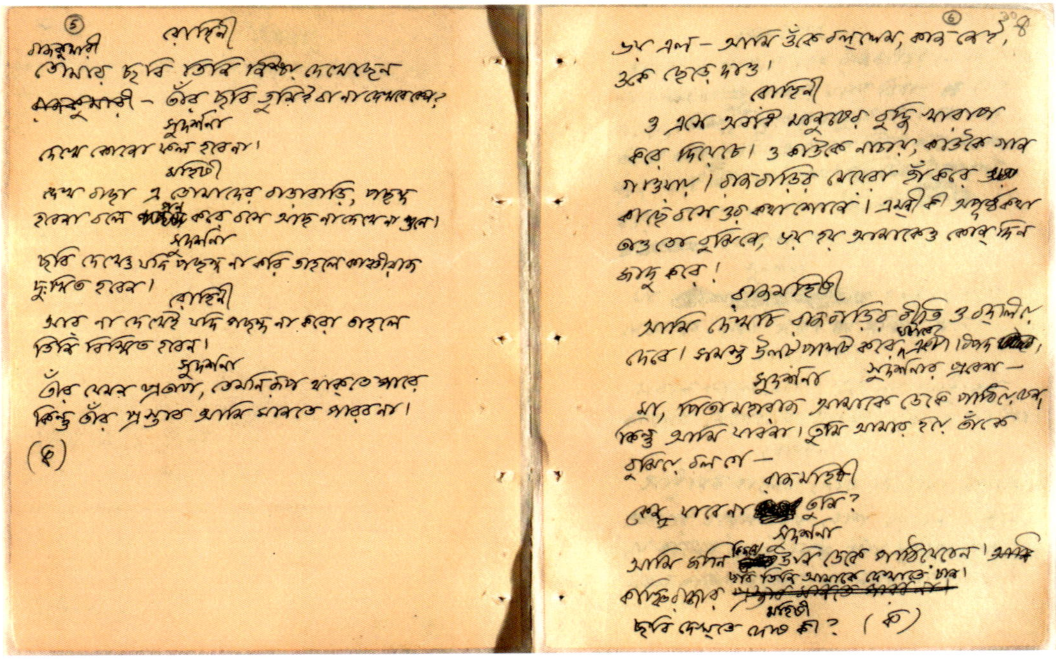

Tagore manuscripts.

poet and dramatist William Butler Yeats (1865–1939) wrote for its 'Introduction': 'These lyrics, which are in original full of subtleties of rhythm, of untranslatable delicacies of colour, of metrical invention display in their thought a world I have dreamt of all my life-long.'

In 1913, there was high praise from the US poet and critic Ezra Pound (1885–1972):

> There is in him, the stillness of nature. The poems do not seem to have been produced by storm or by ignition, but seem to show the normal habit of his mind. He is at one with nature, and finds no contradictions. And this is in sharp contrast with the Western mode, where man must be shown attempting to master nature if we are to have 'high drama'.

Another turning point came in the public arena when in 1915, Tagore received Knighthood from the British Crown. But as a mark of protest to the rulers, post the Jallianwala Bagh massacre in 1918, he renounced the title.

In 1921, Tagore, together with agricultural economist Leonard Elmhirst, set up a centre of rural reconstruction, which he later re-named 'Sriniketan'. It was located in the village of Surul, not too far from Santiniketan Ashram. Tagore sought here to provide an alternative to Gandhi's symbol-based and protest-oriented Swaraj Movement, which he denounced. In the early 1930s, he also grew more concerned about India's abnormal caste consciousness and untouchability—lecturing at its evils, writing poems and plays with untouchable protagonists as well as appealing to authorities at the Guruvayoor Temple to admit *dalits* (untouchables).

In his last decade, Tagore publicly upbraided Gandhi for stating that a massive 1931 earthquake in Bihar was a divine retribution for the subjugation of *dalits*. He also mourned the socio-economic decline of Bengal and the endemic poverty in Kolkata.

'Wanderlust': Love for Wandering

Between 1878 and 1932, Tagore visited more than thirty countries in five continents: many of these trips crucial in familiarising non-Indian audiences with his works and spreading his political ideas. He was in the UK twice in his early youth: in 1878–80 and again in 1890. In 1912, he took a sheaf of his translated works to England, which impressed missionary and Gandhi protégé Charles F. Andrews, the Anglo-Irish poet William Butler Yeats, as well as Ezra Pound, Robert Bridges, Ernest Rhys and Thomas Moore. Poets like Andrews joined Tagore at Santiniketan. In 1912, Tagore toured the USA and the UK, staying in Butterton, Staffordshire, with Andrews' friends who were clergymen.

During 1916–17, Tagore went on lecturing tours to Japan and the US, during which he denounced nationalism—particularly that of the Japanese and Americans. He also wrote the essay 'Nationalism in India', attracting both derision and praise (the latter from pacifists, including Romain Rolland).

Shortly after returning to India, the sixty-three-year-old Tagore visited Peru at the invitation of the Peruvian Government and took the opportunity to visit Mexico as well. Both governments pledged donations of $100,000 to the school at Santiniketan (Visva-Bharati) in commemoration of his visits. In 1924, a week after his arrival in Buenos Aires, Argentina, Tagore, who had fallen unwell, moved into the Villa Miralrio at the behest of Victoria Ocampo. He left for India in 1925. In 1926, Tagore reached Naples, Italy and met fascist dictator Benito Mussolini in Rome the next day. Their initially warm rapport lasted until Tagore spoke out against Mussolini in 1926.

In 1927, Tagore and his companions began a four-month tour of Southeast Asia, visiting Bali, Java, Kuala Lumpur, Malacca, Penang, Siam (Thailand) and Singapore. Tagore's travelogues from the tour were collected in *Jatri*.

In early 1930, he left Bengal for nearly a year-long tour of Europe and the US. Once he returned to the UK, while his paintings were being exhibited in Paris and London, he stayed at a friend's settlement in Birmingham. He wrote there his Hibbert Lectures for the University of Oxford (which dealt with the idea of the humanity of our God or the divinity of Man, the Eternal) and spoke at London's annual Quaker gathering. There, addressing relations between the British and Indians, a topic he would grapple with over the next two years, Tagore spoke of a 'dark chasm of aloofness'. He later visited Aga Khan III and stayed at Dartington Hall (created with Santiniketan as inspiration) in the UK. Then in 1930 itself, he toured Denmark, Switzerland and Germany, as also the Soviet Union. Lastly, in 1932, Tagore—who was acquainted with the legends and works of the Persian mystic Hafez—was invited as a personal guest of Shah Reza Shah Pehlavi of Iran.

Such extensive travels allowed Tagore to interact with many notable contemporaries, including Henry Bergson, Albert Einstein, Robert Frost, Thomas Mann, George Bernard Shaw, H.G. Wells and Romain Rolland. Tagore's last travels abroad, including visits to Iran and Iraq in 1932, and Sri Lanka in 1933, only sharpened his opinion regarding human divisions and nationalism.

Tagore's Oeuvre: A Bird's-eye View

Poetry

Between 1893 and 1900, he wrote seven volumes of poetry, including *Sonar Tari* (The Golden Boat, 1894) and *Kshanika* (Sparks, 1900). This was a highly productive period in Tagore's life and earned him the rather misleading epitaph, 'The Bengali Shelley'! More important was that Tagore wrote in the common language of the people. This also was something that was hard to accept among his critics and scholars.

Much of Tagore's ideology came from the Upanishads and from his own belief that God can be found through personal purity as well as from service to others. He stressed the need for a new world order based on transnational values and ideas—the 'unity consciousness'.

Tagore wrote his most important works in Bengali, but he often translated his poems into English. In 1931, he was also a composer, setting hundreds of poems to music. Many of his poems are actually songs inseparable from their music. Tagore's 'My Golden Bengal' became the national anthem of Bangladesh. Only hours before he died, on 7 August 1941, did Tagore dictate his last poem. His written production, still not completely compiled, fills nearly thirty substantial volumes.

On a closer look, Tagore's poetry—which varied in style from classical formalism to the comic, visionary and ecstatic—reveals a lineage established by fifteenth- and sixteenth-century Vaishnava poets. Tagore was also influenced by the mysticism of sage-authors like Vyasa, Kabir and Ramprasad. Yet Tagore's poetry became most innovative and mature after his exposure to rural Bengal's folk music, which included ballads sung by *baul* singers—especially Lalan Shah. This genre—rediscovered and popularised by Tagore—resembles the nineteenth-century *Kartabhaja* hymns that emphasise on inward divinity and rebellion against religious and social orthodoxy. During his Silaidaha years, his poems took on a lyrical quality, speaking via the *Moner Manush* (the *baul's* 'man within the heart') or meditating upon the *Jeevan Devata* ('the living God within'). This entity sought connection with divinity through appeal to nature and emotional interplay of human drama. Tagore used such techniques in his *Bhanusingha* poems (which chronicle the romance between Radha and Krishna) which he repeatedly revised over the course of seventy years.

Tagore responded to the emergence of modernism and realism in Bengali literature with experimental works in the 1930s. Examples of such works include 'Africa' and 'Camellia', which are among the better-known of his later poems. He also occasionally wrote poems using *sadhu bhasha* (Sanskritised dialect of Bengali); later, he began using *cholti bhasha* (popular dialect). Other notable works include *Manasi* and *Balaka* (Wild Geese—the title being a metaphor for the migrating soul).

Tagore's poetry has been set to music by various composers, among them notable are classical composer Arthur Shepherd's triptych for soprano and string quartet, as well as composer Gary Schumann's *Praan*, an adaptation of Tagore's poem 'Stream of Life' from *Gitanjali*. The latter was composed and recorded with vocals by Pallabsha Siddique to accompany internet celebrity Matt Harding as 'viral video' in 2008.

Novels

Tagore wrote eight novels as well as four novellas, including *Chaturanga, Shesher Kobita, Char Odhay* and *Noukadubi*. *Ghare Baire* (The Home and the World)—through the lens of the idealistic zamindar protagonist Nikhil—flays the rising Indian nationalism, terrorism and religious zeal in the Swadeshi movement. A frank expression of Tagore's conflicted sentiments, it emerged out of a 1914 bout of depression. Indeed, the novel ends with Hindu–Muslim sectarian violence and Nikhil was being (probably mortally) wounded. In some sense, *Gora* shares a similar theme, raising controversial questions regarding the Indian identity. As with *Ghare Baire*, matters of *jati*, personal freedom and religion are developed in the context of a family story and love triangle. Another powerful story is *Jogajog* (Relationships), where Tagore demonstrates his feminist leanings, using pathos to depict the plight and ultimate demise of Bengali women trapped by pregnancy, duty and family honour; simultaneously, he treats the decline of Bengal's landed oligarchy.

Other novels were more diverse: *Shesher Kobita* (translated twice—*Last Poem* and *Farewell Song*) is his most lyrical novel, with poems and rhythmic passages written by the main character (a poet). It also contains elements of satire and post-modernism; the stock characters all seem to gleefully attack the reputation of an old, outmoded and oppressively renowned poet who, incidentally, goes by the name of Rabindranath Tagore! Though his novels remain among the least appreciated of his works, they have been given renewed attention via film adaptations that include *Chokher Bali* and *Ghare Baire*. Many have soundtracks featuring selections from Tagore's own music: Rabindra Sangeet.

Essays

Tagore wrote many non-fiction books, writing on topics ranging from Indian history to linguistics. Beside his autobiographical works, his travelogues, essays and lectures were compiled into several volumes, including *Europe Jatrir Patro* (Letters from Europe), *Manusher Dharmo* (The Religion of Man) and *Sabhyatar Sankat* (Dilemma of Civilisation).

Music

Tagore was a prolific musician writing around two thousand two hundred and thirty songs, collectively known as Rabindra Sangeet, now an integral part of Bengali culture. Tagore's music is inseparable from his literature, most of which—poems or parts of novels, stories, or plays—became lyrics for his songs. Primarily influenced by the *dhrupad, khayal* and *thumri* styles of Hindustani classical music, they ran the entire gamut of human emotion, ranging from the almost dirge-like early Brahmo devotional hymns to quasi-erotic compositions. They emulated the tonal colour of classical *ragas* to varying extents. Though at times his songs followed a given *raga's* melody and rhythm faithfully, he also blended elements of different *ragas* to create extraordinarily innovative works.

Cover design for Shap Mochan *by Tagore.*

The appeal of these songs, stemming from the combination of emotive strength and beauty, described as surpassing even Tagore's poetry, was such that the *Modern Review* observed: 'There is in Bengal no cultured home where Rabindranath's songs are not sung or at least attempted to be sung...Even illiterate villagers sing his songs.' Music critic Arthur Strangways of *The Observer* first introduced non-Bengalis to Rabindra Sangeet with his book *The Music of Hindustan*, which described it as a 'vehicle of a personality...[that] go behind this or that system of music to that beauty of sound which all systems put out their hands to seize.' In this compilation of songs is included Bangladesh's national anthem—*'Amar sonar Bangla'* (mentioned earlier) and India's national anthem—*'Jana Gana Mana'*; Tagore was the only person ever to have written the national anthems of two nations. Rabindra Sangeet influenced the style of rendition of many musicians of succeeding generations.

Paintings

At sixty, Tagore took up both drawing and painting; successful exhibitions of his many works—which made a debut appearance in Paris upon encouragement from artists he met in the south of France—were held throughout Europe. Tagore—who probably exhibited protanopia or partial lack of (red-green, in Tagore's case) colour discernment—painted in a style characterised by peculiarities in aesthetics and colouring schemes. Nevertheless, Tagore took to emulating numerous styles, including that of craftwork by the Malanggan people of northern New Ireland; Haida carvings from the west coast of Canada (British Columbia); and also woodcuts by Max Pechstein. Tagore also had an artist's eye for his own handwriting, embellishing the scribbles, cross-outs and word layouts in his manuscript with artistic leitmotifs, including simple rhythmic designs.

Theatre

Tagore's experience in theatre began at sixteen, when he played the lead role in his brother Jyotirindranath's adaptation of Moiré's *Le Bourgeois Gentilhomme*. At twenty, he wrote his first drama-opera *Valmiki Pratibha* (Virtuosity of Valmiki), which describes how Valmiki, the bandit, having reformed his ethos, is blessed by Goddess Saraswati, following which he sets off to compose the Ramayana. Through it, Tagore vigorously explores a wide range of dramatic styles and emotions, including usage of re-vamped *keertana* and adaptation of traditional English songs and Irish folk melodies. This was followed by *Kal Mrigaya* (The Fatal Hunt) and *Mayar Khela* (The Illusionist Game). Another notable play, *Dak Ghar* (The Post Office), describes how a child—striving to escape his stuffy confines—ultimately 'falls asleep', which suggests his physical death. A story with worldwide appeal (it received rave reviews in Europe), *Dak Ghar* dealt with death as, in Tagore's words, 'spiritual freedom' from 'the world of hoarded wealth and certified creeds'.

Chandalika: *The first protest against untouchability. Artist: Kelu Nair.*

Above: Tasher Desh: *A voice against frozen rituals. Sagarmoy Ghosh and Santidev Ghosh.*
Below: Mayar Khela: *The pioneering opera.*

Left: Chitrangada: *The ultimate feminine persona. Sujata and Haridas.*
Right: Shyama: *Clash between lore and lust. Nandita as Shyama.*

His other works—emphasising the fusion of the lyrical flow and emotional rhythm tightly focussed on a core idea—were unlike previous Bengali dramas. His works sought to articulate, in Tagore's words, 'the play of feeling and not of action'. In 1890, he wrote *Visarjan* (Sacrifice), regarded as his finest drama. The Bengali originals included intricate sub-plots and extended monologues. Later, his dramas probed more philosophical and allegorical themes, including *Dak Ghar* (mentioned above). Another one is Tagore's *Chandalika* (Untouchable Girl), which was modelled on an ancient Buddhist legend. Lastly, among his most famous dramas is *Raktakarabi* (Red Oleander), which is about a kleptocratic king who enriches himself by forcing his subjects to miming. The heroine, Nandini, eventually rallies the common people to destroy these symbols of subjugation. Tagore's musicals and dance-based plays include *Natir Puja* (The Worship of a Danseuse), *Shap Mochan* (Deliverance from Curse), *Tasher Desh* (The Land of Cards), *Chitrangada, Shyama* and *Chandalika* (see Chapter 8).

Short Stories

His short stories usually showcase Tagore's reflections upon his surroundings, on modern and fashionable ideas and on interesting mind-puzzles (which Tagore was fond of testing his intellect with). Tagore typically associated his earliest stories (such as those of the *Sadhana* period) with an exuberance of vitality and spontaneity; these characteristics were intimately connected with his life in the villages of Patisar, Shajapur and Silaidaha while managing the vast ancestral landholdings of the Tagores. There he beheld the lives of India's poor and common people; Tagore thereby took to examining their lives with a penetrative depth and feeling that was singular in Indian literature up to that point. In *Kabuliwala* (The Fruit-Seller from Kabul), for instance, Tagore speaks in first person as town-dweller and novelist who chances upon the Afghani seller and attempts to distill the sense of longing felt by those long trapped in the mundane and hard-scrabble confines of Indian urban life, giving play to dreams of a different existence in the distant and wild mountains. Many of the other *Galpoguchchha* stories were written in Tagore's *Sabuj Patra* period (1914–17; name derived from one of Tagore's magazines).

'Welternshauung': World View

Marked complexities characterise Tagore's political views. He criticised European imperialism and supported Indian nationalists. However, he also lampooned the Swadeshi movement, denouncing it in 'The Cult of Charkha', an acrid essay written in 1925. Instead, he emphasised self-help and intellectual uplift of the masses, stating that British imperialism was not a primary evil but instead a 'political symptom of our social disease', urging Indians to accept that 'there can be no question of blind revolution, but of steady and purposeful education.'

Such views inevitably enraged many, placing his life in danger. During his stay in a San Francisco hotel in late 1916, Tagore narrowly escaped assassination by Indian expatriates. The plot failed only because the would-be assassins fell into argument. Yet, Tagore wrote songs lionising the Indian Independence movement and renounced his Knighthood in protest against the 1919 Jallianwala Bagh Massacre. Two of Tagore's more politically charged compositions, 'Chitta jetha bhayshunyo' (Where the mind is without fear) and 'Ekla chalo re' (If they answer not to thy call, walk alone) gained mass appeal, with the latter favoured by Gandhi. Despite his tumultuous relations with Gandhi, Tagore was the key person responsible for resolving a Gandhi–Ambedkar dispute involving separate electorates for untouchables and ending Gandhi's fast 'unto death'.

Tagore also criticised orthodox (rote-oriented) education, lampooning it in the short story *Totakahini* (The Parrot's Training), where a bird which ultimately dies is caged by tutors and forcefully fed pages torn from books. These views led Tagore—while visiting Santa Barbara, California, in 1917—to conceive of a new type of university, desiring to: 'make [his Ashram at] Santiniketan the connecting thread between India and the world...[and] a world centre for the study of humanity ...somewhere beyond the limits of nation and geography.' The school—which he named Visva-Bharati—had its foundation stone laid on 22 December 1918; it was later inaugurated in 1921. Here, Tagore implemented a *Brahmacharya* pedagogical structure employing gurus to provide individualised guidance for pupils. Tagore worked hard to fund-raise for the school, even contributing all of his Nobel Prize money. Tagore's duties as steward and mentor at Santiniketan kept him busy; he taught classes in the mornings and wrote textbooks for students in the afternoons and evenings. Tagore also travelled extensively in Europe and the US between 1919 and 1921 to raise funds for the school.

Penchant for Dance

Our starting point is the account which Santidev Ghosh—a remarkable chronicler of dance-related events in Tagore's life—has provided, alongside his own account of learning dance in the Indian subcontinent and abroad with Tagore's encouragement. Santidev documented, like a faithful Boswell, what he saw as the process of efflorescence of fifteen Tagore's dance-interests, observed over three decades at Santiniketan. We use many other important sources and examine three key hypotheses: what was the evolutionary nature of Tagore's dance persona? What were its cardinal features? And what kind of cross-cultural liaisons did he undertake to arrive at a clear philosophy and a coherent choreographic mind that could lead to a genre of Rabindra Nritya?

Tagore had a teenage exposure to Western dance in England and retained an obvious interest for the terpsichorean muse all his life. Seminally inspired by Spencer and Wagner, he penned, in the 1880s, two musical dramas and one opera, and encouraged his students in Santiniketan to participate in song and dance, himself participating in these activities wholeheartedly. Once Visva-Bharati was formed in 1921, his interest gathered momentum appointing dance teachers, laying down dance courses a la Dartington Hall, UK, and often appearing on stage as a dancer himself in his plays and musicals. He proceeded to compose several celebrations of the seasons and create musical dramas like *Natir Puja*, *Tasher Desh* and *Shap Mochan*—to be accompanied wherever feasible, by dance. In the twilight years of his life, his enthusiasm for choreography reached its pinnacle in *Chitrangada, Shyama* and *Chandalika*, all fully formed dance-dramas. He never spared any pains to source dance teachers from the four corners of the country as well as abroad. He sent emissaries to and gathered knowledge from Manipur, Cochin and Malabar besides welcoming talent from Kathiawar and Chennai. In the Asian continent, he had close liaison with Java, Bali, Siam (now Thailand), China, Japan, Burma (now Myanmar) and Sri Lanka.

Santidev Ghosh: Iconic disciple of Tagore.

In all these endeavours, he was enviably ahead of his time. In 1919, he had already motivated his young students to dance *en masse* in the seasonal festivities before formally introducing music and dance in the study curriculum in 1925. He was possibly the first virtual choreographer and participating dancer, with an early systemic foray into dance, using the foundation of Bengal's folk-dance ethos, the veneering of classical dances and seminal subcontinental, and later, regional influences of the Asia-Pacific. This was truly remarkable, considering that India's dance-doyen, Uday Shankar, appeared on the scene only in 1929 and founded his Almora training centre almost a decade later in 1938. It was also only in 1929 that Rukmini Devi Arundale, the 'uncrowned queen of Indian dance', was first exposed to Anna Pavlova in Australia and took nearly half-a-decade to establish her school—Kalakshetra—in 1936. Even then, both Shankar and Rukmini Devi aimed at producing trained dancers through their illustrious efforts, while Tagore placed dance in a holistic education approach at Santiniketan, in the teeth of such castigations as revealed in the local reportage: 'The boys are learning musical gymnastics, to the tune of *mridang*'! Finally, Tagore inexorably pruned his dance idiom—including the classical dances—of its mythical links, using it boldly against shibboleths of ritual, upholding gender equality and feminine rights and challenging the scourge of untouchability. His early exhibition of feminine talent on the public stage against heavy cynicism was another pioneering move in the social context.

What Tagore left for posterity is by no means a polished 'grammar' of dance that can be methodically followed by the uninitiated, but a conscientious body of work towards it as well as a few finished products from his last few years that have incandescent designs of music, melody and dance for 'body–mind orchestration'. His musicals and dance-dramas are vastly popular today, but not many try to follow the specific choreographic leads Tagore left, and only a handful of gurus like Valmiki Banerjee are re-constructing the dance vocabulary and set sequences based on his ideation, complete with dance syllabus. Tagore's own dance paintings, rarely analysed, remain indicative of what perhaps he had in mind.

The above is, of necessity, a highly synoptic view of Tagore's unsurpassable genius that is a pointer to a single fact: his was a Renaissance mind. The span of his imagination was incredibly vast, only to be matched by his capacity of articulation and integrity of expressional range. As has been said, he was a colossus bestriding his space and time.

Biographical Notes

Uday Shankar (1900–70)

Uday Shankar ushered in a new era of Indian dance. He choreographed and performed innumerable new dances created in his own style. He lifted the art of Indian dance to a level of universal recognition. As early as April 1934, the *Manchester Guardian* reported:

> The chief dancer, Uday Shan-Ker, is a noble appearance. He can move with the lightness of wind. When he would represent a snake his arms seem to have a thousand joints, so sinuously do they imitate its movements. Every muscle in his body seems to be at his command.

Uday Shankar was born in Udaipur, Rajasthan, as the eldest son of Pt. Shyam Shankar Chowdhury. As a child, Shankar was keener on painting and so he was sent to the Royal College of Art, London, in 1920. The principal of the Art College, Sir William Rothenstein, found tremendous talent in young Shankar and arranged for him to visit the British Museum, encouraging him to go through the section on India, especially Indian paintings and sculptures. During this period in London, Shankar was inspired by the wealth of India's culture and performed at society events, but it was not until his meeting with Anna Pavlova in 1921 that he took up the art form on a more professional level. In spite of a lack of formal training in Indian dance, Shankar performed with Pavlova, choreographing *Krishna and Radha* (in which he played Krishna to Pavlova's Radha) and *A Hindu Wedding* for her. The production ran to considerable acclaim at the Royal Opera House, Covent Garden, in September 1924.

Within less than a decade, Shankar left Pavlova to pursue independent projects with his own cast of dancers. After leaving Pavlova, Shankar went through a period of struggle in trying to establish himself. In 1926, he met a Swiss lady, Alice Boner, who sponsored his subsequent plans. They came to India in 1929 and travelled all over the country. His first troupe at that time consisted of his three brothers, cousin Kanakalata and her father Kedar Shankar Chowdhury; as well as Timir Baran, Ananda Bhattacharya, Brojobehari Banerjee, Simkie and Vishnudas Shirali. As they rehearsed for their first show in Paris, he met Amala Nandi and her father, Akshay Kumar Nandi, who were visiting Paris for an exhibition of Indian jewellery and handicrafts. Amala Nandi joined the troupe for a short tour to Europe.

Between 1929 and 1933, Shankar researched Indian dance, viewing different styles in India and eventually studying Kathakali with Guru Shankaran Namboodiri. At the same time he was evolving his own style, choreographing new pieces and developing his own approaches to training. With financial support from well-wishers like Elmhirst of Dartington, in 1928, he set up his school in the name of 'Uday Shankar India Cultural Centre' in Almora, nestling in the Himalayas. He devised his own method of training, which included essentials such as concentration, observation, imagination and improvisation. At his Centre, there were renowned gurus such as Ustad Alauddin Khan (classical music), Guru Shankaran Namboodiri (Kathakali), Guru Amobi Singh (Manipuri) and Guru Kandappa Pillai (Bharatanatyam). In 1944, he made a legendary film *Kalpana*. Between 1950 and 1968, Shankar travelled extensively all over the world with his troupe. His enchanting style of dance delighted wherever he performed.

It was Shankar who revolutionised the art of stage presentation in India. He was not only a dancer and choreographer, but also a genius of the age. It must be kept in mind that Shankar never formally learnt any classical form of dance. Yet, he was the pioneer in creating a new *gharana* of stage presentation, which is followed by millions of artistes, big or small. Any stage or dance presentation in India that deviates from the pure traditional and classical forms is an offshoot of Shankar's style. One must remember that Shankar was the father of 'Indian Ballet' and the person who brought contemporary dance to India and Indian dance to the world.

About his own work, Shankar said, 'My innovation, if I may put it so, lay in creating an altogether new technique which was no less important than the previous ones of the older schools. I always seek in my dancers, simplicity, power and beauty.'

Between 1930 and 1970, he choreographed nearly ninety new dance pieces, including:

1930s: *Indra, Radha Krishna, Sword Dance, Gandharva, Shiva Tandava, Snanum, Astra Puja, Kartikeya, Rhythm of Life*

1940s: *Ram Leela* (dance in shadow), *Kirat Arjuna, Labour and Machinery, Surya Puja, Bidai*

1950s: *Nirakshan, Lord Buddha, Assam Impression*

1960s: *Samanya Kshati, Prakriti, Ananda*

1970s: *Shankarscope*

Shankar remains a pioneering force in propagating South Asian dance in Britain. Famous music directors who composed music for Uday Shankar—Late Ustad Allauddin Khan, Pt. Ravi Shankar, Late Timir Baran, Late Vishnudas Shirali, Late Pt. Lal Mani Mishra, Shri Kamlesh Maitra—made inroads into popularising the art form for the Western audiences. At the same time, he created a new style of dance which continues to be practised till date.

Rukmini Devi Arundale (1904–86)

Rukmini Devi Arundale was an Indian theosophist, dancer and choreographer in the Indian classical dance form of Bharatanatyam, and also an activist for animal rights, animal welfare and vegetarianism. She is considered the most important revivalist of Bharatanatyam from its original *Sadir* style, prevalent amongst the *devadasis*. She also worked for the re-establishment of traditional Indian arts and crafts. Though she belonged to the Indian upper caste, she espoused the cause of Bharatanatyam, which was considered a low and vulgar art in the early 1920s. Recognising the beauty and spiritual value of this art form, she not only learned the dance, but also presented it on stage in spite of strong public protests.

Rukmini Devi was born in Madurai. Her father was Neelakanta Sastri, an engineer by profession and a scholar. Deeply influenced by the Theosophical Movement, as a follower of Dr Annie Besant, upon retirement, Neelakanta shifted to Adyar, Chennai, where he built his home near the headquarters of the Theosophical Society. Young Rukmini was exposed here, to not only theosophical thoughts but also new ideas in culture, theatre, music and dance. She met prominent British theosophist Dr George Arundale, who was a close associate of Annie Besant and later the principal of the Central Hindu College in Varanasi. In 1920, they got married, shocking the then conservative society. Post marriage, she travelled all over the world, meeting fellow theosophists and also forging friendships with educator Maria Montessori and poet James Cousins.

In 1928, the famous Russian ballerina Anna Pavlova came to Mumbai. The Arundale couple came to her performance and later happened to travel on the same ship as her to Australia, where she was to perform next. Over the course of the journey their friendship grew and Rukmini Devi started learning dance from one of Anna's leading solo dancers, Cleo Nordi. It was later at the behest of Anna that Rukmini Devi turned her attention to discovering traditional Indian dance forms, which had fallen to disrepute and dedicated the rest of her life to their revival.

In 1933, at the Annual Conference of Madras Music Academy, she saw, for the very first time, a performance of the dance form called *Sadir*. Later she learnt the dance from Mylapore Gowri Amma, and finally with the help of E. Krishna Iyer from Pandanallur Meenakshi Sundaram Pillai. In 1935, Rukmini Devi gave her first public performance at the 'Diamond Jubilee Convention of the Theosophical Society'. In 1936, she along with her husband, established Kalakshetra, an academy of dance and music, built around the ancient Indian Gurukul system, at Adyar, near Chennai. Today the academy is a deemed university under the Kalakshetra Foundation and is situated in its new hundred-acre campus in Tiruvanmiyur, Chennai, where it shifted in 1962.

Originally known as *Sadir*, the Indian classical dance form of Bharatanatyam owes its current name to E. Krishna Iyer and Rukmini Devi, who has been instrumental in modifying mainly the Pandanallur style of Bharatanatyam and bringing it to the global attention, and removing the extraneous *sringaar* elements from the dance, which were the legacy of its *devadasi* association in the past, thereby raising it to the status of puritan art form. Soon she changed the very face of the dance by introducing musical instruments like the violin; set and lighting design elements; and innovative costumes and jewellery inspired by the temple sculptures. Just as for her teacher she approached noted gurus in various arts and classical dances, for her productions, Rukmini Devi approached noted scholars for inspiration and classical musicians and artists for collaboration. The result was the creation of some of the pioneering dance-dramas based on Indian epics like Valmiki's Ramayana and Jayadeva's Gita Govinda. Starting with famous dance-dramas like *Sita Swayamvaram, Sri Rama Vanagamanam, Paduka Pattabhishekam* and *Sabari Moksham*, they were followed by *Kutrala Kuruvanji, Kumara Sambhavam* and *Usha Parinayam*.

In 1977, Morarji Desai offered to nominate her for the post of President of India, which she turned down. Rukmini Devi Arundale passed away on 24 February 1986 in Chennai.

Nature obviously provided the first spark of inspiration for Kalidasa and Tagore to spread out their many-splendoured poetic genius

Tagore's Milieu

Japan, 'the Land of the Rising Sun', known to have four distinct natural seasons, is marked by twenty-four micro-seasons. India, in contrast, has the full panoply of six seasons—summer, rains, autumn, frosts, winter and spring—and nobody has really counted how many micro-seasons there are: weaving in the early cyclones, scorching summer and the abating heat; the early showers, the torrential downpours and the suddenly vanishing rains; the floating nimbus clouds and the carpet of falling leaves and all-white blooms; the foggy mornings and the all-enveloping shroud of white mystery; the first simmering shiver and then the biting cold; and the flippant tone of spring with its humming bees and fragrant blossoms. And talking about blossoms, while in India one does not witness the post-winter suddenness of cherry trees bursting into flowers heralding the Ohanami festival, nonetheless there are millions of multi-hued flowers with their heady fragrances, besides all the colourful festivals virtually in every nook and corner of this vast land!

Clearly, two of India's most luminary poets could not be mere spectators to nature's riotous celebrations, ever renewing itself. In the early Middle Age (in the absence of an accurate chronicle of anybody's life by a historically amiss nation), Kalidasa did not forget to celebrate India's all six seasons: with twenty-eight poems on summer, twenty-eight about rains, twenty-six on autumn, eighteen on frosts, sixteen about winter and twenty-eight on spring: a tally of one hundred and forty-four poems in *Ritu Samharam* (The Bouquet of Seasons). Coming a millennium and half later, his worthy successor Tagore penned a total of one hundred and eighty-three odes to nature: nine in general, seventeen on summer, a mind-boggling one hundred and fourteen on rains, thirty on autumn, five on frosts, twelve on winter and as many as ninety-six on spring, besides a myriad allusions and resonances of nature strewn all over his lifetime's work. Nature obviously provided the first spark of inspiration for both Kalidasa and Tagore to spread out their poetic genius.

Milieu in Santiniketan

Kinship with Nature

After a sequestered urban upbringing, Silaidaha and its contiguity, in the river-studded East Bengal, provided Tagore a window to nature at its manifold splendour. After founding Santiniketan in 1901, Tagore's exposure to nature continued at its best and was all-pervading: with vast open meadows, occasional sweltering heat and pre-monsoon cyclones, sudden storms and torrential rains, forests and tall sal trees, gardens aglow with flowers, the *khoai* of the Kopai River, groves of plants and creepers. Nature, in its abundant expressions, provided him the best fillip to his creative genius.

His outpourings were continuous and in extravagant abundance: lilting songs paying odes to seasons in the scorching summer, dripping-wet rains, fleet-footed autumn, mysterious frost, shivering winters and flower-bedecked spring. This brought the denizens of Santiniketan their best gifts in their weal and woe, offerings to gladden their hearts and soothe their frayed moods. The nectar of his music was ambrosia to the lucky inmates of the Ashram who, in turn, gave the Poet their abundant love.

Khoai, *Santiniketan.*

The cycle of village life in our country revolves around nature. On one hand, while the rural environs—of which the then Santiniketan was a prime example—blessed with natural resources is a source of inspiration aesthetically, on the other hand, its large proximity to nature is celebrated through several festivities. Both are expressions of man's kinship with nature, which did not leave Tagore untouched.

So grew Santiniketan under Tagore's benevolent guidance: with nature at the core of its education system. The *guru–shishya parampara* evinced its best façade not merely in the teaching–learning situation, but also in co-habitation of the guardians and their wards. Keeping out excesses of life's luxuries, Tagore allowed every season to be welcomed through poetry and songs, drama and dances, visual and manifold performing arts. The seasonal festivals were an all-absorbing activity in a very organic sense, touching everybody, not excluding Tagore.

The milieu provided encouragement not merely to celebrate the six seasons in all their variegated beauty as in *Nataraj–Riturangashala* (see Chapter 7), but also to combine the students and teachers alike in successfully devising blended forms of dance, music, acting, costume and decorations in such celebrations. Some excellent examples were the group dance in folk form along with Tagore's song on planting saplings: 'Fly high in the sky your banner of conquering deserts, O the vibrant life; sanctify the dust below with your empathy, O the graceful soul' and the song on spring festival: 'O the householders, open your doors, "Dol" festivity is on; it has begun swinging the woods and plains, earth and the seas'.

Ashram's Fledgling Denizens

Since in Santiniketan, from the very outset, Tagore had made music and dance inseparable from academics, rigours of studies were invariably punctuated by incidences of singing and traipsing around. Nobody remembered since when festivities like hailing the seasons, welcoming the respected guests, tilling the land, singing in the New Year and myriad other celebrations began in the Ashram. But among the youngest participants were senior girls—Amita Sen, Jamuna Sen, Nandita Thakur (Kripalini) and Nibedita Basu, who were the main *dramatis personae* and juniors—Sukriti, Mamata, Sunipa, Anu and Tultul, who would furtively imitate the performance of their predecessors.

This was around 1915–16 when senior boys from Kala Bhavan included Sudhir Khastagir, Ramkinkar Baij and Satyen Bishi. They were among the early 'pioneers' who left their mark in stage-setting and decorating. The young lot would stage *Lakshmir Pariksha* and *Valmiki Pratibha* (see Chapter 4) under the elders' supervision from time to time, while *Dak Ghar* would be showcased by Dinendranath Tagore with Maya Mazumdar as Amal and Anu Chakrabarti as Sudha, with possibly the first sampling of free-style dance by Sukriti, Mamata and Sunipa for the song: 'The brick-red path that meanders away from the village entices my mind, too; whom does my heart long to touch by extending its reach on the dusty walkway'.

Ashram's Adoring Housewives

The Puranas of Shrimat Bhagavat and Harivamsa are replete with the *Dwapara*-era mythology of the youthful Krishna playing on his flute and dancing on the banks of River Yamuna in Vrindavan with his cowherd friends as well as *gopis* surreptitiously congregating around and standing enraptured at the pranks of the young Krishna.

There is nothing quite as romantic in our modern times but perhaps there is a very distant echo of a mystical encounter of the Poet and his cohorts on one end and the enchanted Ashram-wives on the other that comes through in Amita Sen's lyrical words:

> It was 1915 in a luminous spring evening. The walkway through

the sal trees was all aglow with the moonlight shimmering on the fresh, young leaves, the aimless breeze, blowing from the south, was driving the Santiniketan residents crazy with the heady aroma of *shirish, bakul* and *mahua* flowers and mango-buds. And, in the early spring breeze, they heard the refrain of the Tagore song—'Dear brothers, *Fagun* has plunged into the forests—in their myriad branches, leaves and blossoms—invading every crag, crevice, every nook and corner'.

It was no longer possible for the young Ashram wives—Kamala Devi, Labanya Devi, Manorama Devi, Surabala Devi, Sukeshi Devi, Kiranbala Devi and others—to stay at home. They trouped out and gathered in the walkway shaded by the sal trees to advance, step by step, towards the precincts of the 'Santiniketan' house. There the rehearsal of the play *Falguni* (The Early Spring) was taking place on the first floor. They picked up their ears and listened to the acting instructions given by Tagore for *Falguni*. Soon the absorbing choral song: 'Let's go, let's go, let's go away—leaving the lit-up lamp on the wayside under the open skies; we'd play our wayfaring song, scatter forth the wayfarer's laughter and fly aloft the banner of our colourful clothes in water and on earth' would commence.

The wives lost hold of their patience, noiselessly walked up the stairs to the first floor and stood transfixed on one corner of the darkened veranda. In spellbound surprise and with thumping hearts, they witnessed Tagore singing: 'Let's go, let's go, let's go away'.

And traipsing forward in dance rhythms, following behind him with dancing steps, were the youthful contingent that comprised the *Falguni* actors—Dinendranath Tagore, Ajit Chakrabarty, Kshitimohan Sen, Kalimohan, Santosh Mitra, Santosh Mazumdar, Asit Halder—and a few other residents of the Ashram. What a lovely scene it made! What a colourful gathering! We used to listen to this story from our mothers as a fairy tale.

We also heard from our mothers the stories of Tagore essaying the role of the blind *baul* and showing others the way, while singing: 'Slowly, my friend, slowly lead me to your lonely temple'.

We used to hear about Tagore's ethereal dance as the blind *baul* playing an *ektara* in hand and leading others with songs on his lips: 'Let me surrender my all to the One to whom everyone is giving away their belongings; let me open up on my own, before I am told and beseeched...The spring has woven me its garland of triumph; it has let loose a blazing southern breeze into my soul'.

The stories of how Tagore danced his extraordinary dance with these lilting songs—bearing the dancing resonance of waters spouting from Gangotri—would come down to us in our early childhood. We could eerily listen to them and our minds would then begin to jump in joy with those dancing rhythms... .

Ashram's Indulgent Guardians

The first couple of decades of the Ashram (from 1901–21) were fraught with resistance against dance from the teachers themselves, who came to stay and study there, let alone the guardians of the pupils. When Tagore introduced the Manipuri teacher Nabakumar (see Chapter 6), there were adverse remarks in the Ashram mouthpiece that the boys were learning musical gymnastics to the tune of *mridanga*!

Again, when he attempted to teach dance to girls—almost a first, in India—the early magazines would carry sarcastic remarks: 'Rabindranath Tagore must be getting old. It is learnt that he has opened dance classes for women in Visva-Bharati. What is this education that he is imparting to the simple-hearted and socially inexperienced girls?' Even many teachers were averse to let their wards being called for dance rehearsals and although they were unable to prevent it, they often made caustic comments—in words and in writings.

In these years, between Tagore at forty and sixty, he made unceasing efforts to let dance be accepted as part of the academic discipline and a source of pure enjoyment. Slowly the resistance melted away and gradually dance was accepted as a valid form of self-expression, thanks to the Poet's endeavour. While appreciation grew, it was quite another matter when Tagore proposed to take the girls as performers in his outstation tours. It went to the redounding credit of the parents and guardians at the Ashram to repose their entire faith in Tagore and allow their female wards to go out to different parts of the country for performance and fund-raising missions. Such help and kind support must have been invaluable for Tagore to fulfil his mission and give full expression to his abiding creative genius outside Santiniketan.

Ashram's Foreigner Aficionados

Tagore attracted many well-qualified foreigners to Santiniketan: some for brief visits and others for extended assignments, almost all of whom later became part of the school faculty. These visits could be by virtue of Visva-Bharati's wide academic and cultural mandate, or for the lure of personally working with Tagore, or due to the sheer attraction of Tagore's persona. Several foreign students also enrolled in Santiniketan for studies from time to time. Again it was the magnetic power of Tagore's works and the Poet's unique way of enthusing them, if not providing only the background (or just innate flair) for dance, that made some of them participate in dance-related roles, add new colours and even earn success!

In 1914, *Achalayatan* (The Frozen Citadel; see Chapter 4) was staged in Santiniketan where William Pearson not only danced with abandon as one of the under-privileged tribals, *Shonpangshus*, with a distinct Western touch with the Poet's express consent, but taught under his vigil. In 1916, Pearson again danced for *Falguni* (see Chapter 4). Pearson was not merely Tagore's friend and an early resident of Santiniketan, but he also occasionally helped out as Tagore's secretary and accompanied him in foreign tours.

In 1923, *Vasanta* (The Spring) was staged in Kolkata where the last song was earmarked for a collective dance in entirely free style. The song: 'O the wayfarer, O the lover, separation will consummate your fractured union; come all, join in the grand celebration of the music of dissolution' was the only one in the whole play calling for dance.

While all the actors, young and old, romped and jumped and danced on the stage, Tagore himself joined in the dance and held hands with Leonard Elmhirst. The two of them were in such a jubilant mood that everybody was highly inspired, creating a very lively atmosphere. Elmhirst (see Chapter 1) was not merely the founder of 'Sriniketan' in 1921, but also—with his multimillionaire wife—its largest donor.

In 1931, Dr Harry Timbers and his wife came into Santiniketan's dance scene, with their background in Russian folk dances. While Timbers was into academics, Ms Timbers gave her time to initiate Santidev into her dance style, as witnessed later in a dance celebrating *Maghi* (full moon) in February. In the same year, owing to Santidev's sudden illness, Timbers was inducted by Tagore to do the male protagonist's role in *Shap Mochan*. As Timbers had no grounding in Bengali, Tagore painstakingly translated Aruneshvar's songs into English and using Timbers' background in other European dances as well as Russian folk dances, the Poet initiated him to inculcate *bhava* so that there could be both miming and dance with the protagonist's songs. The result was very rewarding and Timbers succeeded in introducing an altogether new flavour to the evolution of dance in Santiniketan.

There were notable dance inputs from some foreign students too. In 1926, the Dutch girl, Hjordis, was on board the ship with Tagore and his family on their return journey home and, in keeping with the Poet's penchant for naming persons, Tagore called her 'Haimanti': much to her liking. Once she joined Santiniketan, she learnt Bengali—from none other than the Poet—and was induced by Tagore to learn Manipuri dance along with other girls. One of her first forays into dance was with the Tagore song: 'Her anklets are ringing on and their resonance tells me I do know her', which proved to be a success. Ever since, she participated in all dances along with other Ashram girls and developed a

Natir Puja: *Tagore as Upali and Gouri as Nati lying at his feet.*

knack for expressing the poems' mood very well, with the advantage of Tagore personally explaining her the meanings and nuances. Once she was urged by Tagore to compose a dance with his famous poem 'Dussamay'— 'Even though the evening is descending slowly and all songs have been signalled to cease' —and out of concern for perfection, he had the poem repeated to her several times by Amiya Chakrabarti (her future husband)! The dance eventually passed off well to Tagore's immense liking.

Another foreign girl, Karen (named 'Karuna' by Tagore), accompanied Haimanti in 1927 in the play named *Natir Puja* (see Chapter 4) in the dance scene as *pratiharini* or the royal female guards at Tagore's specific instance. The duo, with their statuesque lissome figures, registered an impressive presence. Karuna later married Arnold Adrian Bake, the musicologist for Tagore songs in Santiniketan. Elizabeth Sass Brunner, a Hungarian girl (who was an ace painter and had joined Santiniketan on an impulse, having 'seen' Tagore in a dream), also was a dancer known for her dance with the Tagore song: 'I recognise you, O the foreign maiden; you are a denizen from beyond the high seas'.

Since Santidev's trips to Sri Lanka (then Ceylon), there were many students who had come to Santiniketan for studies. Anangalal was a student well versed in Kandyan dance who came from Sri Lanka in 1938, when the dance-drama *Shyama* (see Chapter 8 for its blend of many dance-forms) was staged. Essaying the role of Kotal, he executed a heroic dance in Kandyan style. Towards the end of the scene of Uttiyo getting killed, he would jump vigorously upon the hapless youth brandishing a sword and the lights would go off instantly, leaving a deep impact on the spectators. Incidentally, dance with open sword was an innovation for Kandyan style too. Anangalal also did the curd-seller's role in *Chandalika* (see Chapter 8), after making his Kandyan style a little softer. Many Kandyan troupes continued to visit Santiniketan in the later years.

In 1940, Maki, a Japanese youth, was studying dance and instrumental music in Santiniketan. When *Chitrangada* (see Chapter 8) was being staged, he was asked to do the role of Madan (the Cupid) and was urged to use the ancient dance forms of Japan—Noh and Kabuki—with the songs of Madan. Maki also did the role of the curd-seller in *Chandalika* (see Chapter 8). Tagore, Nandalal, Pratima Devi and other residents of Santiniketan were very impressed with his Japanese mode of dance. Since Maki was conversant with European forms, he blended some Western touches as well. Maki's stay in Santiniketan had a sad end as, at the peak of World War II, in 1941, he was put under house arrest by the colonial police and was deported later to Japan.

The practice of the foreign students participating in dance at Santiniketan was a continued one and there were many who kept up the tradition. They included a Malaysian girl, trained in European ballet, who danced with some of Tagore's songs and etched the role of Madan in *Chitrangada*; an American girl, trained in Thai dance, who also did Madan's role; and a Javanese youth, Sukarna, from Tamanshishya School in Java, who was also associated with the dance movement in Santiniketan.

Ashram's Ace Catalyst—Pratima Devi

It was to Tagore that the world of literary and performing arts owes their outstanding oeuvre of music drama, recitative drama and finally dance-drama, but it was Pratima Devi, his vastly talented daughter-in-law, who single-handedly prodded him and provided him with a most sincere initiative and abiding enthusiasm to see them come to fruition. In the last fifteen–sixteen years of Tagore's life, the Poet was motivated to create his incomparable performative works and it is quite doubtful if he would have undertaken this venture without Pratima Devi playing the catalytic agent.

Pratima was herself not a dancer and had only a rudimentary training in Manipuri dance from Nabakumar Singha, in June 1927, when she was staying in Shillong with Tagore—perhaps just enough to give her an insight into the dance. But she was the prime mover in not merely suggesting new themes to Tagore, but also in making the preliminary planning for what would later flower—from Tagore's pen—into a full-fledged work ready for performance. Even in the rehearsals, while the main aim would always be to structure dance on the songs in the drama and Santidev would instruct the dance teachers how to frame the compositions, it would be Pratima who would supervise the whole affair. Only the finished product would be shown to Tagore for his final touches, for he would always have the last word.

There was also the question of finesse. For instance, in Tagore's dance-dramas, Kathakali or Manipuri styles were used, but always without their respective costumes, facial make-up or the veil, as typically used in Manipuri dance. Only the nature of characters dictated the relevant costumes and décor. Pratima would ordain bright stage and gorgeous costume for *Chitrangada*, whereas *Chandalika* would deserve an overall rustic mood and village ambience. While this followed common sense, the ultimate subtlety—even after Santidev or Atamba Singh had taught the item—was according to her dictates. For example, that the song: 'My companion, what's that touch of light that radiates on my eyes' would need a sitting posture with head lowered at the beginning, but would call for rising up gradually with outstretched hands and with a radiant face later on was something which only she would decide.

Pratima's catalytic role in Tagore's creativity could be best illustrated from the few events narrated below.

■ In 1926, arrangements were on to celebrate Tagore's birthday and since Tagore was away from Santiniketan, there was little chance of getting a new play from him. Pratima was planning to do a mime performance based on his poem *Pujarini* (inspired by the annals from the Buddhist *Abadanshataka*, about a legend on the killing of a female worshipper at the Buddhist stupa in the ongoing Hindu–Buddhist confrontations). As Tagore returned by chance, Pratima appealed to him to do a new play with only female characters that could be enacted on Tagore's birthday. In the middle of the communal violence rampant then—which pained Tagore no end—the Poet took the peg of the *Pujarini* theme and went ahead to pen *Natir Puja* (see Chapter 4). The rest is history.

■ Again in 1929, *Sundar* (The Beautiful, see Chapter 7) was staged in Kolkata as a new song-and-dance ensemble act (different from the previous *Sundar* of 1925), for which Pratima guided all the dances with Dinendranath directing music. Tagore, despite his ill health, arrived from Santiniketan and made a few minor alterations and the ensemble was performed in public.

■ Later in 1929, when Tagore produced his prose-play *Tapati* in Kolkata, there were songs by Bipasha, the companion of the female protagonist Sumitra. Pratima took over the responsibility of arranging dances by the Ashram girls to accompany all of Bipasha's songs like: 'Look at the thief come to pilfer the light, where are you all who'd conquer the darkness'; 'Wake up, O the terrible One, we can't bear any longer the prevailing dark webs strung by slumber'; and the famous ditties like: 'When you executed your terrible dance of deluge, oblivious of everything, O the master dancer [Shiva], your matted hair furled down unfettered' and 'Your throne is vacant today, O my hero, come and take its possession; do look at the whole world trembling in your anticipation'.

■ In 1930, Pratima accompanied Tagore, with the rest of the family, on his UK tour. They stayed for a while at the Dartington Hall, established by Elmhirst—Tagore's Santiniketan cohort—following the Poet's ideals. Since the school had good arrangements to teach ballet, Pratima made an in-depth study of its teaching methodology for dance. In particular, Pratima was keen to learn how a dance theme was structured in different parts; how instrumental music was composed for dance; and how a ballet teacher integrated that music with dance choreography and action. This helped her considerably to modulate the dance teaching process in Santiniketan later on (see Chapter 8).

■ In 1931, Pratima arranged *Shishu Tirtha* (The Child; see Chapter 3) through music and dance and did the entire planning. Her initial idea was to showcase Tagore's 'The Child' in English through mime action along with dance. Tagore took over, rendered the poem into Bengali and divided it into ten stanzas, more or less following its European version that was done in ballet form. This was another consummate success story.

■ In 1933, Pratima selected out of Tagore's *Galpoguchchha*, the collection of short stories, a story called 'Ekta Ashadhe Galpa' (A Cock-and-Bull Story) that describes an isolated island inhabited by card-like creatures who follow strict rules and rites to the hilt and whose strictly disciplined existence is suddenly dislocated by three shipwrecked youths—jolting them back to human normalcy. Pratima intended to use only girl students who knew dance to enact the story through dance and mime. Perhaps inspired by her exposure to the Dartington methodology, she made out an elaborately written plan: dividing the story into a few scenes, narrating the storyline for each scene and outlining the process of each scene's visualisation through dance

Tasher Desh:
Deriving inspiration from the stage.

with Tagore songs. Following the earlier Santiniketan practice, her idea was that the text would be recited by a narrator (probably by Tagore himself) and dances would be used for all the songs.

■ Pratima's structured format was a wake-up call for Tagore's ever-alert creative instinct! Once her notebook reached the Poet, he took one long look at it and called for the poem 'Vanijye Vasati Lakshmi' (the Goddess of Wealth Resides in Commerce) from *Sanchayita*, his collection of select poetry. Obviously, Tagore's writing acumen worked overtime and by the second day, the fifteen-page draft for a brand new play, later named: *Tasher Desh* (see Chapter 8), saw the light of the day. The poem—around the same theme as the story selected earlier—had obviously suited Tagore quite well for quickly transforming the text into songs. Melodies were set forthwith and rehearsals started without ado by the Poet: with boys and girls selected by him to enact the male and female roles. This was the genesis of what went on to become what is considered one of the most successful of Tagore's musical dramas.

■ In early January 1936, Pratima chose *Chitrangada*, to be enacted through dance by the female students. Again, akin to the Dartington approach, she made out a formal structure by detailing the story into six scenes, filled with song and dance that captured the essence of Tagore's theme, namely, the awakening of femininity in Chitrangada, dressed as a male, while gazing at Arjuna; the latter's refusal to accept Chitrangada as she was and her dogged meditation to the God of Love; the union of the lovers with Chitrangada's changed femininity; Arjuna's distraction; and the final union of the lovers without any pretences at the end. Once Tagore was persuaded to compose songs for Pratima's plan of action, he became enthusiastic to create a completely new dance-drama and began working on the play from January second week. Songs cascaded one after the other and the dance choreography was completed by the beginning of February 1936: barely within a month!

■ In 1935, Pratima had selected the Tagore poem 'Samanya Kshati' (The Minor Loss) about the whimsical queen setting up a bonfire out of the peasants' huts to warm her body after a river bath and being punished by the enraged king to re-build the same huts solely on her own. When she requested the Poet to compose a song for the queen's bath, hence came the song: 'I can hear in my mind's ears, every moment, the call of fathomless waters', followed by a fast-tempo *antara*: 'Waves have broken on the waters, like the waves they're surging in my innermost mind'. In 1936, Tagore had it added to *Chitrangada* for a tumultuous dance effect. There was indeed a rare resonance of mind between Pratima and the Poet!

■ In August–September 1936, Pratima chose another Tagore poem 'Parishodh' (the Redress) for a sequel of song, mime and dance, and submitted it to Tagore. Initially the Poet had confined himself to compose songs, but soon he changed his mind and turned the story around in his own way, added songs and made it a full-fledged dance-drama—*Shyama* (see Chapter 8). The story hinged on a handsome stranger falsely accused of a royal theft; the beautiful courtesan taking a fancy to him and making her youthful lover sacrifice himself in place of the stranger; and eventually, spurning the courtesan's amours. This was yet another brilliant dance-drama from Tagore's stable that germinated from Pratima's initial sketch of ideas!

■ In early 1938, Pratima took up Tagore's prose-play *Chandalika* (originally inspired by *Shardula Karnavadana* from the Buddhist literature in Nepal) and was keen on depicting it through dance. In the original story, Ananda, the disciple of the Buddha, feels thirsty one afternoon while returning to the *vihara* and seeks water to drink from an untouchable girl. The latter falls for the handsome Ananda and urges her mother to use her magic to pull the Buddha's disciple to her. This happens and when the girl prepares the bed for the union, the Buddha rescues his agonised disciple from the predicament. Tagore had sublimated it into the girl repenting her carnal desire and even convincing the girl's mother to eventually follow the Buddha's path.

■ Again, Pratima arranged the play, a la Dartington process, into a few scenes and wrote them precisely down in her notebook to indicate how each portion would be enacted through dance. She later used white cards, of postcard size, to break the scenes into smaller parts and draw them out in colour. Her visualisation comprised: the market-place and the festive dances there among the Santhals with the protagonist Prakriti; her mother's intervention, followed by Prakriti's dance to draw water from the well; the arrival of the Buddhist *bhikshus* and the last one seeking drinking water; and rhythmical mime-action of Prakriti giving water after the initial hesitation and the monk's assurance on their common humanity. Pratima had conceived this far and Tagore—after looking at her manuscript—decided to convert it into a full-length dance-drama, starting then to compose songs. Interestingly, Tagore took the creative action as a willing imposition by his daughter-in-law and, later, awaited her arrival for the ultimate *manjuri*—so strong was the bond of creative understanding between the two!

■ By the end of 1938, Pratima urged Tagore to change the half-century-old *Mayar Khela* opera (see Chapter 3) into a complete dance-drama and the ever-affectionate Poet abided by this request to 'reform' the play, change some 'immature' portions and add new songs, often composing several each day, for days together. The older play had songs for every character, which were changed; some lyrics were altered; some characters were brought down in importance; and a few male characters were planned to be reduced. There were many incipient difficulties, as a result of which only its first part was staged in 1939, and the rest given up. This was the last foray of the exemplary 'networking' between Pratima and the Poet, never repeated afterwards.

Ashram's Prime Sparkler—Santidev Ghosh

Santidev was the 'dancer extraordinaire' of Santiniketan all his life. Brought as a mere stripling, he matured and spent his total career here. All along, although an outstanding singer, a first-rate actor and highly conversant with a variety of musical instruments, he was—first and foremost—a dancer, a choreographer as well as a dance teacher. Above all, he had the extraordinary ability to literally 'soak up' disparate styles of dance from widely diverse sources both in India and abroad, and was supremely confident to mould as well as modulate the prevalent dance forms in Santiniketan to bring about a new lustre and sparkle in them.

In the above sense, he was an abiding asset to Tagore who could implicitly and explicitly trust Santidev to bring in the best in dance—from wherever and whenever available—that would suit Santiniketan's innate genius and utilise him to take the legacy forward. If Pratima was the catalytic agent at the creative end of Tagore's mind, Santidev was the kindling agent at the performative end of his creativity: as the terpsichorean torch-bearer of whatever had to be expressed and delivered. One could almost say that had Pratima and Santidev not been there, one would have to invent the duo for Santiniketan and Tagore!

While Santidev was dancing away all his growing years in childhood and early adolescence in the Ashram milieu, it again needed the synergy between Pratima and Santidev: to let the latter bloom in formal dance. It so happened in 1927 that Pratima was directing *Rituranga* (The Playful Domain of Seasons, see Chapter 7) and young Amita Sen was preparing, under her baton, the storm dance for the song: 'O my heart, there comes probably the early cyclone of summer; the ecstasy of tearing away fences is descending with its orgiastic abandon'. It did seem that the storm's momentum was not coming through in the dance and Santidev—as the main singer but only an onlooker for the dance—was giving armchair advice to Amita how to dance. Amita, although junior in age, remonstrated volubly and challenged him to dance on stage and prove his worth! Santidev responded in heated words, but Pratima picked up the idea quickly and called upon Santidev to dance in partnership with Amita. The *pas de deux* worked remarkably well and, for Santidev, there was no looking back since.

As subsequent chapters would recount, Santidev was the heart and soul of the entire dance evolution in Santiniketan and he was associated in all dance-related productions from the very beginning to end: either as chief producer or as choreographer or as adviser to the classical dance teachers or as the counsellor for the finished productions. These were besides his frequent assumption of direct roles as principal dancer, singer or instrument player, on 'as needed' basis—all under the direct care of Tagore. The following illustrative summary of Santidev's dance career (detailed in Chapters 4, 5, 6 and 7) would be illuminating:

Left and facing page: Santidev Ghosh: The virtuoso dancer in Kandyan style.

■ His exposure to Baul dance, in 1924 and 1925, when he was fourteen or fifteen years old, on the festive grounds of Kenduli in Birbhum was seminal—imbibing their stepping rhythms and body postures.

Later in 1931, he learnt some vigorous dances: Raibenshe of Birbhum and Jari of Mymensingh districts.

■ Until 1931, he learnt dance at his own volition. From 1931 onwards, he was associated with composing dance for Tagore's songs. But the enthusiasm for learning new dances continued undiminished in his mind, alongside his desire to experiment, blending them with Tagore's meters and rhythms. He received Tagore's unstinted support in such efforts.

■ Tagore encouraged him to visit new places to learn new dance forms and utilise them to interpret his songs. This helped to enrich the dance tradition of Santiniketan.

■ He was first associated with Manipuri dance in 1920 and took no respite from his learning practices of the form till 1940.

■ He began learning Kathakali dance (really a dance theatre) and a few other folk forms of Kerala. For this purpose, he made three trips to Kerala—in 1931, 1932 and 1937.

■ He made four trips to Sri Lanka between 1936 and 1938, in close proximity to each other, to learn the virile and masculine Kandyan dance of that country.

■ In 1937, he stayed for a month in the capital Yangon (then Rangoon) of Myanmar to learn hand gestures and movements from an aged local dancer.

■ In 1939, he stayed for three months, from May onwards, in Indonesia (then Java-Bali-Sumatra) to learn, first, the dance of the royal palace and, later, the popular dances of the Bali Island by staying there for another month.

■ There was, however, a clear caveat from Tagore in such learning and subsequent enrichment exercises. While absorbing dances from elsewhere within a limited time, Santidev was advised by the Poet to concentrate only on their rhythms and footsteps. Here was Tagore's specific instruction excerpted from a letter:

> Complete learning of the dances from the other regions would take considerable time. But picking up a few (significant) gestures may not be a difficult task. This is because it will do more harm than good, if we try to imitate the others in order to supplant our own dances...

Santidev followed religiously Tagore's words and always attempted first to assimilate in himself forms like India's Manipuri and Kathakali, Kandyan of Sri Lanka, Ram Poye of Myanmar and varied dances of Java and Bali, and then, use them in dance compositions in Santiniketan.

■ The other onerous task that Santidev continually carried out was to compose dance according to the mood and feelings that Tagore's songs evoked. He had this responsibility since 1931, starting from *Natir Puja*. Again from 1934 to 1940, he had to train the Manipuri teachers as to how that style was to be adapted to Tagore's songs. This was also his given task for the Kathakali teachers. As regards to the group dances of Kerala taught by those teachers, he had to arrange the dances sequentially according to the lines of Tagore's songs so that they would not be forgotten later in the absence of the mentors. For all the foreign students (mentioned earlier), he had to mould their latent dancing talents (for Noh, Kabuki, ballet and so on) to the needs of the song and the characters of a particular dance-drama.

■ Finally, in his trips to Sri Lanka, Myanmar and elsewhere, Santidev was always the 'ambassador' of Tagore's dances—performing himself or teaching the locals to perform, often colouring these dances strongly with the local fervour and flavour. Apart from the fact that it was no mean achievement (considering the time usually available at his disposal), Santidev was an incredible multi-tasking persona!

The above account does not dilate the contribution of the Indian students at the Ashram towards Tagore's dance movement. Among four of them, the first was Srimati Devi (Thakur) who came from a rich family of Ahmedabad and joined Visva-Bharati in 1920 at Kala Bhavan. She was intimately connected with all dances from *Shesh Varshan* (The Last Rains) to *Nataraj* (The Lord of Dance) performances. In 1927, she went to Germany and learnt European 'Modern Dance' as established by Rudolf von

Above and below: Drawings by Ramendra Nath Chakraborty.

Laban (of famous 'Labanotation'; see Chapter 12), Merry Wigman and Kurt Juss. On return in 1930, she went to Darjeeling and danced to a Tagore poem 'Jhulan' as recited by the Poet, who also was present, in 1931.

Varsha Mangal (name changed to Geetotsav) saw Vasudevan—the talented Kala Bhavan student from Chennai who was conversant with rudimentary Bharatanatyam—perform to the song: 'O the clean and the incandescent one, all salutations go to you! O the gentle and the serene one, all salutations go to you!' This was followed by the celebrated *Shishu Tirtha* (The Child) with Tagore's reading touched off by Srimati dancing 'in her own style', followed by Vasudevan dancing with the song: 'We salute you, salute you and salute you, O the cruel one, for your endless mercies' and Srimati coming back dancing after the seventh and eighth stanzas for the two songs: 'There will be victory, only victory, and nothing but victory' and 'Who's the one who drives us crazy'.

In the late 1930s, Bharatanatyam and Kathak were the two emerging classical styles to which Tagore was privy only in the last few years of his life. Yet he was receptive enough to let Mrinalini Swaminathan (nee Sarabhai), a trained Bharatanatyam dancer, dance in her own style in *Shyama* as the protagonist and in *Chandalika* as mother, before she left for Indonesia and later for the USA. As regards Kathak, it was Asha Ojha, the talented Kathak dancer from the North, who was a sensation in the role of Uttiya for the dance-drama *Shyama*. They were only 'flashes in the pan' for Tagore.

On the whole, Santiniketan provided Tagore a favourable milieu: with Mother Nature's uninhibited exuberance, with students eager to follow his lead in song and dance, with teachers and guardians—over a period of time—lending him full indulgence, with visitors from abroad to fall in line and absorb the ambience and with Pratima Devi and Santidev Ghosh extending rock-steady support. Tagore was unmistakably a Titan, but the environment in which he manifested his genius was also all set to foster his creativity in whichever way he chose. Not all maestros in all times and climes—in recorded history—have received such a fostering atmosphere and Tagore was fortunate to receive all-round approbation and accolade in his creative growth, in all the four decades he lived in and nourished Santiniketan.

Biographical Notes

Santidev Ghosh (1910–2000)

Santidev Ghosh, the great exponent of Tagore's music and dance, was a legendary figure in his lifetime. The story of his dedication to understand the works of Rabindranath Tagore, particularly his music and dance, survives in the history of Bengali culture as an instance of what specialisation is and how difficult are the ways to lead on to that stiff target. Santidev was brought to Kolkata from Santiniketan as a child where he lived eighty-nine years of his life shaping up his career as a musician, writer and performer. Santidev was born in 1910 in Bajapti village, now in Bangladesh. Kalimohan Ghosh, a hard-core Swadeshi activist came close to Tagore and helped him materialise the Sriniketan concept. Kalimohan brought his son Santimoy to Santiniketan for a visit when he was six months of age. Tagore affectionately changed the middle part of his name and called him 'Santidev' instead of 'Santimoy'.

Settled in Santiniketan, Santidev revealed excellence in music at an early age. Tagore asked his father to educate Santi in music and himself shared some responsibility of training him. The illustrious Dinendranath Tagore also trained him in the art of singing Tagore songs. He learned Hindustani classical music from Bhim Rao Shastri who came to Santiniketan as a classical music teacher.

Santidev had a keen fascination for dance. Rabindranath took interest in this aspect of his talent, because he really required a dependable exponent of the concept of dance which he was going to build. Santidev began to take lessons on dance from 1926. Tagore sent him to South India in 1931 to learn the art of Kathakali dance. He spent three years, 1937–39, in Sri Lanka, Burma and Indonesia to learn Kandyan dance and the dance forms of Java and Bali.

In 1930, he was appointed as music teacher in Visva-Bharati, the university founded by Tagore as an extended version of his Santiniketan school. Santidev became the director of the Sangeet Bhavan in 1939. He was made the principal of the Sangeet Bhavan in 1945 and he held tenure between 1946–68 and again 1971–73. He retired in 1974. As Visva-Bharati was made a central university of India, Santidev was appointed the head of the department of Tagore music and dance. Afterwards he worked with the University Grant Commission for two years as a research fellow. The Government of India conferred the Padmabhushan on him in 1984. The same year, the Visva-Bharati awarded him with its highest title: Deshikottama.

Apart from his autobiography, Santidev Ghosh wrote many important books on Tagore's music and dance. In fact, his works made ready the background for Tagore's music and dance criticism. Santidev was one of those rare scholars as well as performers whose only object of life-long attention was Tagore alone. He was taught and brought up by Tagore and lived a long chequered life for his sake only.

Initially Santidev's activities as teacher and performer were limited to the environment of Santinikaten. But after the birth centenary of Tagore in 1961, he was introduced to the larger environment as a great performer of Tagore's songs. The wealth of his voice and his great insight into the aesthetics of Tagore compositions was greatly felt by his listeners all around.

Pratima Devi (1893–1969)

Pratima was the daughter of Binayini Devi, sister of Gaganendranath and Abanindranath Tagore. Brought up in a family of artists, Pratima developed a keen aesthetic sense. If as a child she imbibed artistic qualities from her family; as the daughter-in-law, she developed her mental and spiritual faculties with guidance from Rabindranath Tagore. He personally looked after her education, recommending books for her to read. His letters to the young bride show how anxious he was that her personality should outgrow the narrow mould within which women were held.

Pratima was one of the first students of the Bichitra club and studio. She learnt painting from Nandalal Bose and this interest in art remained with her till the end. Accompanying Rabindranath and her husband Rathindranath, she had travelled to many distant places. She would try and learn a new craft wherever she went and would incorporate these into the curriculum at Shilpa Sadan.

She assisted Rabindranath in the production of dance-dramas and plays. She was always consulted when a stage was being designed for a performance.

After Manmayee*, Tagore never went back to pure Western dance, but moved forward to successive generations (and unique blends) of 'free movement', classical dance, South-Pacific dance and finally to new idioms of dance-drama*

European Fount

Tagore's dance consciousness had a cross-cultural dimension from the very beginning. But while he had sound training and consistent exposure to quality music since his childhood (see Chapter 10); he had no such luck in dance. Nevertheless, as a teenager during his eighteen-month stay in England, in 1878–80, he came in touch with the British urban society and picked up Western social dances of the time. That he attained some success in learning these forms is recorded in his own memoirs.

Tagore recounts that he tried his hand in such esoteric dance forms as Galop and Lancer. During dance invitations on particular occasions, he danced his best (or not quite his best), depending on the suitability of his female partners, apart from his own predilections. Interestingly, both Galop and Lancer were pretty fast-paced dances and needed considerable skill, which on Tagore's own admission, he seemed to have acquired. But, as to what prevented him to learn—and excel in—more slow-paced easier dances like Waltz, one can only speculate.

Western Dance Milieu in Tagore's Time

Galop

Galop was named after the fastest running gait of a horse (that is, gallop). A lively country dance introduced in the Parisian society in the 1820s, it became popular in Vienna, Berlin, as well as London, where Tagore had learnt the form. The steps combined a *glissade* (sliding step of the ballet) with a *chasse* (hurried pursuit) on alternate feet, ordinarily in a fast 2/4 time, in the same closed position as in Waltz. The Galop was a forerunner of the Polka, introduced in Prague ballrooms in the 1830s and made fashionable in Paris in the 1840s. The Galop was particularly popular as the final dance of the evening. The post-Horn Galop, for instance, was first introduced in London in 1844 and became a way to indicate that the dancing at a Ball or wedding reception has ended. Numerous Galops had been composed by Waltz king Johann Strauss II.

Lancer

The elegance and rich tradition of the Polish military was brought to stage in this spectacular and beautiful suite of dances. The men dressed in their full military regalia and the women in their elegant Empire dresses re-lived a grand ball in honour of the Polish Lancers who would be off at sunrise to the battlegrounds. The steps comprised, first, a stately Polonez performed to the music of Fryderyk Chopin followed by a romantic Waltz also by Chopin, with the suite finishing with a fiery Mazur; in fact, the last Mazur before the Lancers must leave for battle. Polonez, the Polish national Grand March, was Poland's oldest dance in 5/4 times, dating back to the fifteenth century.

Mazur

The Mazur was also one of the Polish national dances that originated in the plains of central Poland. Later, the nobility embraced and polished the Mazur when it reached the palaces and spread to European courts. In a still more refined form, it was adopted by the ballet and was an inspiration for many composers. Chopin's Mazurkas were the most striking examples. As a social dance, it reached its peak of popularity during the nineteenth century and was made part of the Lancer's suite.

Waltz

Waltz was a dance born in Vienna suburbs and the Alpine region of Austria. While Waltz was danced in the ballrooms of the royal court in the seventeenth century, Weller or the turning dances were danced by peasants in Austria and Bavaria even before that time. By the end of the eighteenth century, the 3/4 rhythm was here to stay. However popular Waltz was, opposition was not lacking. First, dancing masters saw Waltz as a threat to the profession, as the basic steps of Waltz could be learnt in a relatively short time, whereas the minute, complex postures and deportment of other court dances required considerable practice. Second, Waltz was criticised on moral grounds by those who were opposed to its closer hold and rapid turning movements. Religious leaders almost unanimously regarded it as vulgar and sinful, and in England—a land of strict Victorian morals—Waltz was accepted still more slowly.

In 1816, Waltz was included in a ball given in London by the Prince Regent. A blistering editorial followed in the venerable *Times*:

> We remark with pain that the indecent foreign dance, called the Waltz, was introduced in the English court... It is quite sufficient to cast one's eyes on the voluptuous intertwining

> of the limbs and closed pressure on the bodies in their dance, to see that it is indeed far removed from the modest reserve...hitherto considered distinctive of English females. So long as this obscene display was confined to prostitutes and adulteresses, we did not think it deserving of notice; but now... we feel it a duty to warn every parent against exposing his daughter to so fatal a contagion...

Even as late as 1866, the English magazine *Belgravia* stated:

> We who go forth at nights and see without the slightest discomfiture our sister and our wife seized upon by a strange man and subjected to violent embraces and cantering round a small-sized apartment...

But as history repeats itself, the antagonism only served to increase the popularity of Waltz and Paris alone had nearly seven hundred dance halls for Waltz in the early nineteenth century! Around the close of the nineteenth century—nearer Tagore's time—two modifications came up. The first was Boston—an even slower Waltz with long gliding steps—and the second was the Hesitation—taking step to three beats of the measure.

Tagore's Choice of Western Dance

Tagore could not have been unfamiliar with the prevailing easy-paced and vastly popular Waltz, but would have given it a long rope for its mute tone of social disapproval. This is despite the fact (and he would have been scarcely unaware of it) that Queen Victoria, the reigning queen, had been a keen and expert ballroom dancer who had a special love for Waltz! Whatever the reason, the act of forsaking Waltz would perhaps be understandable, yet the fact that he chose to learn more complex postures, some elaborate suites and far faster forms of Galop and Lancer would only prove that he must have had a passion, attended by stamina, for such dances. If anything, this early taste for highly structured dance would put a stamp on his life-long love affair for dance, even amidst myriad other preoccupations! After returning from England, he immediately applied his Western dance skills to a song he wrote: 'Come, the ladies' maids, let's hold hands and dance round and round' for *Manmayee* (1880)—a play written by his brother Jyotirindranath—and choreographed as a dance. The play was performed once again in 1889, now under a changed name *Punarvasanta*, and Tagore taught the ladies' maids the same song and dance—with the clapping of hands—at the rehearsals.

Interestingly, after *Manmayee*, Tagore never went back to pure Western dance, but moved forward to successive generations (and unique blends) of 'free movement', classical dance, South-Pacific dance and finally to new idioms of dance-drama. As we shall see, this was, in essence, an evolutionary process in his dance thoughts that always opted for 'natural selection' for what seemed best to survive and suited available talents.

Tagore, Western Music and Herbert Spencer

The incredible variety in Rabindra Sangeet (Tagore songs, see Chapter 10) covered an enormous range of subjects of human interest. He brought into Bengali music, virtually single-handedly, songs of patriotic fervour, vigorous songs, battle songs, humorous songs, lamentations on death, celebration of marriage, welcome songs, welcome tributes, songs on rituals and festivities, songs on sowing and harvesting, songs on entering a new home and digging a tube-well, songs on ironsmith, songs on tea drinking and playing games—in fact, songs for all seasons and every occasion. These songs seeped into his dramatic oeuvre, including musicals, recitative drama and eventually dance-drama, describing all situations and emotions.

One may note that music pivoting around human interests is typically a genre of Western origin. The Indian traditional music, in vivid contrast, thrives on a *sthayee bhava*, capturing the briefest of moods in an extraordinarily variegated exposition. This usually is a foray into the ineffable domain of boundless beauty of an individual pouring his heart out in near solitude that transcends all barriers of petty human concerns. The European songs and melodies, on the contrary, contribute to bring in daily-life realities far more into the domain of music than their Indian counterparts do.

Tagore's inspiration for the diversity of subjects, in all probability, came from his familiarity with the Western genres. Herbert Spencer (1820–1903), English sociologist and philosopher, was a single major influence on him and the intelligentsia of his time. The extract below catches a few of Spencer's seminal thoughts:

> Music is but an idealisation of the natural language of emotion: and that consequently music must be good or bad according as it conforms to the laws of this natural language. The various inflections of voice that which accompany feelings of different kinds and intensities are the germs out of which music is developed. It is demonstrable that the inflections and cadences are not accidental or arbitrary; but that they are determined by certain general principles of vital actions: and their expressiveness

Herbert Spencer: The inspiration behind Tagore's musical thoughts.

> depends on this, whence it follows that musical phrases and the melodies built of them, can be effective only when they are in harmony with these general principles...

These scientific principles were exemplified by Spencer as follows:

> The 'staccato', which is appropriate to energetic passages—to passages expressive of exhilaration, as well as of resolution and confidence.
>
> 'Slurred intervals' expressive of gentler and less active feelings...The difference of either resulting from difference of time in music is also attributable to the same law.
>
> More frequent changes in 'pitch' ordinarily resulting from passion are imitated and developed as song.
>
> The slowest movements, 'largo' and 'adagio' used where such depressing emotions as grief or such unexciting emotions as reverence, are to be portrayed, while the more rapid movements, 'presto', represent successfully increasing degrees of mental vivacity.

Tagore adopted and virtually re-wrote in Bengali the points brought up by Spencer. This was the time when he was busy writing *Valmiki Pratibha* and wrote in particular the following, in support of the characteristics of European music:

> When we weep, the contiguous notes have little interval between them. The weeping notes glide over the semi-tones and the melody is a very continuous one. When we laugh—ho, ho, ho, ho, there is no semi-tone in between, the neighbouring notes are apart from each other and the melody follows the stroke of rhythms. The *raga* of sorrow is a very slow-moving one like the night of melancholy; it has used the glide over semi-tones. And

Tagore as Valmiki in Valmiki Pratibha*: an artist's colourful impression.*

> the *raga* of contentment resembles the days of happiness, moving fast and skipping two or three notes. The boisterous joy arises spontaneously. We suddenly break into laughter and are not sure where it begins and where it ends. It does not fade away imperceptibly like weeping...
>
> Rapid rhythms are no doubt a means of expressing feelings, the rhythm must keep pace with the change in mood equally fast or slow—it is not necessary to maintain an even pace of rhythm at all...
>
> In the music drama which is recitative from the beginning to the end, rhythm must be skipped at specific times—otherwise the acting would not be effective...

This was the Western ideal that was kept upfront by Jyotirindranath when he was experimenting with music compositions based on *ragas* but on the piano during the period of *Valmiki Pratibha*. Tagore wrote:

> Jyoti-dada was busy in those days with the deliberate churning of classical music on the instrument of piano... Those melodies which normally are rendered at a slow pace would be played arbitrarily fast. That was a revolution adding extraordinary energy to them and would hugely move our heart. We clearly felt that the melodies were speaking to us in multiple voices...

While writing *Valmiki Pratibha*, Tagore acknowledged explicitly his indebtedness to Spencer and wrote: 'I wondered why I should not follow his ideas in letting the entire play be sung in different melodies for different moods and be expressed and enacted accordingly'. The only departure from Spencer was that the songs were not Western, but essentially based on Indian *ragas*. Tagore said further: 'This play is not an "opera", but "music drama", that is, a play which lets its theme to be enacted through melodies—but seldom bears the beauty of independent songs...'

Tagore, 'Music Drama' and Richard Wagner

Tagore's specific distinction drawn between opera and music drama was very prescient. European opera had earlier been entirely melody-dominated, an extended dramatic composition in which all parts were sung to instrumental accompaniment. Such singing normally comprised arias, choruses and recitatives. Out of them, an aria was an elaborate melody sung solo with accompaniment and a recitative was a style of vocal music intermediate between speaking and singing—for a passage or a part. All these were musical compositions with no doubt a text (mainly with sketchy religious themes), but not necessarily very dramatic in character.

Music drama, on the other hand, was primarily a play in which a clear storyline was interspersed with, or developed by songs, choruses and the recitatives. This form—adopted consciously by Tagore for both *Valmiki Pratibha* and *Kal Mrigaya* (1882)—was a distinct phenomenon set in motion by Richard Wagner (1813–83), the German composer, who brought a revolution in the world of European opera. As observed by critics (cited by Santidev Ghosh),

> He did give the world a new and perfect form of 'music drama'. He broke completely with older compositions according to which an 'opera' had been merely an opportunity for a few strong-lunged singers to see how they could juggle their high Cs while paying absolutely no attention to the text.

Wagner's music drama followed musically almost the same melodic theory of Spencer, as observed by the cognoscenti:

- Abolition of a set form (that is, ending as one began) and the use of any shape that the poem suggested.

- Absolute unity of the entire work; no division into songs, duets, choruses, with applause between and sometimes even encores; complete continuity from beginning to end.

- Music is always used to interpret the poetry. Its entire character is to be directed by words. 'In the wedding of the arts, poetry is the man, music the woman'; 'Poetry must lead, music must follow'; 'Music is the handmaid of poetry'—are a few of Wagner's aphorisms.

Richard Wagner: The German composer who gave the world the perfect form of 'music drama'.

- Abolition of mere tune and substitution of a melodic recitative, also known as the melos.

- Excellence of libretto. No book is fit to be used for the text of an opera unless it would be a successful drama by itself.

- Music, when united with poetical and dramatic literature, expresses everything of which it is capable.

Wagner, besides being a composer, was a conductor, theatre director and essayist—primarily known for his music dramas for which he wrote both scenario and librettos, very similar in temperament to Tagore. Wagner transformed through his idea of *Gesamkunstwerk* (total artwork) the synthesis of all poetic, visual, musical as well as dramatic arts, as was pre-eminently done by Tagore in his own oeuvre.

Wagner, even though while agreeing with Schopenhauer's doctrine that music had a supreme role among all the arts, strongly held that music in opera was subservient to the cause of drama. Music dramas remained his primary legacy, divided into three periods. His early-phase operas included *The Fairies* at the age of nineteen. His middle-phase output, considered to be of remarkably high quality, began to show his powers as a dramatist and composer, in works like *The Flying Dutchman*.

Wagner's late-phase operas were his masterpieces that advanced the art of opera, as in *Tristan and Isolde, The Mastersingers of Nuremberg* as well as the lengthiest opera still performed, *The Ring* (the latter, taking twenty-six years to complete, requires, in fact, fifteen hours to perform). Both his youthful work and later flowering were remarkably similar to Tagore's own!

Drawing largely from North European mythology and legends, Wagner exerted a strong influence on the operatic medium and his music drama fused together all the musical and dramatic elements. Wagner wrote his own libretti, referred to as poems, akin to Tagore. Both Wagner and Tagore achieved astonishing levels of emotional expression and introduced new ideas of musical form, including elaborate chromaticism (with scales ascending or descending by semi-tones). Both successfully explored the limits of the traditional tonal system.

Tagore's Opera Trilogy

As mentioned before, both *Valmiki Pratibha* and *Kal Mrigaya* were composed following clearly the tenets of Wagnerian music drama, with dialogue passages as recitatives (expressed between speaking and singing). Operatic music in both plays—strung around many singing styles and woven with many *ragas*—created entirely new paradigms of Bengali music drama, tightly knit around dramatic themes. The first play is the saga of a dreaded dacoit who rampages the woods with his gang until he comes across a cruel tribal hunter killing the male of a copulating bird-pair. He bursts unknowingly into a poetic curse (probably giving birth to India's first poem in Sanskrit) and is hence blessed by the gods. Tagore essayed the eponymous role with great aplomb, with some hand gestures of dance while the marauding dacoits, holding their swords high above their heads, pranced along the stage in rhythmic trots (reminding one of the quaint practices of a Christian marriage procession under an arcade of raised swords) and sang: 'Chant aloud thrice the name of "Kali", "Kali", "Kali": we'll achieve our goal by the force of her holy name'. The play, truly speaking, had no organised dance.

Kal Mrigaya, the second play, was another mythical legend of King Dasharatha coming with his companions to hunt and shooting an innocent hermit-boy with a fatal arrow, thinking him to be a deer drinking at the river. The king then carries the dead son to his blind father in deep repentance. Again, the play was full of recitatives and had no dance element. Later, there were repeated thoughts of converting these two plays into full-fledged dance-dramas, but they never really fructified, barring stray attempts.

Mayar Khela (1888), on the other hand, harked back to the pre-Wagner opera form of Europe: principally with recitatives and songs, but grafted only on a tenuous theme of love, suffering and separation. Tagore admitted: 'When I wrote this play, my mind was entirely submerged in musical emotions…' There was no freedom available for dramatic enactment and certainly no dance. After almost half-a-century, Pratima Devi proposed the musical to be made into a dance-drama and Tagore began composing many new songs and re-writing many others—with songs interchanged among characters and reducing the number of male roles. At some stage, the Poet toyed with the idea of pure mime-action. The preparation suffered from some long gaps and only the first modified portion was briefly staged in 1939. The remaining acts were never taken up afterwards (see Chapter 8).

Tagore, Lieder and Franz Schubert

Both Spencer and Wagner averred that melody should follow the spirit of what poetry could do to form the libretti. Tagore supported this in early life by saying:

> It's the purpose of music to express the text of the song through its melody… and, I intend to let the song's words stand on the shoulders of its melody.

Mayar Khela: *Enacted in Santiniketan's milieu.*

> I craft my melody in order to express the text's meaning...

This Western model of adding melody to libretti was modified over time by Tagore, when his lyrical poetry began gradually to lend beauty and grace to his songs with both meaning and tune. Incidentally, Indian classical music has always been the vehicle of lyrical expression of inner feelings, but not necessarily with highly meaningful libretti. While letting his music and dance foray into his recitative drama, music drama and dance-drama, Tagore urged that his poetry was already the perfect language of feelings, as his music was the language of mood and emotion. Blending the lyrical language of poetry with the melodic one of music—for expressing feeling, mood and emotion—would help to enhance the beauty of music, and allow the limited joy of reading poetry increase manifold by the joy of listening to meaningful music, without any one medium dominating the other.

This was already happening in the West and the German *lieder* or *lied* or art song was one of the great glories of music, with Franz Schubert (1797–1828) as one of its undoubted masters. Joseph Haydn (1732–1809), Amadeus Mozart (1756–91) and Ludwig van Beethoven (1770–1827) certainly composed some fine songs, but it remained for Schubert to achieve real perfection in a previously unattained unification of poetic text and music. His wonderful sense of melody and expressive harmony combined to explore the text of a poem to a much greater depth than ever before. The incredible variety of mood, feeling, emotion, and above all, the profound drama achieved by Schubert in his more than six hundred art songs were unprecedented. The similarity between Tagore's dramatic song literature and the German *lieder* has been noticed by the cognoscenti and it is most unlikely that Tagore could have been immune to the upsurge of *lieder* in Europe in his time. The uncanny resemblance between Schubert and Tagore in composing beauteous art songs was merely 'two great men thinking alike'!

The texts Schubert set to music came from some of the greatest of German lyric poets—Johann Wolfgang von Goethe (1749–1832), Friedrich von Schiller (1759–1805) and Heinrich Heine (1797–1856)—and Schubert's very first compositional masterpiece was a song: 'Gretchen at the spinning wheel', based on Goethe's poem from his *Faust* (1814). In a brilliant stroke, Schubert took the rapid spinning of the wheel as the basis of his piano accompaniment, unifying the song through its changing moods and capturing all the complex emotions as Gretchen recalls her lover. The vividly intense emotions of the young girl were captured perfectly by Schubert's music at his age of only seventeen! This *lieder* would be perfectly comparable to Tagore's art song 'Krishnakali' (written 1901, set to music 1931)—'I call her Krishnakali, named just "the black one" by the villagers; I saw the black girl's dark doe-eyes on the meadows

The Erl King

Who rides, so late, through night and wind?
It is the father with his child.
He holds the boy in the crooks of his arm
He holds him safe, he keeps him warm.
'My son, why do you hide your face so anxiously?'
'Father, do you not see the Erl King?
The Erl King with crown and cloak?'
'My son, it's a wisp of fog.'
'You lovely child, come, go with me!
Many a beautiful game I'll play with you;
Some colourful flowers are on the shore,
My mother has many golden robes.'
'My father, my father, can't you hear?
What the Erl King quietly promised me?'
'Be calm, stay calm, my child;
The wind rushes through dry leaves.'
'Do you want to come with me, fine lad?
My daughters should be waiting for you;
My daughters lead the nightly dances
And will rock and dance and sing you to sleep.'
'My father, my father, can't you see there,
The Erl King's daughters in the gloomy place?'
'My son, my son, I see it well:
The old willows seem so gray.'
'I love you; your beautiful form entices me:
And if you're not willing, I shall use force.'
'My father, my father, he's grabbing me now!
The Erl King has wounded me!'
The father shudders; he rides swiftly,
He holds in his arms the moaning child.
Barely he arrives at the yard in urgency;
In his arms, the child was dead.

one clouded day'—equally vivid, equally intensely felt and as romantically dramatic as ever.

Schubert achieved the proportions of an epic drama in a song like 'The Erl King', again by Goethe. The song was unified by having the piano imitate the galloping of the horse, as it did with the spinning wheel earlier. In 'The Erl King' too, there was a slow build-up of tension: with four separate voices of the narrator, the frightened child, the reassuring father and the chillingly seductive Erl King—none but Death—brilliantly contrasted. Reproduced here is a literal translation from: *Wer reiter so spat durch Nacht und Wind?*, to give a flavour of Goethe's art. It was a tour de force of concentrated high drama, breaking new ground in song literature and showing Schubert's ability to respond so passionately to imaginative poetry.

A fascinating comparison is possible between 'The Erl King' and Tagore's 'The Child' written in Munich in 1930—with poetry, music and European ballet—for UFA, a German film company, after he had witnessed the decennial 'Passion Play' (an enactment of Christ's life in real-life setting, much akin to India's 'Ram Lila' at Ramnagar) in the picturesque locale of Oberamargau in Germany. 'The Child', metaphorically based on Christ's life, was rendered in Bengali by Tagore as 'Shishu Tirtha' in Kolkata in 1931. It was an epic poem starting: 'What's the hour at night? There isn't any response' and ending: 'Victory is to man, to that newborn, that ever-alive one'. Tagore transformed it into a ten-part art tableau to be recited by Tagore first; the mood to be carried through choreography and movements by the dance-group, thereby building up the action; and finally rounded off by a song for almost every part, on the following lines:

> Opening—Tagore's recitation and Shrimati Thakur's Western dance in her own style; the song: 'My threefold salutation to you, for your benevolence, O the merciless one';
>
> Part one—anarchy, fear, greed, anger, excitement, crazy laughter—collective *abhinaya;*
>
> Part two—the song: 'What can be the fear, my king, in your fearless abode, fear disappears in your name';
>
> Part three—the song: 'Raise thunderous sounds tearing the sky, whoever is awake, look east and call loudly the slumbering ones to wake up';
>
> Part four—group dance along with miming with the song: 'Who's the wayfarer on sojourn to ambrosia, it's the deep dark night, the sky is asunder with the hurrahs of victory; a procession scene';
>
> Part five—action to depict fatigue and suspicion;
>
> Part six—the song: 'My lamp died out when I was trudging on the lonely path; the storm has begun raging and is my companion now' with Vasudevan's dance, which is followed by the song: 'My death shall signify your triumph; my life will bear your identity';
>
> Part seven—the song: 'There'll be victory, only victory and nothing but victory, O the brave one, the fearless one', with dance by Srimati Thakur;
>
> Part eight— the song: 'Who's the one who drives us crazy and where does he hide himself' with dance accompaniment by Srimati;
>
> Part nine—the song: 'It's dawning, the journey's over—hark to the music of light in the celestial spheres', is the dancing entry of all participants and sitting down; the second song: 'Open the doors of darkness—do enter with silent footsteps, my mother, appear in this nascent radiance of the sun', when everybody slowly rises up in slow motion;
>
> Part ten—the song: 'Victory, O victory to the new dawn, let the eastern horizon be lit up effulgent radiance' with everybody dancing; repetition of the opening song: 'My three-fold salutation' with everybody paying ovation with folded hands.

This art tableau was far more elaborately woven than could be achieved in the rise and fall of a single art song.

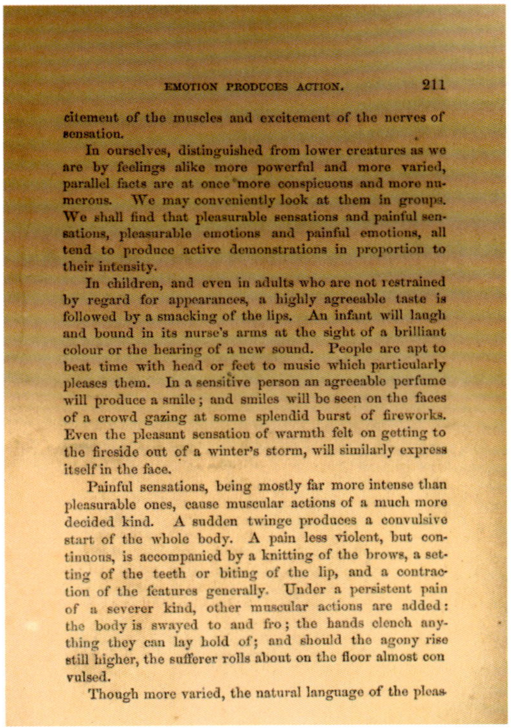

EMOTION PRODUCES ACTION. 211

citement of the muscles and excitement of the nerves of sensation.

In ourselves, distinguished from lower creatures as we are by feelings alike more powerful and more varied, parallel facts are at once more conspicuous and more numerous. We may conveniently look at them in groups. We shall find that pleasurable sensations and painful sensations, pleasurable emotions and painful emotions, all tend to produce active demonstrations in proportion to their intensity.

In children, and even in adults who are not restrained by regard for appearances, a highly agreeable taste is followed by a smacking of the lips. An infant will laugh and bound in its nurse's arms at the sight of a brilliant colour or the hearing of a new sound. People are apt to beat time with head or feet to music which particularly pleases them. In a sensitive person an agreeable perfume will produce a smile; and smiles will be seen on the faces of a crowd gazing at some splendid burst of fireworks. Even the pleasant sensation of warmth felt on getting to the fireside out of a winter's storm, will similarly express itself in the face.

Painful sensations, being mostly far more intense than pleasurable ones, cause muscular actions of a much more decided kind. A sudden twinge produces a convulsive start of the whole body. A pain less violent, but continuous, is accompanied by a knitting of the brows, a setting of the teeth or biting of the lip, and a contraction of the features generally. Under a persistent pain of a severer kind, other muscular actions are added: the body is swayed to and fro; the hands clench anything they can lay hold of; and should the agony rise still higher, the sufferer rolls about on the floor almost convulsed.

Though more varied, the natural language of the pleas-

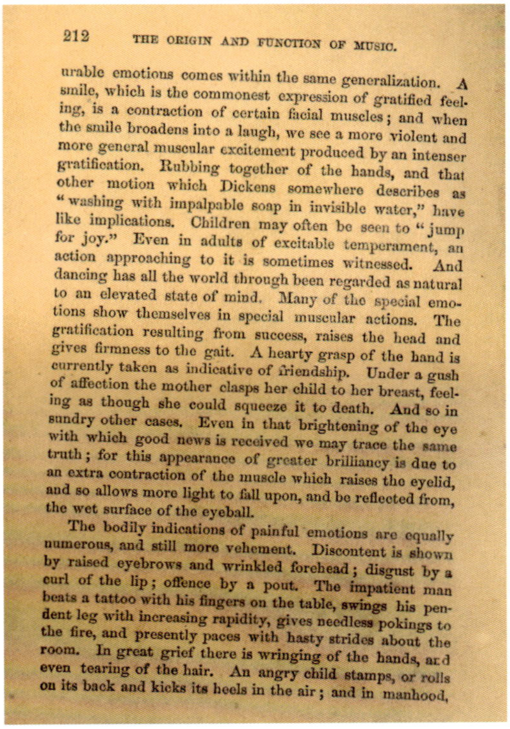

212 THE ORIGIN AND FUNCTION OF MUSIC.

urable emotions comes within the same generalization. A smile, which is the commonest expression of gratified feeling, is a contraction of certain facial muscles; and when the smile broadens into a laugh, we see a more violent and more general muscular excitement produced by an intenser gratification. Rubbing together of the hands, and that other motion which Dickens somewhere describes as "washing with impalpable soap in invisible water," have like implications. Children may often be seen to "jump for joy." Even in adults of excitable temperament, an action approaching to it is sometimes witnessed. And dancing has all the world through been regarded as natural to an elevated state of mind. Many of the special emotions show themselves in special muscular actions. The gratification resulting from success, raises the head and gives firmness to the gait. A hearty grasp of the hand is currently taken as indicative of friendship. Under a gush of affection the mother clasps her child to her breast, feeling as though she could squeeze it to death. And so in sundry other cases. Even in that brightening of the eye with which good news is received we may trace the same truth; for this appearance of greater brilliancy is due to an extra contraction of the muscle which raises the eyelid, and so allows more light to fall upon, and be reflected from, the wet surface of the eyeball.

The bodily indications of painful emotions are equally numerous, and still more vehement. Discontent is shown by raised eyebrows and wrinkled forehead; disgust by a curl of the lip; offence by a pout. The impatient man beats a tattoo with his fingers on the table, swings his pendent leg with increasing rapidity, gives needless pokings to the fire, and presently paces with hasty strides about the room. In great grief there is wringing of the hands, and even tearing of the hair. An angry child stamps, or rolls on its back and kicks its heels in the air; and in manhood,

The 1888 article by Herbert Spencer.

As seen from 'Gretchen...' and 'The Erl King', it was Goethe—as seminal to German literature as Shakespeare is to English—who was the very wellspring of the German *lieder*. A total of fifty-nine poems of Goethe were set to music by Schubert, with an amazing variety of melodies. Their warmth, pathos, directness and strength were as far-reaching as was the fertility with which Schubert poured forth so many masterpieces of the genre of *lieder*. On the contrary, it goes to Tagore's credit that he combined both the poetic prowess of Goethe for his own art songs as well as the musical acumen of Schubert to compose his astounding variety of melodious music—since he not only penned his own exquisite poems but set them to ethereal music himself. What was even more, he was also a highly accomplished singer who could regale one and all and set fire to their imagination, as was evident during the patriotic movements. Little wonder that he was such an inspirational figure of not only his own time, but for all times!

Seminal Influence on Tagore

by Herbert Spencer from 'The Origin and Function of Music'
(written in1888)

Emotion in Natural Language and Music–I

These vocal peculiarities which indicate excited feeling *are those which especially distinguish song from ordinary speech*. Every one of the alterations of voice which we have found to be a physiological result of pain or pleasure *is carried to its greatest extreme in vocal music*. For instance, we saw that, in virtue of the general relation between mental and muscular excitement, one characteristic of passionate utterance is loudness. Well, its comparative *loudness* is one of the distinctive marks of song as contrasted with the speech of daily life; and further, the *forte* passages of an air are those intended to represent the climax of its emotion. We next saw that the tones in which emotion expresses itself, are in conformity with this same law, of a more sonorous *timbre* than those of calm conversation. Here, too, song displays a still higher degree of the peculiarity; for the singing tone is the most resonant we can make. Again, it was shown that, from a like cause, mental excitement vents itself in the higher and lower notes of the register; using the middle notes; but seldom. And it scarcely needs saying that vocal music is still more distinguished but its comparative neglect of the notes in which we talk, and its habitual use of those above or below them and, moreover, that its most passionate effects are commonly produced at the two extremities of its scale, but especially the upper one.

Emotion in Natural Language and Music–II

In respect alike of *loudness, timbre, pitch, intervals and rate of variation*, song employs and exaggerates the natural language of the emotions—it arises from a systematic combination of those vocal peculiarities which are the physiological effects of acute pleasure and pain.

Tremulousness of Voice in Singing

Certain passions, and perhaps all passions when pushed to an extreme, produce (probably through their influence over the action of the heart) an effect the reverse of that which has been described: they cause a physical prostration, one symptom which is a general relaxation of the muscles, and a consequent trembling. We have the trembling of anger, of fear, of hope, of joy; and the vocal muscles being implicated with the rest, the voice too becomes tremulous. Now, in singing, this tremulousness of voice is very effectively used by some vocalists in highly pathetic passages.

Slow and Fast Movements in Music

The more frequent changes of pitch, which ordinarily result from passion, are imitated and developed in song; and here we have to add, that the various rates of such changes, appropriate to the different styles of music, are further traits having the same derivation. The slowest movements, *largo* and *adagio*, are used where such depressing emotions as grief, or such unexciting emotions as reverence, are to be portrayed; while the more rapid movements—*andante, allegro, presto*—represent successively increasing degrees of mental vivacity; and do this because they imply that muscular activity which flows from this mental vivacity. Even the *rhythm*, which forms a remaining distinction between song and speech, may have a kindred cause.

Music vis-à-vis Emotion and Passion

What we regard as the distinctive traits of song are simply the traits of emotional speech intensified and systematised. In respect of its general characteristics, vocal music, and by consequence all music, is an idealisation of the natural language of passion.

Musical Recitation

Recitative, or musical recitation, is in all respects intermediate between speech and song. Its average effects are not as *loud* as those of song. Its tones are less sonorous in *timbre* than those of song. Commonly it diverges to a smaller extent from the middle notes—uses notes neither so high nor so low in *pitch*. The *intervals* habitual to it are neither so wide nor so varied. Its *rate of variation* is not so rapid. And at the same time that its primary *rhythm* is less decided, it has none of that secondary rhythm produced by recurrence of the same or parallel musical phrases, which is one of the marked characteristics of song.

Lyrical Music

Lyrical poetry differs from epic poetry; just as lyrical music differs from recitative: each still further intensifies the natural language of the emotions. Lyrical poetry is more metaphorical, more hyperbolic, more elliptical, and adds the rhythm of lines to the rhythm of feet; just as lyrical music is louder, more sonorous, more extreme in its intervals, and adds the rhythm of phrases to the rhythm of bars. And the known fact that out of epic poetry the stronger passions developed lyrical poetry as their appropriate vehicle strengthens the inference that they similarly developed lyrical music out of recitative.

Sensibilities of Music Composers

Instances in abundance may be cited, showing that musical composers are men of extremely acute sensibilities. The life of Mozart depicts him as one of intensely active affections and highly impressionable temperament. Various anecdotes represent Beethoven as very susceptible and very passionate. Mendelsson is described by those who knew him to have been full of fine feeling. And the almost incredible sensitiveness of Chopin has been illustrated in the memoirs of George Sand. An unusually emotional nature being thus the general characteristic of musical composers, we have in it just the agency required for the development of recitative and song.

Physiology of Music–I

If music, taking for its raw material the various modifications of voice which are the physiological results of excited feeling, intensifies, combines and complicates them—if it exaggerates the loudness, the resonance, the pitch, the intervals, and the variability, which, in virtue of an organic law, are the characteristics of passionate speech—if, by carrying out these further, more consistently, more united, and more sustained, it produces an idealised language of emotion; then its power over us becomes comprehensible.

Physiology of Music–II

There is a physiological relation, common to man and all animals, between feeling and muscular action; that as vocal sounds are produced by muscular action, there is a consequent physiological relation between feeling and vocal sounds; that all the modifications of voice expressive of feeling are the direct results of this physiological relation; that music, adopting all those modifications, intensifies them more and more as it ascends to its higher and higher forms, and becomes music simply in virtue of thus intensifying them; and that, from the ancient epic poet chanting his verses, down to the modern musical composer, men of unusually strong feeling prone to express them in extreme forms, have been naturally the agents of these successive intensifications.

Music's Impact on Speech

Beyond the direct pleasure which it gives, music has the indirect effect of developing language of the emotions. Having its root in those tones, intervals, and cadences of speech which express feeling—arising by the combination and intensifying of these, and coming finally to have an embodiment of its own; music has all along been reacting upon speech, and increasing its power of rendering emotion. The use in recitative and song of inflections more expressive than ordinary ones must from the beginning have tended to develop the ordinary ones.

Musical Culture

In its bearings upon human happiness, the emotional language which musical culture develops and refines, is only second in importance to the language of intellect; perhaps not even second to it. For these modifications of voice produced by feelings, are the means of exciting like feelings in others. Joined with gestures and expressions of face, they give life to the otherwise dead words in which the intellect utters its ideas; and so enable the hearer not only to *understand* the state of mind they accompany, but to *partake* of that state.

Musical Ethics

If it is the function of music to facilitate the development of this emotional language, we may regard music as an aid to the achievement of that higher happiness which it indistinctly shadows forth. Those vague feelings of inexperienced felicity which music arouses—those indefinite impressions of an unknown ideal life which it calls up, may be considered as a prophecy, to the fulfilment of which music is itself partly instrumental. The strange capacity which we have for being so affected by melody and harmony, may be taken to imply both that it is within the possibilities of our nature to realise those intense delights they dimly suggest, and that they are in some way concerned in the realisation of them. On this supposition the power and the meaning of music become comprehensible; but otherwise they are a mystery. Music must take rank as the highest of the fine arts—as the one which, more than any other, ministers to human welfare.

Since Tagore loved dance himself, he was keen to ensure that others accept it as a means of unsullied joy and entertainment

Era of 'Free Movement'

Since the early years at Santiniketan, Tagore had accepted that painting, music and dance had their special place alongside general education and laboured hard to realise this ethos in practice. He would dance himself alongside the male and female students; encourage them to participate in dance; compose songs and plays suitable to incorporate dance; as well as tirelessly conduct rehearsals day after day, without showing the least fatigue. Since he loved dance himself, he was keen to ensure that others accept it as a means of unsullied joy and entertainment.

Dance in Tagore's Eye

The following excerpts reveal how he would view dance. First, identifying himself as dancer:

> I am the messenger of the many-splendoured. I dance and make others dance; I laugh and make others laugh; I sing; I paint. The *Abih* (Supreme Soul), restless in his spontaneous joy to bring forth the universe, has me as his torch-bearer. The splendorous spirit—having its playful multifarious expression in every direction; every melody and every song, every picture and every colour; in weal and woe; in strife and conflict, in bloom and gloom, in boom and doom—has appointed me his mount for all his variegated moods and tastes. I longed to be the companion of these innocent boys and girls in all their playfulness in the Ashram precincts under the blue firmament lit by dawn and dusk. Cadences from the Ever-Playful One reverberates within these children through song and dance—my entity and utility lie entirely in having their minds triggered in this joyous resonance...

Then, the *raison d'etre* of dance and what it comprises:

> The art of dance expresses, first and foremost, the inchoate beauty of our body movements that mirror only the joy of rhythms...Our body bears the burden of all its limbs and is, in turn, propelled by their movements. When these two opposites coalesce with one another, the dance is born. The body's movement gives the body's burden a dynamic form of art: not for a livelihood but for a creative intent. We call it dance then...
>
> None of the dance gestures is a still frame; they keep getting many-hued. Yet the observer is thrilled and exclaims in glee that he is witnessing dance. All the transient gestures of dance, stuck together in rhythms and intervals, are expressing an unbroken truth. We do not look at the separations of multiple facets of dance—we witness its whole truth and are therefore delighted...
>
> The girls keep drawing a filigree of patterns with the curving lines of their supple limb movements upon the melody of the song, making us wonder what the sense could be of it all. We quiz it with the everyday existence of sullied, fractured, criss-cross routines and try to find consistence. If the daily deprivations were the unique verities, we would've detested this dance and called it madness. But, when the complete play of the rhyming beats and notes emerge, our mind resonates to that whole truth—far more deeply and intently than the soiled surroundings that attract our attention...

About his personal knowledge of dance:

> I had earlier witnessed the art of dance while travelling around in the country—in Java, Bali, Cambodia, China and Japan as well as in our own land in Cochin, Malabar and Manipur. I'm familiar with the folk dance and other forms of Europe. I've experience as well as the right to speak about them. Let me not hesitate to tell you that all streams of dance have a confluence in our Ashram. The preparations and the artistic sense that inform them and manifest the beauty of the whole would be rare anywhere...

And, finally, about dance in education and society:

> Dance is included in all countries in the academic discipline of the arts and receives respect as a tool of expressing inner feelings. In our land, since it has disappeared from the urban civil society, we presume that it doesn't exist. But, for the common men, the art of dance is still prevalent in many forms—but then they belong to the lower class! Therefore, what they possess is not ours! Even if it's

> skilled and beautiful, it's a matter of shame for us...

He had nonetheless realised that the Indian urban culture would not approve of dance and by going severely alone, he introduced the practice of dance among the students and teachers of Santiniketan. The dance movement that he initiated in the Ashram culminated in the full-bodied dance-dramas that he composed in the sunset years of his life. Only through an understanding of his relentless effort and involvement, one can appreciate his love for dance: not as an isolated gush of his poetic self or a momentary spurt of enthusiasm, but what he would treat as part of development and fulfilment in life and civilisation.

Nascent Stirring

The story begins when Tagore founded Santiniketan in 1901, catering to students from the educated middle-class of Bengal and later, from other parts of India. The prevalent school curriculum in the land not only prohibited the art of dance, but also forbade vocal or instrumental music. Yet, right from the first day of establishing the school at Santiniketan, Tagore brought in music, theatre and fine arts as an important part of the teaching process. While he could not arrange for the practice of dance from the Ashram's very beginning, he would enthusiastically dance with the students himself during the performance of his plays and would encourage the students to dance to the tune of his dramatic music.

Here is a connected account of how dance slowly acquired a local habitation and a name at Santiniketan:

Raja (The King of the Dark Chamber, 1911) by Tagore was enacted before an invited audience. The play, originally based on the Buddhist *Kush Jataka*, found its recurring occurrence in Tagore's dramatic oeuvre. The story revolves round a highly metaphorical theme of a disfigured king who would remain invisible even to his queen, with their union only in the dark. The listless queen is mislaid by her insistence on seeing the king, plumping for an impersonator and ashamedly leaving the kingdom. After many tribulations, she is chastened and re-united with her consort. The role of Thakurda (grandfather), known for his wise cracks and a ubiquitous one

Garba dance: Folk idiom of Gujarat.

in many of Tagore's plays, is almost built around Tagore's own persona. He is virtually the absent king's alter-ego in this play.

Tagore himself essayed the part of Thakurda, singing with children his own songs, such as: 'The southern gate is open today—come, my Spring, and rock our hearts;... Who is dancing in my innermost heart with his cadenza of Ta-Ta Thai-Thai for ever and ever?' The fifty-year-old Tagore, dancing as the grandfather with a bevy of dancing and prancing boys in festive mood, in a tailor-made role, was an instant hit remembered by viewers long afterwards, especially with his songs: 'Southern gates' and 'Ta-dhin Ta-dhin'. This was beside the madman's song: 'Whatever you may say, I hanker after the golden deer' with dance resonance.

Sharadotsav (The Autumn Festival, 1911) was another allegorical play by Tagore that showcases grandfather and his young brigade again, pitted against the ever-worrying rich miser (reminding one of Moliré's eponymous play), the visiting boy steadfast in paying back his dead master's loan and the local king worried about the absent emperor's visit. To everybody's consternation—and the boy's delight—Thakurda turns out to be the disguised emperor, with a visiting sage whom the miser wishes to adopt as guru and get redeemed.

The boys joined steps in *Sharadotsav* in 1911 but more systematically in 1919 during the second performance. Under Tagore's direction, the two songs selected were: 'We've tucked together the bunch of *kaash* flowers and made garlands with *shefali* blossoms, with our trays bedecked with fresh paddy seedlings' and 'What's it I'm witnessing, my bewitching master, you've arrived at last'. The well-tuned boys fell in line and circled the stage in step with the songs, holding in hand baskets of *kaash* and *shefali* flowers. As regards to the other songs of the play, the boys endeavoured to maintain the songs' rhythm in their footsteps and follow an unregulated style. In 1922, the play—now called *Reenshodh*—was staged a couple of times and the boys followed Tagore's direction to dance in rhythmic steps and catch the mood of the song.

Achalayatan (The Frozen Citadel, written in 1911–12), enacted first in 1914 and repeated several times afterwards, was yet another highly metaphorical play about a cloistered monastery where dreary routines and rituals had brought time to a standstill. Panchak, who had made friends with the marginalised and deprived *Shonpangshus* living outside the closed citadel in joyous abandon, is the one whose protestations cannot be quelled. The great king, in the guise of grandfather (here Dadathakur), rescues the stultified lot by leading a revolt of *Shonpangshus* and liberates the domain.

Under the Poet's personal instructions, the dancing steps for the *Shonpangshus* were created and William Pearson, as one of the tribals, executed a dance in the so-called 'Western style' with Tagore's consent. This dance was done by *Shonpangshus* from behind Panchak to the tune of his song: 'Who knows, O who knows where meanders this ever-stretching path—from which source to which destination' and was actually performed with full abandon!

Falguni (1915) was repeated twice: in Santiniketan, in 1915 and in Kolkata, in 1916. Another of the deeply symbolical plays from Tagore's treasure-trove, it hinges on the fulsome spirit of Spring when people, while talking, burst into songs at the slightest pretext and wished to convert the non-believer into believing, making the taciturn and the morose happy, celebrating alongside the all-round festivities in nature. Led by a blind *baul* who finds his way through his inner eye, they are looking for a mythical old man who would show them the way to salvation.

Little girls were to symbolise nature—as river, the *champak* bower, flute, and so on. A ten-year-old boy enjoyed a flower bedecked swing ride and sang intently the bamboo-wood song: 'O the southern breeze, the wayfarer breeze, rock me please to and fro'. Girls with tucked up buns moved within undulating blue clothes to sing: 'O river, you're all astir in your ceaseless crazy flow; I'm the silent *champak* tree carrying my fragrance through a sleepless night with a movement hidden deep within'. The play was the vehicle for Tagore's appearance, as the Poet-laureate entered with dancing steps for his own song: 'Who's the one driving us crazy and yet keeping himself hidden' and then led a bevy of followers with the song: 'Let's go, let's go, let's go away—leaving the lit-up lamp on the wayside under the skies'.

To cap it all, he danced as the blind *baul* while singing meditatively: 'Slowly, my friend, slowly lead me to your lonely temple' but then again with gusto to songs like: 'Let me dedicate my all to the One to whom everyone is bestowing their belongings' and 'The Spring has woven for me its garland of triumph and let loose a fiery southern wind in my soul'. The other *baul* song: 'Victory, the final victory will be decidedly ours, O my hero, O the brave one' was the clarion call while 'I lose you every other moment only because I yearn to discover you ever anew, my beloved one' was on a contemplative note. The play, with Tagore dancing as the blind *baul*, was an all-time hit and was made memorable by the sketches of the Poet drawn by the famous maestros: Abanindranath Tagore (his nephew) and Nandalal Bose (his disciple).

Vasanta (The Spring, 1923) was a string of songs, interspersed with dialogue, to celebrate Spring: with a specially created royal court, a seated king surrounded by courtiers, and a poet in conversation with the king. Tagore essayed the role of the poet, with the play almost personifying the woods, bamboo forest, *Rituraj* (The King of Seasons, namely, the Spring), posse of flowers, southern breeze, river and so on. The finale was a choral song:

'O the wayfarer, O the lover, separation will consummate your fractured union; Come all, join in the grand celebration of the music of dissolution'. The high-point of the play was Tagore's own dance with the last song, with everybody—including the king and the courtiers—joining in. It was not done in any structured form, with actors and youngsters leaping and moving with the music rhythms and miming the mood, unlike the rest of the twenty-one songs meant for singing alone sans dance. In the finale, Tagore and Elmhirst (see Chapter 2) held hands with each other and filled up the stage in a festive mood.

Arup Ratan (The Eclectic Treasure, written in 1919–20) was staged in 1924 as an abridged and re-written version of *Raja*. The king, albeit in darkness, is not present here at all but becomes a disembodied voice. There were also major changes in songs: thirty-eight songs in all, with eight for grandfather, twenty-six for chorus groups and the rest for *baul*, boys, queen's maid as well as the madman, with only one song for the queen. Staged in 1924, its metaphor of spirituality was far more pronounced than in *Raja*. All the songs of the play were accompanied by mime with simple footwork rhyming with the songs.

Mamata Shankar's visualisation of Tagore's Hori Khela.

As has been observed by the cognoscenti, with the performance of *Arup Ratan* in 1924, the era of 'free movement' virtually ended in Santiniketan where miming the meaning of the songs had predominated earlier, but with only the simplest of footwork and movements. Indeed, this was the era of unstructured dance. Any partial grammar or incidence of folk forms, let alone classical codification, had still to await their advent. But one cardinal feature of this period was Tagore's own dance activity in his plays, with the inspiration doubtless dating back to his dance training during the late 1880s in the UK (see Chapter 3). His major free-style dance as Thakurda, for instance, was with the mnemonic-based song: 'Whoever dances in my heart for ever and anon with the cadence: Ta Ta Thai Thai, Ta Ta Thai Thai, Ta Ta Thai Thai'. This was wonderfully resonated by Santidev singing and dancing as *baul* for: 'My inner being resides deep within me, and hence I keep finding him everywhere' and also for: 'Whatever seemed black and white is now tinged in vivid colour'.

This era was also marked by Tagore's personal initiative to bring dance into the academic milieu of Santiniketan, not replicated in any other institution of India then. Spread over two decades, this era also helped to break the mental barriers in Santiniketan itself: between 1901 and

1921 (between his ages of forty to sixty) and a little beyond, when he would create many occasions in his plays for dance and would participate in dance himself to prove the point that the art of dance is as noble as other academic pursuits.

Links with Folk Forms

Tagore's association with folk forms had a gradual and sporadic beginning. In 1923, Tagore had been to Kathiawad, Gujarat and was most impressed with the finger-tied cymbal dance performed by girls belonging to the working class. Tagore invited a mother–daughter duo from Kathiawad and had their dance demonstrated in the Ashram. The technique of playing the cymbals was quite unique: not holding the cymbals in hand but having them wrapped round the fingers of both left and right hands and having the hands twisted and turned in a most aesthetic fashion, in tune with an undulating body.

Tagore wrote and composed an inspirational song: 'The two hands play on cymbals of eternal time, left and right, for ever and anon, breaking slumber and creating dance with each of its clapping, always afresh'. The senior girls—Manju, Minu, Manasi, Gouri, Babli, Baasu, Amita Sr., Amita Jr., Laabu and Sabita (a newly-wed girl) among others—learnt the style well, with the bride Sabita coming out the best of all! Pratima Devi gave her a reward: a hand-made boat made of tender sticks, woven with green grass and adorned with many colourful flowers! It was but one instance of Tagore fetching whatever was beautiful for the Ashram girls, having their mind trained and vision broadened, leading them to new creativity with Tagore's prodding.

In 1924, Prof. Jehangir Vakil came from Mumbai to teach English at Visva-Bharati. Mrs Vakil was well trained in Garba, the traditional folk dance of Gujarat. Tagore and Pratima Devi requested her to teach Garba to the Ashram girls. It was an established folk form, danced by the upper and middle-class women of Gujarat—standing in circles, clapping hands or clicking fingers in unison, occasionally holding two short sticks (or small brass-plates) in two hands and beating them, moving round and round with great joy and vigour. Pratima Devi and Mrs Vakil had the dance adopted with alacrity for *Shesh Varshan* (see Chapter 7), a celebration of the last rains and made it into a principal dance style while miming the action.

Induction of other folk forms in Santiniketan was more indirect. In 1924 and 1925, young Santidev went with his father and other senior students of Visva-Bharati to the Jayadeva Fair at Kenduli village of Birbhum District on the banks of the Ajay River. While working as volunteers, Santidev availed of the opportunity of listening to the *baul* singing: both in the mornings and evenings. Their dances were well structured in different rhymes and beats, and would allow a variety of footwork. The dance had masculine virility too, and he followed their stance. Later, he choreographed the Tagore song: 'Where have I been called at this time, to the tune of *Falgun's* last melody in her tired hours'. On another occasion, he danced with *ektara* in hand, in *baul* style to the Tagore song: 'In the mad breeze blowing in *Falgun*, I've given up my selfless soul, my undeterred spirit'.

In 1931, Santidev went to attend the festival of folk songs and folk dances in Siuri of Birbhum District, held under Gurusaday Dutta, the well-known founder-promoter of Bengal's folk forms in an organised manner. Along with other students, Santidev witnessed Raybenshe dance there, a totally male dance form, originating from the erstwhile martial traditions of that region. It was performed as a group dance by the lower-caste *doms*. The other folk form that drew his attention was Jari dance executed by the Muslim youth from Mymensingh District—basically with Jari songs and performed with vigorous steps, holding handkerchiefs in hands.

On return, Santidev assimilated both forms into the Santiniketan milieu. For staging the song-and-dance ensemble *Naveen* (see Chapter 7), he transformed the dance for: 'Where have I been called this time' into an amalgam of Raybenshe and Jari, along with a male partner. Tagore was very enthusiastic and for the repeat performance of *Naveen*, increased the dance numbers. Much encouraged, Santidev composed another male dance in the dual style for Tagore song: 'O my heart, it's perhaps the great maelstrom that's descending on you, forcing you to break all barriers in a fierce abandon'.

In 1931, mid-April, Santidev attended a three-day folk festival of Chhau dance in Baripada of Mayurbhanj District. (This is, incidentally, the gentle variety of Chhau without mask, which has since acquired national popularity; the other two variations being masked—vigorous Chhau from Purulia District and soft and gracious Chhau from Seraikela District, also with mask.) Organised under the patronage of the local king, Santidev found it performed by the local youth with good physique, to the rhythm of big and small drums—with undulating body and circular footsteps. The young dancers with bare torso obviously enjoyed their performance and looked like stone-sculpted figures. Tagore made sincere efforts to get Chhau teachers from Baripada, but did not eventually succeed.

Folk dances in our land are inalienably connected with folk songs. Santidev was singularly responsible to induce a lot of the folk culture to Santiniketan which enriched its dance elements. After Kshemendranath Sen brought in the troupe singing songs of the saint-poet Lalan Fakir, Santidev followed up with groups singing Aul-Baul, Fakir-Peer, Murshid, Bhaoaiya and Bhatiyali forms, giving them a respectable platform for performance in Santiniketan. On the whole, Santiniketan's dance was not much exposed to the folk styles beyond the above categories, partially because

Tagore was relatively unfamiliar with the rest of the folk forms in the country and much of cross-fertilisation did not take place.

A-B-C of Mood Dance

What Tagore termed *bhao nritya* (mood dance, see Chapter 7) germinated in 1918–19, fairly inconspicuously, with the student plays—*Lakshmir Pariksha* (Trial of Goddess Lakshmi, 1897) and *Valmiki Pratibha*—to be staged during VIP visits to the Ashram. The *dramatis personae*—both boys and girls—sang their own songs and took their first steps towards rudimentary facial expressions and hand gestures while emoting with the songs.

Lakshmir Pariksha was a versified farce for young girls about a mock trial of an avaricious woman, on the extent she could go on her greed. In *Valmiki Pratibha*, the junior girls, for instance, would begin the first scene, dressed as *Vanadevis*. By standing at one spot and singing: 'We can bear no more and our souls are anguished to see the woods turned into crematorium, with bandits violating peace and scaring everyone', they would shake their hands saying 'no' and place their hands on the chest to express their 'anguish'. Amita, as the little girl, would enter the stage with scared eyes and hands stretched skywards, singing: 'Look at the sky gathering clouds and darkness spreading around with the nightfall, how shall I get back home?' She would then show explicit tiredness and collapse on the floor, while singing: 'The legs are refusing to go on, the body is wearied'. In the very next moment, she would clamber up, look frantically on all sides and go round desperately: 'What a deep forest! Where have I strayed?'

In the fourth scene, the *Vanadevis* would enter shaking their hands vigorously to show the heavy rainfall, while singing: '"Rim Jhim" sing the torrential rains from dark clouds, the sky is overcast, the trees and plants quiver, and the peacock-duo are dancing gleefully'. In the sixth (and last) scene, Goddess Lakshmi (enacted by Labu) would appear, holding a gold chain in her two hands and ask the highly depressed Valmiki with genuine concern: 'Why are you roaming around in the forests distractedly, with tears welling up in your eyes?' This would be in a beautiful questioning gesture, with a tilted head, to ask 'why'. Then, she would kneel down, extend her hands towards Valmiki and offer the gold chain to him, singing: 'Kamala [Lakshmi] is herself here to bestow on you her heaps of jewels—do now break into smile and wipe out the sad face'.

In the last scene, Saraswati [Vasu], dressed in a white costume, would enter with her *vina* in hand and sit down on her knees, to sing melodiously to Valmiki with hands folded: 'I came into this deep wood in the guise of a poor maiden, only to melt your stony heart! I'll tell you why. As Vinapani [Saraswati] I was keen to teach you how to sing mellifluously'. With the words on her lips, she would present her *vina* to Valmiki and sing again: 'Here, do accept my *vina* as a gift for you—whatever you long to sing would be echoed in its chords'. Valmiki would lift the instrument to touch his forehead when the final curtain would come slowly down.

Inspired entirely by Tagore, this was the early beginning made by the Ashram girls for their *bhav nritya* that took concrete shape later (see Chapter 7) and this could be termed as its A-B-C.

Tagore's Dance followed an entirely evolutionary process. Out of the two streams of rhythm-based 'free movements' and the expressional gestures to follow the meaning of his sterling songs, a 'natural selection' came through, favouring more the latter and was refined over time. This was remarkably similar to Darwin's prescient ideas on 'evolution' and 'natural selection', under which only the organisms (here, the organic song-based choreography), best adopted to their environment (here, the songs' milieu) would tend to survive and transmit their characteristics (here, Tagore's inherent thought process) in increasing numbers to succeeding generations while those less adopted would be eliminated.

For Tagore, the era of 'free movement' with prose-play was succeeded by generations of song-and-dance ensembles; music drama; semi-operatic dance-drama; and finally, full-fledged dance-drama (with inherent recitative drama). In this evolutionary process, as we shall see, 'natural selection' went from rhythmic group dances in favour of incorporation of classical dance elements of India, graceful male and female dance elements culled from South and Southeast Asia towards the well-structured organic compositions imbibing dance and music in the last decade of the Poet's life. It was a remarkable free play of 'evolution' and 'natural selection' that informed a highly productive life, spanning many decades.

Folk Dances

Influencing Santiniketan

Folk Dance: How folk dance was initially introduced and accepted in the emerging dance milieu in Santiniketan was principally one of attitude. Unlike classical dance, there is no deliberate attempt in artistry in folk dance. No audience, in the usual sense of the term, is implied and those who gather round to watch are as much part of the collective self-expression as the dancers themselves. Again, the concept of 'portraying' emotion is foreign to folk dance since what is expressed is natural and original. What is important is not the grace or virtuosity of the individual dancer, but the eloquent, effortless ease with which it is expressed.

Garba: Garba is a popular folk dance from Gujarat which depicts the rich tradition of song, dance and drama. It is a unique graceful and undulating dance form: associated with the *Ras Lila* of Krishna and the *gopis*. According to legends, while Krishna popularised *Ras*, his grand daughter-in-law, Usha, got the credit in introducing *Lasya Nritya* or gentle dance in the form of Garba dance. Garba is performed by ladies of the middle and upper middle-class on the Nava Ratri days, Sharad Purnima, Vasant Purnima and other festive occasions. The word 'Garba' is derived from *garbha* meaning deep, alluding to a lamp inside a perforated earthen pot. The flickering light inside the pot symbolises the embryonic life. In the folk dance, ladies place the pot with the lamp on their heads and move in circles, singing in unison in time measure and clapping their hands or snapping their fingers, to the accompaniment of folk instruments. Although associated with Krishna mythology, Garba is now a regular feature during the Nava Ratri Puja, when the celebration covers all the nine nights in honour and worship of Goddess Durga. Garba songs praise Mother Amba (Durga), describing her form and power, and invoke her blessings. There are also Garbas describing seasons and social themes of domestic ends and married life. Musical instruments in Garba are *damru, nagara* and *tabla* for percussion; *ektara, raven hatta* as stringed instruments; and *pavo, shehnai, murli turi, taturi* as wind instruments.

Baul: This dance forms part of the religious rites of *bauls*. Their songs are spiritual in nature and, while singing these songs, *bauls* start dancing in ecstasy. They hold an *ektara* in their left hand and often a small drum attached to the waist-front, played by the right hand. Usually, Baul dances are performed as solo, but at times they also perform duets or group dances at their *akhada*. Some *bauls* wear *ghumur*. While dancing, *bauls* shake their heads and locks of hair, or twirl around and move their arms and feet. But there are no ritualised gestures. The *ektara* plays a prominent part in the dance, sometimes being held close to the ears and sometimes high up. The Baul dance is very popular in Kusthia and Jessore Districts in Bangladesh and Burdwan and Birbhum Districts in West Bengal. Here are usually annual meeting grounds of *bauls* when certain earmarked fairs take place, among which the fair at Kenduli village, commemorating the poet Jayadeva's birth in the twelfth century, is the most prominent one.

Jari: This dance accompanies Jari singing and is usually performed by Shia Muslims. It is organised during Muharram (not participated by Sunni Muslims) around October and recounts the mournful death of Imam Hussain at Karbala Desert. About eight to ten youths form a Jari dance group with the leader called Ustad and the others *dohars*. The dancers wear everyday garments, but tie red handkerchiefs around their wrists and brows, perhaps to remind one of the colour of gory bloodshed at Karbala. In some areas, they also wear strings of bells round their ankles. The Ustad claps or plays the *chati* and the *dohars* play an instrument made of bamboo called *jharni* to maintain rhythm and keep up the beat. In some places, the beat is also maintained by clapping. The Ustad stands at the centre and sings, while the *dohars* move in a circle round him, singing the refrain of the song. The dancers express their grief by the movements of their heads, hands and feet. Jari dance performance starts with the sighting of the Muharram moon. Jari groups go around different houses of the village. They are paid in cash or given some food in lieu of their performance. The various dance groups assemble at a place designated as Karbala for a final performance.

Raybenshe Dance: This is a war-like dance, reminiscent of the battle traditions of yore. The dancers carry poles of large strong bamboo, known as Raybenshe. The warrior-like dancers also carry swords and spears. Drums and brass cymbals are used to maintain the rhythm and tempo. The youths wear close-fitting garments, tying at times strings of bells round their ankles. The performance is half-dance and half-sport. With spears and swords in their hands, the youths demonstrate their valour by way of a mock battle. The fierce clashes of the poles create a battle scene. The drummers play an important role in the dance, guiding the moves, tempo and rhythm of the dancers. The dance is divided into several sections: an introduction, different war-like stances, the fight, the resolution and the rest. The tempo is slow at first, but picks up and ends on a crescendo. Both Hindus and Muslims take part in this dance and it is mainly popular in Burdwan, Birbhum and Murshidabad Districts. The main attraction of the dance lies in the dexterity with which the artists use their hands and bamboo poles. The latter is used in different ways by the dancers: to climb up and down and to hold on heads (tightened by hand grips) and other interesting ways.

Tagore with child artists of Kal Mrigaya.

Part Two

Cross-cultural Horizons

As Tagore noted, an enlightened atmosphere was being created in the country for teaching and learning dances. But the forms themselves needed guided discipline under qualified teachers

Indian Subcontinental Influences

From the mid-1920s, Tagore recognised the need for a formal initiation process in dance in two streams. These were: gradual incorporation of group dances from Indian folk forms and codified classical dances, brought in by teachers to Santiniketan and both streams vitally resuscitated by his faithful associate Santidev Ghosh. With regard to the first stream, he introduced dance as a subject for Santiniketan's holistic teaching. Rhythmic steps—with swaying bodies but without *abhinaya*—were introduced in group dances for all items and festivals. This was primarily culled from Baul, Jari and Raybenshe of Bengal (see Chapter 4) and adjacent regions. Over time, Manipuri rhythms and later Kathakali rhythm-based dances were added in group dances as well, but the *joie de vivre* of the group dances reigned.

Regarding the classical stream, it must be understood that in the Indian subcontinent any attempt at teaching and incorporation of styles would involve intense inter-cultural dialogue among far-flung regions. In Tagore's time, when communication was physically difficult, this meant a three-fold process: gathering first-hand information about the classical forms; inducting suitable classical teachers in Santiniketan; and above all, assimilating the forms appropriately with the corpus of Tagore songs for purposes of dance-based expression, especially in solo dances. As Tagore noted, an enlightened atmosphere was being created in the country for teaching and learning dances. But the forms themselves needed guided discipline under qualified teachers.

In this context, the contribution of Santidev Ghosh in bringing in dance-related material had been immense as whenever he had gone outside Santiniketan, he had the intention to witness dance or learn it.

Tagore would ask him to give a detailed description. He would also brief Pratima Devi about his experience. They would discuss among themselves the different dimensions of these dances.

Induction of Manipuri Dance Style

In 1917, Tagore visited the village of Macchimpur in the Sylhet District where many Manipuris were settled. The community boys received him with a cowherd dance and in the evening, Manipuri girls staged a dance for him. A happy Tagore resolved to teach Manipuri dance to Santiniketan boys and looked for a teacher, but nobody agreed to leave their settled community. On his return journey, Tagore stopped at Agartala in Tripura—which also had a large settlement of Manipuris—as a guest of the king, Virendrakishor Manikya and, at his request, the king spared Buddhimantra Singh (along with a Manipuri drum player) from his court as a Manipuri dance teacher for the Santiniketan boys. This was to mark the beginning of Manipuri dance in Santiniketan.

Teaching of this dance form was confined to boys, who would have a bamboo strip strapped behind their back from shoulder to waist so that they would not dwarf down. The stance followed was to keep the legs apart, bending the knees slightly and tilting a little forward, while standing in a circle. A straight chest was essential for the dancer who would alternately lift his legs and follow the clapped rhythm of the dance.

Manipuri dance: Classical window on Manipur. Artist: Charu Matthur.

One of the introductory dances was with the Tagore song: 'Come you, the crazy one, forget your little self and stop moving round in its futile whirlwind'. But Tagore's effort at teaching regular dance at the school was not received kindly by his compatriots and the school's monthly organ *Santiniketan* carried the news, 'The Tripura king has sent two artists to the Ashram and they are teaching *musical gymnastics*, along with drums, to the Ashram boys' (emphasis added).

Despite opposition, Tagore found the classical Manipuri form deeply attractive because of its common roots in Bengal's Vaishnava tradition—in terms of its religiosity, music, supportive treatise and aesthetic taste. The corpus of music came from Jayadeva, Chandidas, Vidyapati and Govindadas's *padavali keertan*. Of late, Manipuri songs have been translated into Manipur's Maitai language, but their musical genesis was, no doubt, predominantly in Bengal.

Since Tagore found Manipuri dance congenial in its graceful elements to women, he took the brave decision to teach the form to Santiniketan's female students. This was in 1925 when, at Tagore's request, the Tripura king sent the Manipuri dance teacher Nabakuma Singh and his brother Vaikunthanath Singh for playing the *mridanga*. Girls selected to learn this dance comprised Haimanti (a foreigner), Gouri Basu (Nandalal Bose's daughter), Labu, Fullarani, Kundarani, Kusumika, Angshalekha, Jyotsna, Uma, Amita Sr., Amita Jr., Lalita, Sumita, Lalita, Jamuna and perhaps a few others. This was easily the female 'pioneer brigade' to learn a codified classical dance for the first time in Bengal (and India).

The teaching of girls, done on the quiet, observed all the necessary rituals associated with Manipuri, along with its deep religious base. On the very first day, two girls were adorned as Radha and Krishna, and were paid their ritual obeisance before starting with the teaching. Tagore was enthused enough to bring them out in the open and the festival of Holi was chosen to be the first public occasion. Tagore wrote a specially lilting song: 'Her anklets are tinkling away and my heart throbs to find her so familiar'. The dance became a hit, repeated often. On the whole, Manipuri got its pride of place in Santiniketan's scheme of things, with the generally soft temperament of Tagore's actors and dancers matching with the classical Manipuri *lasya*. In particular, its codified dance items such as *Chali, Achouba Bhangi Pareng* and *Vrindavani Pareng* struck the right mood for Tagore and its soft *gamaka* rhythmic steps—with *mridanga* percussion but without any *abhinaya* since accompanying songs are devotional or descriptive—appealed to Tagore's dance spirit.

A spin-off from the Manipuri teaching was that Tagore's personal involvement in teaching dance became less and less. Of course, till the last day, he would personally direct the dances, but the time came when he would explain verbally while sitting down and would only occasionally get up; however, the days of having him alongside from the beginning till the end of learning a dance were finally over. This was perhaps as expected of him, for Tagore, respected a qualified teacher and considered it prudent to hand over the teaching responsibility wielded by him earlier.

Spread of Manipuri Style

From 1920 onwards and until Tagore's death, he would engage qualified teachers for dance in Santiniketan. A succession of Manipuri teachers came following Buddhimantra Singha and his brother, Nabakumar Singha and his brother, and then, Senarik Singha, Mahim Singha and Nilambar (or Nileshwar) Mukherjee. The teachers would have an assistant for the rhythmic instruments, but no classical singer. This was only because Tagore's own music was to be used and was eminently suitable for the dance movement he initiated, which was based on his songs and poems. This too, was a pioneering venture launched by him in the early twentieth century.

Tagore sent Santidev to Manipur in 1932 and 1933 with a special permission collected earlier. Santidev used his contacts with former Santiniketan teachers there since the 1920s and was inducted to witness the girls dancing *padavali keertan* and the vigorous *Pung Cholam*, a male dance of Manipuri drummers in joyous abandon. Santidev's many subsequent visits to Manipur helped to strengthen its theory and practice in Santiniketan.

In Shillong, Tagore met Ambalal Sarabhai, a rich businessman from Ahmedabad and invited him to witness *Natir Puja* (see below) and *Rituranga* (see Chapter 7) at Santiniketan. Sarabhai was so impressed that he wanted to introduce Manipuri dance in Gujarat and invited Nabakumar to teach. Thus Bengal and Gujarat became the only two states in India—outside Manipur—to have strongholds for Manipuri classical dance, thanks to Tagore's initiative!

Ineffable Memory of Natir Puja

Although *Natir Puja* made quite a dance history in 1926, its beginning was a low-key one; an attempt by Pratima Devi to convert Tagore's classic poem *Pujarini* (The Female Worshipper, 1899), originally inspired by a story from the Buddhist collection *Abadana Shataka*, into a mime enactment to celebrate his birthday. The story revolved round Ajatasatru, a Hindu king of sixth century BC, who wanted to erase vestiges of the worship of the Buddha from his kingdom. The devoted courtesan Srimati persisted in carrying out the ritual worship at the votive sanctuary against specific palace exhortations and premonitions of dire consequences and, eventually, fell prey to the royal army, who killed her on the spot. The story had many nuances of fanaticism that extends beyond its ancient origin and continues till date, although in different garbs. Even in

Jamuna, daughter of Nandalal Bose.

Tagore's time, there was communal riot that was rending the country asunder. A pained Tagore readily agreed to the effort and eventually made it into a full-blooded new play meant only for girls—in dialogue, songs and the crucial final dance by Srimati in Manipuri style.

Tagore took upon himself the task of directing the play, selecting the appropriate girls for the play and teaching them acting. Dinendranath was responsible for music, while Pratima Devi and Nabakumar were responsible for dance—with the master painters Nandalal and Surendranath Kar responsible for costumes and stage décor. Boys like Santidev were inducted as Hindu and Buddhist citizens, belonging to opposite camps, enacting a 'religious war' with swords, sticks and lighted torches. Even two foreign girls, given names of Karuna and Haimanti.

There was one group dance by boys in Manipuri style for the song: 'There would be the quest now for severing bonds and leaving the safe coast behind with a clarion call against all fears'. But it was Gouri, as the dancing Srimati, who gave heart and soul to her role; practised her dance quietly in the derelict basement-room of Tagore; and used her Manipuri lessons tinged with a devotional fervour, all her own, to dance for the epiphany (with the Ashram girls providing the accompanying song): 'beseech your forgiveness and offer you my obeisance, O the Unequalled One, for, my thoughts on you infuse my mind with throbbing emotions of dance; my entire body vibrates with the boundless sounds of prayers towards you, sans all chants'. In her own words, 'Tagore had indicated the meaning of the song. To visualise that meaning was my only goal. It was not to be merely through hand gestures and footwork, but also through expression as the cardinal feature.' To forestall the criticism of girls taking part in a public theatre, Tagore introduced the Buddhist monk Upali, the only male character, and essayed the role himself. He would enter the dark stage with a morning song on his lips: 'The eastern horizon is lit up with nascent sunrays in their effulgence'; then urge Srimati to prepare for her supreme sacrifice; and would exit with his song still reverberating in the Jorasanko precincts of Kolkata.

The outcome was a highly successful performance, for the following reasons:

- Its theme was a very relevant one in the social context and carried a clear message against communal violence as prevalent in prehistoric times, translating it in the contemporary context.

- The production combined some of the best talents in the novel experiment, reminiscent of the multi-disciplinary Bauhaus experiment as practised in Germany at that time, in the early 1920s (with architect Gropius, painters Picasso and Kandinsky, dancer Nijinsky and composer Stravinsky, among others), with which Tagore was familiar; he was even instrumental in holding a Bauhaus Exhibition in Kolkata, in 1922.

- It was the first public performance which highlighted the classical dance of Manipuri and also put it up on a public proscenium stage.

- The girls were the principal *dramatis personae*, something unheard of till then.

- Above all, Gouri's passion as a female solo dancer, highly appreciated by one and all, was unthinkable earlier as it shattered the prejudice of girls dancing in public, once for all.

The play—repeated several times later, using different casts and mixing Kathakali with Manipuri under Santidev's inspired guidance—left an indelible mark on public conscience and was made into a movie by New Theatres in 1931. It was filmed at their studio in Tagore's presence, perhaps another first for a classical dance-related production.

Induction of Kathakali Style

Kathakali was another classical dance whose rhythmic dance components like *kalasam* and *saari*—with only a veneer of gestural *abhinaya*—attracted Tagore. The beginning of this affair was unspectacular; Tagore's encouragement to Santidev to learn some virile masculine dance after his Baul folk form, brought in a variety in Santiniketan's prevalent dance practice. Another inducement came from the demonstration of a rudimentary form of Bharatanatyam by Vasudevan, a student at Kala Bhavan from Chennai's Theosophical Society. The opening, however, came after Santidev spotted good quality male-dances' pictures in a French journal, followed by its detailed coverage in Mumbai's *Illustrated Weekly of India*. This was the genre of Kathakali dance from Kerala.

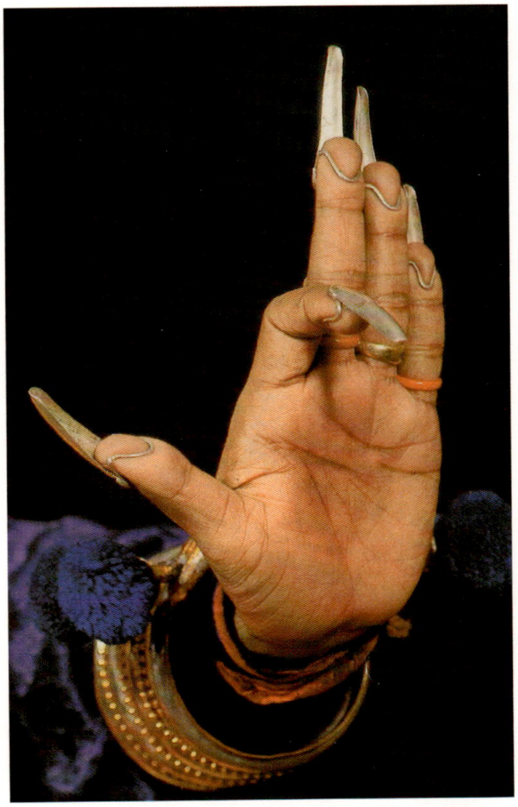

Kathakali mudra, *a vignette of Kerala.*

In 1931, Santidev—with a lot of personal initiative—reached the village of Mulkunnathakava in Cochin where the Malayalam poet Vallathol Narayana Menon had, just a few months ago, opened Kerala Kalamandalam, a school for Kathakali. Santidev joined under gurus Kunju Kurup, Konnan Nair and Samikutty Bahgavatar alongside junior students like Krishnan Nair, Madhavan, Kelu Nair and Ananda Shivam. A three-month stint with rigorous physical exercise, rhythmic practice and verbal learning of *bols* equipped him with an introduction to some rhythm-based items, besides a few hand gestures and their application in dance. Since this would be not enough and time-consuming in any case, he selected a few words from Tagore's songs and tried to learn to express them through Kathakali's broad gestural language, apart from a good initiation into rhythmic dance. There was active encouragement from Tagore.

On return, the first Tagore song with Kathakali gestures was: 'There comes the summer cyclone enveloping the evening sky', used for *Varsha Mangal* (see Chapter 7). This was followed by Srimati's dance in *Natir Puja*, essayed by Lalita Sen this time, which combined the movements and footsteps of Kathakali, Baul and Manipuri, in keeping with the rhythm of the song. Interestingly, this was objected by some people who wanted to revert back to pure mime action, when Tagore intervened and—having witnessed both earlier and later versions—approved of the changed production, with the comment that the dance climate of the country is improving and he would like to move with the times! This was the production that was filmed by New Theatres.

In 1932, Santidev made his second trip to Kerala, after attending a month-long summer school of learning *vina* in the Carnatic style. His stay for another month at Kalamandalam was fruitful to pick up some more threads in Kathakali. In 1937, Santidev made his third—and final—trip to Kalamandalam at the instance of Tagore, to select a Kathakali teacher for Santiniketan. This time, the institution had moved to its new and spacious location, and poet Vallathol helped him to select Kelu Nair, a recent alumnus. Kelu Nair, with his open-mindedness, was a great success in Santiniketan and took an initiative in blending Kathakali with Manipuri. He enacted several main roles of the later dance-dramas composed by Tagore.

Keeping his interest unabated in Kathakali, Tagore invited its many votaries to Santiniketan as described below.

■ In 1935, Guru Gopinath and Ragini Devi brought their troupe to perform in Kathakali style, by holding a colloquium on the first day and staging many episodes —based on *abhinaya*—as separate items on the second day. They had substantially simplified the gestural vocabulary, made several changes in traditional costumes and had used removable white paper as facial masks instead of the traditional, elaborate painting.

■ Later, Shankaran Namboodiri, the guru of Uday Shankar, came to showcase the solo form of Kathakali. *Putana Badh*, a charming mythic legend of the demon Putana trying to kill baby Krishna by suckling and, in turn, getting sucked to death, was most painstakingly enacted by him: in *ekaharya abhinaya*—single dancer enacting multiple roles of Putana, baby Krishna and Gokul women.

■ In 1939, poet Vallathol brought his own Kalamandalam group and showed pure Kathakali dance and *abhinaya*.

Between 1931 and 1941, till Tagore's death, Kathakali and other Keralan forms were intermingled with Manipuri and prevailing folk forms, to give the dance movement of Santiniketan a special character. Among Kathakali teachers, there was Velayudha Menon and then Kelu Nair who greatly contributed to this transformation—and was continued after Tagore, by Govindan Kutty, Krishna Kutty, Balakrishna Menon and Haridas Nair, the latter an outstanding disciple of Guru Kunju Kurup. Tagore wanted his girls and boys to learn Kathakali as well as one could, but drew a line in emulating the eyes and facial expression. He ordained that his songs should define the basic framework of how to build up the total image.

The remarkable point is that Kathakali existed as a village art till the time of Vallathol and with Tagore' active persuasion and involvement, the two brought it up to a classical, structured form.

Induction of Mohiniyattam Style

The Mohiniyattam form, recognised as a classical form today, had a debased existence right up to 1930. Considered as a developed style in the reign of King Swati Thirunal of Kerala, in the middle of the nineteenth century, it fell into its evil days after his demise and the artistes found it difficult to sustain themselves except by performing on the public streets for the common man and earn a livelihood by showing cheap items like *Polikali, Esaal, Mukutti, Chandanam* and so on. In 1930, Vallathol resolved to restore this street dance to its pristine form and after much search located Kalyani Amma, a middle-aged dancer, whom he brought to Kalamandalam. Unfortunately, she had left behind her Mohiniyattam style after her prime and was unable to fetch students.

At that stage, Tagore, who was looking for a female teacher for girls in Santiniketan to teach a soft form of dance, came in the picture and invited Kalyani Amma to Santiniketan. She stayed there for a year. This was in 1933 with the munificence of the king of Cochin. Kalyani Amma was able to teach many Kerala folk dances to the Ashram girls like *Swaram, Kaikuttikali* and *Kalammuli*, in which she was particularly adept. However, as there was no singer or instrument-player with her, she was unable to teach *abhinaya*.

Utilising the gestures and movements taught by her, the group dance for the

Tagore song: 'O the beauteous bride, you are the honeysuckle of the bower; Do receive congratulations from the delighted *champaka* flower' took shape. Today, Mohiniyattam is as accepted as Kathakali in modern India and Tagore's name should figure alongside Vallathol's in the resurrection of both these classical styles, especially for Mohiniyattam.

Bala Saraswati: The legendary dancer from South India.

Other Classical Styles

Bharatanatyam

This was the regenerated form of another despised form, called *Sadir Nauch* or *Dasi Attam*, until the 1920s, when the lawyer-cum-dancer E. Krishna Iyer started waging a relentless battle to bring it back to its lost glory. Iyer was a patriot and ardent admirer of Tagore and at his invitation in 1935, Tagore was present at the All-India Music Conference in Varanasi where Bala Saraswati, coming from the class of *devadasis,* performed the dance form.

Perhaps it was in the same year, in 1935, that Santidev saw for the first time a recital of Bharatanatyam by Bala Saraswati and that of Kathakali by Gopinath and Ragini Devi, and was most enamoured. Especially, he realised by seeing Bala's dance how much labour and concentration had gone behind her gestural *abhinaya*. But his presence there, without Tagore's consent, did not seem to take his exposure and endeavour too far. Much earlier in 1927, Vasudevan (mentioned above) was regarded as a phenomenon in Santiniketan when he staged his energetic dance in bare torso, with a glowing dark complexion resembling a bronze statue. Tagore was highly appreciative and Nandalal thought his appearance was like Nataraja Shiva! The Ashram boys, who had a dim view that practice of dance was only suitable for girls, flocked to him to learn the masculine form. But Vasudevan proved to be a poor teacher as his own knowledge was confined to the pre-Iyer era of Bharatanatyam when its grammar was yet to be codified only in 1933 onwards; it was yet to be re-named as 'Bharatanatyam' from 'Sadir dance' and Rukmini Devi's 'Kalakshetra' was yet to come up in 1935. Though Vasudevan was successful as a soloist, his foray into teaching did not take off.

On the whole, Tagore was in the scene though it was too early for Bharatanatyam to have emerged as a proper style, but when it did in the latter half of the 1930s, he encouraged Mrinalini Swaminathan (nee Sarabhai), a student in Santiniketan and a trained Bharatanatyam dancer, to evince her consummate classical skills in his dance-dramas—in 1939 as Prakriti in *Chandalika* and as Uttiya in *Shyama*, and in 1938 as Vajrasen in *Parishodh* (The Redress), the earlier version of *Shyama* (see Chapter 8).

Kathak

Originating from the song-and-dance narratives of the *kathakar* prevalent in North India, especially in temples, it received its great boost in the middle of the nineteenth century when Nawab Wazed Ali inspired by the Vaishnava *Ras Lila*, wrote a musical skit *Radha Krishna ki Kahani* in 1843 and set in motion the Lucknow *gharana* of Kathak. Binda Din, the principal dancer of his court, was a devout Vaishnava and used songs by Haridas, Govinda Swami and Tansen, while the king would enact *Darbari Ras* as Krishna with royal women as *gopis*. Jaipur *gharana* came from Shiva-worshipper Bhanu-ji who initiated *Shiva Tandava*, though his progeny converted to Vaishnava faith, promoting *Radha-Krishna Lila*.

By the twentieth century, Kathak had fallen into the hands of *Bai-jis* and was not encouraged by the educated gentry. Kathak's formal entry in Santiniketan was through Asha Ojha, a qualified Kathak dancer, as Uttiya in *Parishodh* (later *Shyama*) in 1938. Dr Ojha, Asha's father, was an arts enthusiast and had sent his family to Santiniketan to learn Manipuri. After Asha demonstrated her Kathak talents especially to Tagore for a considerable duration and impressed him, Tagore inducted her in the role of Uttiya: after having every song and, in turn, every line explained to her with *bol* and *tehai*, and allowing the subsequent line (or the subsequent song, as the case may be) to be sung in that sequence.

Both *bols* and *tehais* were made to interpret the facial expression, hand gesture and body movement of the previous line. This was an unusual format for Tagore's dance and although Asha proved a resounding success to have impressed everybody—including Tagore, Nandalal and Pratima Devi—the innovation was not repeated later. This was mainly because a Kathak dancer of Asha's calibre did not join Santiniketan later. Another valid reason for Kathak's absence in Santiniketan could be as for Bharatanatyam, that is, it was too premature for Tagore to get in touch with qualified gurus in Kathak or its institutional structures in North India. For Kathakali and Mohiniyattam, it was fortunately not so, as the poet Vallathol and his Kalamandalam were there. And as for Manipuri, it was well preserved for long in that secluded part of the country.

Although not exposed to dance since childhood, Tagore took enormous interest in classical dances as performing arts and was among the first to champion their cause in every way he could. He was the one who showed the way to poet Vallathol, E. Krishna Iyer, Rukmini Devi Arundale, Uday Shankar, Madam Menaka and many others to come forward and

Tagore surrounded by danseuses during Geetotsav.

become pioneers in their chosen paths. He happened to be a votary at the altar of dance and wherever he went or sent his emissaries, he made it a point to cull what was beautiful and have it woven in the fabric of Santiniketan.

Odissi, Kuchipudi and Sattriya were the styles that escaped his patronage because these forms received recognition as classical arts only after his death. Odissi was resurrected from the dance of *maharis*, who as *devadasis* performed in the temple sanctums, and of the *gotipuas*, who as boys impersonated girls and danced in the public arena. Odissi as a dance form received recognition in 1972. Kuchipudi was a male dance in Andhra performed by village *Bhagavatar* Brahmins, admitting women in their ranks much later, and became a recognised dance form in 1952. Sattriya was, till very late, a male preserve in the Assam *sattras* and received its classical status in 2000.

Technical Details of Classical Styles that Influenced Santiniketan

Manipuri Style

One of the major Indian classical dance forms, Manipuri dance originates from the north-eastern state of Manipur: surrounded by mountains and isolated geographically. The form developed its own specific aesthetics, values, conventions and ethics. Although the style draws its inspiration from pre-Vaishnava days of Manipur, its present form owes its introduction to Krishna Bhakti in the fifteenth century. The cult of Radha-Krishna, particularly the *Ras Lila,* is central to its theme. Lyrics used in Manipuri dance are usually from the classical poetry of Jayadeva, Vidyapati, Chandidas and Gyandas, in languages like Manipuri, Sanskrit, Maithili or Brij Bhasha.

King Bhagyachandra (1759–98) codified the style, composed three of its *Ras Lilas: Maha Ras, Vasanta Ras* and *Kunja Ras* (performed at Sri Govindaji Temple in Imphal) and the *Achouba Bhangi Pareng* dance. King Gambhir Singh (1825–34) composed two *Parengs* of *tandava* type: *Gostha Bhangi Pareng* and *Gostha Vrindavan Pareng*. King Chandra Kirti Singh (1849–86), a gifted drummer, developed at least sixty-four *Pung Cholams* or drum dances and two *Pareng* dances of lasya type: *Vrindavan Bhangi Pareng* and *Khrumba Bhangi Pareng*. *Nitya Ras* was also his creation.

Traditional Manipuri style embodies delicate, lyrical and graceful movements. Pounded movements and avoidance of jerks, sharp edges and straight lines give Manipuri dance its undulating and soft appearance. The dancer's feet are neither lifted up nor put down at the precise rhythmic points of the music, but rather earlier or later: to express the rhythmic points more effectively. Manipuri dancers do not wear ankle-bells to accentuate the beats tapped out by the feet, in contrast to the other Indian classical forms. The dancer's feet never strike the ground hard. Movement of the body and feet, and facial expressions in Manipuri dance are subtle—aiming at devotion and grace.

Musical accompaniments for Manipuri dance are percussion instruments like the *pung* or drum and small cymbals; stringed instrument like the *pena;* and wind instrument like the flute. The drummers are always male artistes and are trained to dance *Pung Cholam*, while drumming.

Kathakali Style

Kathakali is a form of highly stylised Indian dance-drama that is noted for its ample make-up of characters, their elaborate costumes, detailed hand gestures and well-defined body movements: presented in tune with the elaborate music and complimentary percussion. It originated in the southern state of Kerala during the sixteenth century. Kathakali owes its origin to dance-dramas like *Ramana Attam* and techniques like *Krishna Attam* that dealt with Rama and Krishna, with *Attam* meaning enactment.

Kathakali also shares similarities with *Koodiyattam* (a classical Sanskrit drama of Kerala) and *Ashtapadiyattam* (an adaptation of the twelfth-century Gita Govinda), besides incorporating elements from traditional and ritualistic art forms like *Mudiyettu, Theyyam* and *Padayani*. The usual medium is Malayalam, although a mix of Sanskrit and Malayalam, called *Manipravalam*, is more common. The characters—with painted faces and elaborate costumes—enact advanced choreography around stories from the Indian epics. Kathakali, now performed on proscenium stage, was traditionally performed in temples (especially in Padmanabha Swamy Temple in Thiruvanathapuram) and palaces, also finding venues in post-harvest paddy fields.

Traditionally, Kathakali themes were staged to last a whole night, although severely pruned nowadays to three to four hours. Stories find stage presentations in parts, rather than in totality, with the selection based on criteria like choreographic beauty, thematic popularity and melodramatic elements. Kathakali entails an elegant look of its characters, their abstract movements and synchronisation with the musical notes and rhythmic beats. The most popular stories, mainly from the Mahabharata, veer round *Nalacharitam*—the story of love and sufferings of Nala and Damayanti; *Duryodhana Vadham*—focusing on the Kurukshetra and its aftermath; *Kalyana Saugandhikam*—story of Bhima going to get flowers for Panchali and meeting Hanumana half-way; *Keechaka Vadham*—story of Bhima and Panchali in disguise; and *Kiratham*—the story of Arjuna's fight with Shiva. Kathakali music has songs set in *ragas* based on the microtone-heavy Carnatic music. There is a distinct style of plain-note rendition, known as

'Sopanam' style. Like its acting style, Kathakali music has also singers from the northern and southern schools. Traditionally, Kathakali performance is conducted at night, in front of the huge oil-lamp, *Kalivilakku*. The percussion instruments used are *chenda, maddalam* and *edekka*. Singers use *chegila* and a pair of cymbals. A Kathakali actor uses immense concentration, skill and physical stamina, gained from training (based on Kerala's martial art *Kalaripayattu*) often lasting eight to ten years.

In Kathakali, the story is enacted purely by *mudras, rasas* and bodily movements. Dancers, in particular, undergo special practical sessions to learn the control of eye movements. There are twenty-four basic *mudras*, the permutation and combination of which add up to all the hand gestures in vogue. The main facial expressions are nine *rasas*, as per the *Natya Shastra*. An interesting aspect of Kathakali is its elaborate make-up code, classified into five basic sets, namely, *pachcha, kadu, kari, thaadi* and *minukku*—laying down the pious, heroic, evil and anti-hero characteristics. Kathakali is still largely a male domain, although females have made an entry of late.

Mohiniyattam Style

Mohiniyattam is an age-old female dance form from Kerala, reckoned among the most graceful of Indian classical dances. According to legends, *mohini*, the enchantress, was the form assumed by Vishnu to deceive the demons in yore, to distract them from eating the coveted ambrosia. Historically, it was well established by the sixteenth century and received great encouragement from the royal family of Travancore, as performed in front of the temple-deities by *devadasis*.

In the nineteenth century, King Swati Thirunal of Kerala patronised and stabilised Mohiniyattam as an art form. He composed a number of *varnams* and *padams* to make the music of this art form lyrically rich and attractive. He also brought about reforms in the style and included its recital on festive occasions, besides having a dance troupe under his patronage. In his attempts to revive Mohiniyattam, he took help of the Thanjavur Quartet, the famous composer-brothers in the Bharatanatyam style of classical dance, and could undoubtedly be called the pioneer of Mohiniyattam.

The beauty of Mohiniyattam dance is its costume: white with gold. The dancer usually wears gold ornaments, symbolising purity of the dance of celestial maidens. The dancer also wears a pair of large round ear ornaments—in the shape of a snake's hood—and the nose is adorned by nose-ring, apart from a bungled bun at the left side of the head. The distinctive style of Mohiniyattam is the complete absence of heavy stamping and sliding. The movements are never abrupt, but dignified, easy and natural. As the most graceful of Indian classical dances, the style is eminently suited for showing *shringara rasa*.

Biographical Note

Vallathol Narayana Menon (1885-1985)

The litterateur Vallathol was one of the most famous poets of Kerala. He wrote predominantly in Malayalam. Along with Kumaran Asha and Ullur Paramaeswara Iyer, he was part of a highly creative period of Malayalam literature of Kerala. Influenced by Tagore, Gandhi and Marx, as well as the Sanskrit classics, his poetry evolved from its classical beginning to an increasing expression of nationalism and socialist sentiment. He wrote in a variety of forms, using both Sanskrit and Dravidian meters.

Vallathol's many works include the epic poem *Chitrayogam* (1914) and the narrative poems like *Magdalena Mariyam* (Mary Magdalene, 1921) and *Kochu Sita* (1928), as well as eleven volumes of romantic poems, entitled *Sahitya Manjari*.

In addition to subjects from Nature and the lives of ordinary people, themes of Vallathol's poetry voiced opposition to the indignities of the caste system and the injustice suffered by the poor. Vallathol translated the Sanskrit Rig Veda and Valmiki's Ramayana into Malayalam verse. He also produced a prose translation of the Puranas.

Vallathol played a prominent role in setting up the Kerala Kalamandalam at Cheruthuruthy, on the banks of the Bharathapuzha River. Later, this place was re-named Vallathol Nagar. He raised Kathakali, a great art form, to the level it has achieved today. He married the Mohiniyattam dancer Chittaur Madhavi Amma, who was probably responsible in influencing him to resurrect Mohiniyattam which had fallen in evil days. He lived to be a centenarian of Indian literature.

Tagore's Dance Syllabus at Santiniketan

Original Syllabus, 1936

The Course is for four years.

1st Year: Elementary classes in Manipuri dancing.

Elementary classes in South Indian dancing.

2nd Year: Manipuri "Tala" dances.

South Indian "Tala" dances.

Training in "Bol" and symbolic "Mudra".

3rd Year: South Indian Kathakali and Ceylonese dance.

Rendering of Bengali songs to dances.

Study of poses from old paintings and frescoes.

4th Year: Mimicry and expression. Composition. Dramatic interpretation.

Special advanced classes may also be carried on for those who have finished the four years' regular course or are trained for some dramatic performance.

A special class will be held for those who want to learn to play 'khol'.

Revised Syllabus, 1941 (before Tagore's death)

Kathakali Dance (for Boys):

1st Year: 10 exercises and 7 steps.

Dance: (1) Toream; (2) Purapar; (3) Kalasams—6.

2nd Year: 15 exercises and 12 steps.

Dance: (1) Peacock dance; (2) Hunter's dance; (3) Harvest dance.

Kalasams—15; Asta Kalasams and 200 mudras.

3rd Year: Dance: (1) Tandav; (2) Ekalabya; (3) Kamdeva; (4) Suvadra-Arjun; (5) Flower dance.

4th Year: Dramatic Plots.

700 mudras and all the exercises.

Student's own composition.

Kathakali Dance (for Girls):

1st Year: 10 exercises and 7 steps.

Dance: (1) Flower dance; (2) Nrityanjali; (3) Toream.

2nd Year: 15 exercises and 12 steps.

Dance: (1) Purapar; (2) Hunter's dance; (3) Harvest dance. About 200 mudras

3rd Year: More exercises and steps.

Dance: (1) Peacock dance; (2) Kalasams—15; (3) Asta Kalasams in Jhaptal; (4) Vastra-haran. 300 mudras with steps.

Expressions with eyes and few dramatic plots.

4th Year: (1) Kalasams—15; (2) Putanam; (3) Suvadra-Arjun; (4) Sati-Shiva; (5) Vasanta dance. Three of the main expressions: (1) Sringara; (2) Vira; (3) Karuna; (4) Adbhut; (5) Hasya; (6) Bhayanak; (7) Bibhatsa; (8) Rudra and (9) Shanto.

All the 700 mudras.

Regular practice of exercises will be compulsory.

Manipuri Dance:

1st Year: Dances of 1st Chali, 2nd Chali, 3rd Chali, 4th Chali;

Dance of Lalita in Dadra and Trital.

Dance of Bishakha in Dadra and Trital.

2nd Year: Dance of Lalita in three different Bols and Chautal.

Dance of Bishakha in three different Bols of Chotta-Dashkushi and Bols of Chautal.

3rd Year: Shri Krishna dance in Dadra and Trital;

Shri Radha dance in Dadra and Trital;

Bhangi dance in Lopha Dadra and Jat.

4th Year: Khurambapareng in Lopha, Dadra and Jat.

Shri Krishna dance in Chautal, Chotto-Dashkushi.

Shri Radha dance in Chautal, Chotto-Dashkushi.

Dance of eight Sakhis in Panchamswari and Teora.

If Tagore was deeply impressed by Indonesian dances of grace and lucidity, Indonesia too paid back his benign interest with passion, building an institution for dance

Winds of Asia-Pacific

From the Asia-Pacific region, a transcultural wind blew to Santiniketan in two different ways: first, through Tagore's own travels in those countries and, second, through Santidev's visits and dance apprenticeships in that region under Tagore's active vigilance so that the former could prune and absorb the essential India-friendly elements from the local dance forms in the Asia-Pacific. The most fruitful gain was perhaps Santidev's trips to Sri Lanka from where he could collect a wealth of material, followed by his visit to and stay in Indonesia.

Dance Linkage with Asia-Pacific

As recorded in his *Japan Yatri* (a sequel to his travels in Japan in 1916 during his three-month stay there), Tagore somewhat disliked contemporary Western dance, particularly the type that was: 'half a physical exercise and the other half a dance, comprising vigorous leaps, lightning rotations and kicks into the air...' Japan, on the contrary, offered him 'a dance of delicate physical gestures which left no gaps within their gestural variety... Swinging together, their dancers virtually rained gems of beauty...'. This was far nearer to his creative foray into dance-dramas, in his mature age, which were an approximation to 'dance of delicate physical gestures'.

Tagore left on a sea-voyage to Malaysia, Java, Bali and Thailand in mid-July 1927, returning by the end of October to Santiniketan. His entourage comprised Suniti Kumar Chattopadhyay (the renowned professor of linguistics and philology from Calcutta University), Surendranath Kar and Birendrakrishna Roy Burman (well-known artists, both of Kala Bhavan) and two foreign academicians from Santiniketan. Knowing Tagore's exceptional keenness to observe regional dances, his hosts, mostly royalties of the land, arranged cultural soirees. To Tagore's own visual appreciation were added meticulous notes as kept by Suniti Kumar (whom Tagore credited highly for his photogenic memory!) and a collection of visuals and narratives (including drawings of dancers and their costumes) related to the dance forms of these countries, which were archived later at Santiniketan.

Through his extensive travels, Tagore had a wide exposure of the various dance forms of the Asia-Pacific region, which included the following:

- Ronggeng of Malaysia: primarily female dance, which is performed to the tune of the *pantum*, moving in circles in fast tempo, maintaining distance from each other and expressing emotions in delicate shades;

- Legong of Bali: performed by gorgeously-dressed girls in their pre-teens, carrying Japanese fans;

- Haja of Bali: short humorous dance skits with music;

- Golek solo dance of Bali: with the rhythmic music of *gamelan*, orchestrated with both five notes (pentatonic) and all seven notes (the latter possibly influenced by India), marked by fast melody and is very different from European instrumental music;

- Kambong of Java: floating rhythmically, with superbly graceful body movements;

Legong dancer from the Indonesian coast.

- Tembem and Batjak-dojok of Bali: with gracious movements;

- Bedojo of Bali: performed by masked females who were dressed in male attire, on humorous themes.

Other traditional male dances that Tagore witnessed were: Wireng Pandji Henem (on Javanese historical episodes); Wireng Raden Hindrajit Kalijan Wanara Hanoman (duels between Indrajit, the demon-prince and Hanumana, the monkey from the Ramayana); Wireng Panah Hoedara (dance with bow and arrow on a theme from the Mahabharata); Wreng Raden Werkoedorokalijan Praboe Partipejo (fight between Prince Vrikodara and King Prateep); Pentilan Lajendrjo (ancient love stories); the female Wineng (based on martial arts); the most famous Serimpi (which is very graceful and is performed by royal princesses); and Jogjakarta's conversational song and dance. Tagore's immense interest was evident since his exposure to Javanese and Balinese dances was instrumental to bring home a clutch of sketches and photos, and a large amount of dance-related literature, with the overall inspiration derived from Java and Bali's terpsichorean excellence.

If Tagore was deeply impressed by Indonesian dances of grace and lucidity, Indonesia too paid back his benign interest with passion, building an institution for dance. Devantar, a young man, during Tagore's visit, was highly motivated not merely to listen to every lecture of his, but also to be inspired by the Poet's thoughts on national culture. He followed Tagore's ideals on education to establish the first institution—Tamanshishya—in Surakarta city. The Sultan of the township was a patron of the school and was helpful in many ways. Devantar deputed many youths of his institution to Santiniketan who joined its Patha Bhavan (for academic studies) and Kala Bhavan (for fine arts), participating with vigour in all the festivities as well as sharing their experience with Santidev and others.

Remarkably enough, Devantar introduced dance, music, instrument-playing as well as acting as mandatory elements of the curriculum in Tamanshishya, in addition to academics, akin to Visva-Bharati's approach. In consequence, every student of Tamanshishya—which spread around a hundred branches all over Java and Bali before the World War II—was conversant with the classical and performing arts of their country. Tagore sent Mrinalini (see Chapter 2), a Sangeet Bhavan alumnus, and her mother with his credentials to Tamanshishya for learning dance there. They, however, left for the USA thereafter.

Santidev's Learning Foray in Asia-Pacific

Santidev, against great odds, was motivated enough to visit both Java and Bali for an extended period to get exposure to their dance as well as culture. After considerable groundwork, he managed a six-month-long stint for initiation into Java and Bali dances under the management of Tamanshishya, in 1939.

If Tamanshishya was the first institution of the land to introduce performing arts in the school syllabus, its music and dance departments were the agencies responsible for arranging their exclusive performances; with the royal members, adept in these arts, always taking part in the public shows. On two formal occasions, Santidev was invited to the Sultans' palaces to witness a post-dinner dance-drama and a Serimpi dance in Surakarta; and a two-evening programme of Serimpi and other dances in Jog Jakarta.

In the first two months spent for initial learning in Surakarta, Santidev observed that the Serimpi dance-dramas comprised clear-cut entry and exit and dance styles specific to individual characters. The battle scenes were slow-motion dances, almost like pre-arranged games. From the third month onwards, he moved to the capital, Denpasar in Bali, where he learnt their best dances: Legong and Kabyar. The former was executed by beautifully dressed damsels while the latter was performed while seated, expressing through hand gestures, body movements and facial expressions.

Some pertinent observations of Santidev in reference to the dances of Java and Bali, as applied *mutatis mutandis* in Santiniketan later, have been detailed below.

■ The war scenes were highly stylised, bereft of realistic turmoil and physical tussle, which were aesthetically satisfying.

■ In the battles of Rama–Ravana as well as of Sugriva–Subali (our Bali), there were monkey-like pranks and agility (a well-known hallmark in all countries of Asia-Pacific) that were very enjoyable.

■ The Sultan-prince placed the sense of elation and enjoyment above religion and viewed threats as means to the ends of serenity and inner peace.

■ Gamelan music (which was Tagore's special favourite, but considered difficult by him to implant into Santiniketan) had a unique soundscape with a large range of mellifluous melodies.

■ Vocal music (normally on a prolonged tempo and without intricacies) and Gamelan music followed the same *raga* (mostly pentatonic and very limited in number), but *chalan* or progress of the melody was on different tracks, culminating on the same note at *sam*.

■ Javanese dance used rhythmic variations following the drum beats, but Gamelan music stuck to its own basic rhythm and culminated on the same drum beat.

■ Serimpi of Java, confined to the feudal interiors for princesses of royal families, had different groupings: Sharitungal for solo; Rarashri for duet and Batejo for a group of nine, with body style, footsteps, gait, sitting down and getting up being totally synchronised.

■ Sharitungal carried forward an ancient dance tradition based only on Gamelan music, while the other Serimpi style followed local legends or episodes from the Mahabharata.

Javanese dances, in particular, were being played characteristically on a cloth piece, usually red, tied to the waist and extending to the grounds, which was held aloft, or dropped stylistically or thrown in different directions to create variegated patterns, and each move was distinctively named. Tagore must have been particularly taken in by this patterned beauty, as evident in his later paintings (see Chapter 11).

■ Legong of Bali, although belonging to the poor class, was a common heritage of one and all, and despite receiving no

Modern Balinese dancers perpetuating their art.

munificence from the royalty or Dutch rulers, it occurred spontaneously in every village with its own troupe becoming an organic part of the life-cycle ceremonies.

■ Rajjang of Bali was known for its affinity to priestly worships in temples, where the priest would meditatively move in circles round the deity three times, before ending in salutation to the icon and the danseuses would follow carefully behind.

■ Every village had its own community centre, built on common labour, where the evening gatherings were the points of collective participation.

■ Legong, which implies 'do dance', was obviously for public entertainment as evident from the characteristic sidelong glance, smiling visage, fast movement of shoulders and undulation of the hip, yet devoid of lurid hints as the dancers were little girls innocent of such innuendos.

■ Legong was usually performed by three girls, with their hands angularly drawn in and their bodies moving like billowy waves, which is much akin to Manipuri dance, where the head, body and hands move synchronously together.

■ There was careful balance in Legong, with every stance of the dancer perfectly balanced in terms of consistency in footstep, body, hands and head, without using ankle-bells.

■ The girls stood in a particular way, not seen in India or Myanmar, with knees half-bent and with inclined spinal cord, without the body ever fully stretched.

■ Javanese dance was sculptural: slow, serene and solemn, whereas Balinese dance was more poetic: lyrical, lively and agile, perhaps reflecting the nature of their respective people!

■ Kavyar in Bali, evolved from Legong, was danced entirely to the Gamelan music by the youngsters and was of more recent origin.

Dance Linkage with Sri Lanka

In 1934, the rich Buddhist family of Wilmet Perera from Sri Lanka had visited Santiniketan to study Tagore's experiments in the academic arena and left an invitation for the Poet, with his performance troupe, to visit their hometown Horana in the hilly region in the north near Colombo. Accordingly, a large group of fifty comprising—besides Tagore and the artists—Pratima Devi, Nandalal, Surendranath Kar and many students and their guardians—made a sea-cum-surface voyage and eventually performed *Shap Mochan* (see Chapter 8) in Colombo. For Santidev's wrathful dance as the angry Indra as well as his devisive dance with the Tagore song: 'O the mighty sorrow, O the epic fury, O the terrible, O Shankara, O the precursor of deluge' the *kalasam* form of Kathakali style was used. He drew warm approbation from the press for having learnt 'the ancient art of Kathakali from the interior of Malabar', and blending it 'with the precious genius of a master artiste' and having purified the dance 'into something rich and strange'. The foreign girl Haimanti was the male protagonist Aruneshwar.

It was during this visit to Sri Lanka that Tagore (and others) saw the male Kandyan dance in the Buddhist temples. Perera inaugurated Sripalli in Horana after the model of Santiniketan and arranged teaching of Kandyan dance there. This was the green signal for the inveterate dance-learner Santidev to spend his successive summer and autumn holidays of about a month-and-a-half each in Sri Lanka—in four trips over June–July and October–November between 1936 and 1938—to grasp Kandyan dance from the concerned teachers at Sripalli in Horana and bring back its considerable fruits to Santiniketan. The net result was that Tagore's inspirational songs could be given the masculine Kandyan touch and imbued with vigour and virility: for Santidev himself and for others whom he taught.

But there was also a sweet quid *pro quo* involved in the process. If Santidev was an ever-eager learner, he was also an indefatigable teacher. He not only taught Tagore's songs and dances to the students at Sripalli, but also procured for them two *esrajs* from Kolkata, carried them along and used his own *esraj* at Sripalli to impart musical skills to his progeny.

Dance Linkage with Mynamar

Myanmar (then Burma) was not always so far from India: mentally and culturally. Sea voyages were common and had their takers from both sides. In 1937, Santidev resolved to visit Myanmar to get acquainted with Ram Poye dance. Again, using his extraordinary serendipity, Santidev arranged hospitality with, and access to, an elderly male teacher of Ram Poye dance. He also could witness some performances complete with instrumental music. The physical movements and hand gestures were somewhat difficult to assimilate for someone like Santidev whose body was already so well honed. Still Santidev did his best, even learnt Ram Poye's instrumental music and brought the legacy to Santiniketan.

It appeared that Ram Poye, as the national dance of Myanmar, originated in the middle of the eighteenth century. In 1767, the Burmese king had vanquished the king of Thailand (then Siam) and brought many war prisoners to Myanmar, some of whom were great artistes in music, dance and instruments. At the behest of the Burmese king, they displayed the Siamese dance Ram at the royal court and, encouraged by the king, created Ram Poye dance, similar to the Siamese Ram, for Myanmar. The only changes made were to convert the Siamese lyrics into Burmese and add Burmese dialogue to the Siamese drama. Interestingly, the Siamese dance had a lot of resemblance to Bharatanatyam, revealing strong cultural bonding between India and Siam in days of yore.

Impact on Santiniketan

With regard to Kathakali, as taught by Govindan Kutty to the Ashram girls, Tagore's delimiting dictum in Santiniketan was in terms of *mudra*, eye gestures and rhythm, as he said, 'Whenever you learn a style, learn it completely and don't leave anything out. But when you dance to my songs, don't put much accent on *mudra* and eye gestures. Concentrate only on the natural expression of the eyes and that will be well [for my songs]'.

Owing to the linkages established with Tamanshishya, there were also Javanese students in Santiniketan, one of whom was Sukarno. Under Santidev's arrangement, the girls began learning Javanese dance. This did not prove to be much difficult, thanks to their earlier grounding in Manipuri and Kathakali styles. There was similar influx of students from Sripalli and one of the Sri Lankan youths taught Kandyan dance in Santiniketan.

In 1936, Kandyan dance was used in *Chitrangada* (see Chapter 8) for the dance by the villagers, intimidated by bandits, to pick up courage with the choral song: 'The helplessness of the caved-in temperament is an insult to oneself; don't cower under duress by the mere imagining of danger'. This was a bold and vigorous affair, appreciated by all. In *Chandalika* (see Chapter 8), while Mrinalini as Mother danced in Bharatanatyam style, Nandita as Prakriti followed the southern rhythmic forms and performed in the Kandyan style as taught by Santidev for the defying song: 'I refuse, I refuse, I refuse to worship that God who had pushed me into this abyss of ignominy; Why should I offer flowers, why should I, why should I offer flowers to the One who had put down my whole life into this dungeon of humiliation?' after she was humiliated by the upper-caste village belles.

While Tagore was all for 'natural selection' —the best dance being used under the given circumstance—and offered little resistance to the selection process, his dictum still held: no dance would be strictly according to its orthodox grammar, but would follow the *bhava* of the song and would be, first and foremost, clearly expressive. The foundation of the classical form was important for the dancer and certainly essential to learn, but he wanted to break the form creatively so that the dancer's expressions would follow primarily the song's mood.

Such was the spin-off of Tagore's cultural visits to Asia-Pacific and Sri Lanka that they opened a two-way traffic in music and dance between those countries at one end and Tagore's Santiniketan at the other. If it was Tamanshishya in Java, it was Sripalli in Sri Lanka, both of which flowered under Tagore's direct inspiration, both initiated energetic student exchange programmes with Santiniketan and both ushered in a climate of Renaissance in classical dances in their own countries: to survive as well as to flourish. It was a 'win–win' situation for all and was no small wonder that it could take place at all in those pioneering days—from the late twenties to the late thirties, when all communications were so tardy, voyages and travels over sea and land were so time-consuming and an all-empowering English language as a communicating medium was yet to appear on the scene.

Asia-Pacific Dances that Influenced Santiniketan

Kandyan Dance—Sri Lanka

According to legends, the origin of Kandyan dance lay in an exorcism ritual known as *Kohomba Kankariya*, originally performed by Indian Shamans. The latter came to the island upon the request of King Panduwasdev who had been suffering from a mysterious disease called *Divi Dosa*, believed to be the 'black magic' of Kuveni, the Yaksha princess, who had killed her Indian husband and king, Vijaya. After the performance of the ritual dance of *Kohomba Kankariya*, the illness vanished and thereafter, many natives adopted the dance.

Historically, Kandyan dance originated in the central hilly region of Sri Lanka; it is now widespread all over the island. It was earlier performed by dancers from a separate caste under the Kandyan feudal system. They were aligned with the 'Temple of the Tooth' in Kandy and took a prominent part in the procession held annually by the temple. After the support of the Kandyan kings was gone, the dance waned in popularity, but is revived now and adopted for the stage.

Kandyan dance is traditionally performed to percussion only, the most common being its unique drum, *geta beraya*. The twin drums, *tammettama*, are also used at times to assist the dancer to keep rhythm; *thalampeta*, a small pair of cymbals, is also used. Lyrics, sung in tune with the movements of the dancer, are called *Wannamas*, singing about the virtues of *wanna*, the animal. Even though only males were allowed to train as dancers earlier, women also are initiated now, but no separate *ves* or dress has emerged for them yet.

Kandyan dance principally imitates movements of animals like elephant and peacock. Costumes tend to be colourful, mixed with white, red, yellow and black. Male dancers with bare chests are decorated with exquisite silver regalia and spectacular headgear. Silver bangles are also worn on the arms and ankles. Performances are with hectic rhythms of drums. The dances usually begin with the ritual *Kohomba Kankariya* to propitiate the deity Kohomba. There are eighteen main dances in Kandyan style that include: *Mayura Wannama*—dance of the peacock; *Hanuma Wannama*—dance of the monkey; *Gajaga Wannama*—dance of the king's tusker; *Kirala Wannama*—dance of the Kirala bird; *Ukusa Wannama*—dance of the eagle; *Sinharaja Wammana*—dance of the tortoise and the lion; *Turanga Wannama*—dance of the horse; *Uraga Wannama*—dance of the snake; *Musaladi Wannama*—dance of the rabbit and *Eeradi Wannama*—dance of the soldier.

Legong Dance—Bali

Dance is the main art form of Bali Island's culture and is performed at the main temple festivals and ceremonies, especially in the life-cycle rituals. Legong has many forms, the most frequently performed dance being *Legong Keraton* (Legong of the Palace). Legong Keraton is the most graceful of Balinese dances, an epitome of classical Balinese female dancing. A Legong, as the dancer is known, is often a young girl of pre-puberty age, rarely older than her early teens. First created in the eighteenth century, it is usually the first dance taught to the beginners.

According to legends dating back to the twelfth and thirteenth centuries from East Java, the king of Lasem was undertaking a journey when he found the maiden Rangkesari lost in the woods. He took her home and locked the unwilling girl in a stone house. On learning about Rangkesari's captivity, her brother, the prince of Daha, threatened war unless she was set free. Despite Rangkesari's pleadings to give her freedom and avoid war, the king preferred to fight and, on his way to battle, chanced upon a bird carrying ill omens. He, however, ignored the bird, encountered Rangkesari's brother and was killed in the fight. This is the story described in the dance.

Since Legong dance is very stylised and symbolic, the viewer is expected to know the story before watching the performance. Legong dance involves three dancers: two Legongs and the Condong or attendant. The Legongs are identically costumed in gold brocade, which is wrapped and bound so tightly that it remains a mystery to the audience how such agitated and rapid movements could take place. With elaborately made-up faces, plucked eyebrows that are boldly repainted and hair decorated with frangipanis, the dancers relate the story with captivating movements.

Baris, a male equivalent of the Legong, is a warrior's dance. Executed with energetic steps and martial spirit, the Baris dancer conveys thoughts and emotions of a warrior: preparing for action and confronting the enemy in battle. Performed solo and requiring great energy, spirit and skill, the dancer should be able to depict chivalry, pride, anger, prowess and even a little regret. It is one of the most complex Balinese dances.

Serimpi Dance—Java

Serimpi means 'visions of an ideal world'—similar to gods' paradise—as depicted by the Serimpi dancers in their performance. Serimpi is one of the highest forms of classical dance at the Java palace, *Keraton Surakarta Hadiningrat*, and the creation of a new Serimpi dance is always attributed to the ruler. The Serimpi dance is reserved for the royal daughters embodying a clear purity and the dance depicts a picture of its idealised world with dance movements and structures.

The dance begins with balanced static poses, symbolising a moment of rest. This serenity is disturbed by the constant movements and changing positions of the dancers, a situation comparable with the disharmony caused by disparate passions of the human world. In the dance, this is sometimes represented by a struggle. Then this dance structure recovers its balance, as humanity also comes to its senses. These images are emphasised by the fact that Serimpi is always danced by four similarly dressed dancers: dancing as two couples.

The Serimpi dances of the *kreaton* or palace are characterised by a strong spiritual connection with the goddess of the South Sea, Kanjeng Ratu Kidul. The royal family attributes its position to the personal protection from the goddess. The dances are a tribute to the goddess and the dancers open themselves spiritually to a confrontation with the 'higher world'. Often, the dance depicts an episode of the Ramayana, in which the sovereign Ramawijaya (Rama) gives advice to his younger brother on how to become a good king.

Shyama: *Kelu Nair and Nandita perform in front of a rapt audience.*

Part Three

Outcome

Once experimentation began, there was no looking back, leading to what Tagore pithily called: 'surrender of body and mind to a rhythmic unity'

First Flowering

On Tagore's return from Java and Bali, in 1927, the simplistic *Varsha Mangal* (Ode to the Rains), of the earlier years acquired a new veneer—in *Nataraj–Riturangashala* (Lord of Dance–in the Playful Domain of Seasons, 1927)—with both the production and décor acquiring a Javanese nuance; Surendranath Kar designing a stage with pronounced Japanese influence. This was a phase of 'natural selection': selecting the best-suited style from different dance forms. Experimentation had begun already with *Shesh Varshan* (1925) and *Natir Puja* (1926, see Chapter 5) both being choreographed in the Manipuri style, which again had gained a place for itself in Santiniketan's mainstream. *Nataraj–Riturangashala* was performed in various dance formats along with music. In the same spirit there also came: *Sundar* (The Beauteous, 1925, and in a changed garb, 1929); *Naveen* (The Nascent, 1930) as well as *Shravan Gatha* (Ballad of Last Rains, 1934).

It is important to note at the outset that once experimentation began, there was no looking back, leading to what Tagore pithily called: 'surrender of body and mind to a rhythmic unity'. A wonderful medley started taking shape among many streams and many styles: with new forms constantly emerging. Some instances were: use of suggestive Manipuri *gamakas* and *khol* rhythms for group dances; novel Manipuri compositions tinged with Kathakali and Baul for plays like *Natir Puja* and *Nataraj–Riturangashala*; Vasudevan's solo and duet dances with the duets in semi-Bharatanatyam style; Santidev's use of Kathakali along with vibrant gestures of Baul and Manipuri; Srimati Thakur's use of Western modern dance for the enacted poem *Jhulan* (The Swing, 1931) opening with: 'I'll play the game of death staking my life at this nocturnal hour,' and her use of ballet form for the long Passion poem on Christ, *Shishu Tirtha* (1931); general use of the folk forms Baul, Raybenshe and Jari; and a host of other forms in *Sundar, Naveen* and *Shravan Gatha*; 1929–34).

In particular, the large corpus of Tagore songs on nature—complete with planting saplings, ploughing earth and harvesting (even carrying spades and axes, and digging for iron) and celebrating in an ever-colourful way all the six seasons—that could be, in course of time, set to dance sequences, got a tremendous boost in varied footwork as well as resplendent group dances.

Basic Tenets of Evolution

Among the cognoscenti, Pratima Devi viewed the evolution of Tagore's dance in a linear manner. *Varsha Mangal's* earliest celebrations saw the first stirrings of dance: perhaps not so mature, yet its vocabulary desperately trying to establish itself. This dance was like the child's first uncertain steps—holding on to the apron-strings of its nurse, namely music, and still unaware of its own potential to walk independently. Second, *Natir Puja* ushered in a new dance form based on simple rhyme: with a smooth gait that easily enchanted the viewer, even with its unevenly-learnt idiom. Third, the costume and stage-décor at Santiniketan went ahead to achieve its own distinctive stamp.

Finally, *Nataraj–Riturangashala* came with its own décor of music and created new aspirations in the art of dance. Gestures excelled and simultaneously dancers were made aware of the need for perfection. Choreography appeared to play its role, especially in the songs like: 'Remove all obstacles, O the Lord of Dance, with your mighty cadenza, Traversing the lonely furrows, and O the serene-bodied, do take my salutations'. The quality of the artistic structure of *Rituranga* laid down a format to be followed for quite a while, as evidenced in *Sundar* (1929), *Naveen* (1930) and *Shravan Gatha* (1934). Meanwhile, the individual events of excellence were Srimati Thakur's: 'Come to the *neepa* woods under its shady bowers; Swing me hard, swing me fast' and the celebrated *Shishu Tirtha* (discussed in Chapter 3).

It was, however, still not clear what the dances should really express and the experimentation persisted with some plain miming, some miming with songs and some with sheer body movements—not leading to an integrated whole. The dances were item-based and although aesthetically satisfactory, did not leave a lasting impact on the viewer. This phase dawned with *Shap Mochan* (1934, see Chapter 8) when dance was the harbinger of dramatic events. Here dance followed the narrative text and accentuated the dramatic conflicts through facial *abhinaya*: to express the *bhava*. This was no doubt a music drama, but not yet a full-fledged dance-drama, much like the other music drama *Tasher Desh* (1933, see Chapter 8). Still, their poetry, music and mime-acting made up for the whole and opened up the vista for the later, more organic and fully recitative dance-dramas, namely,

Chitrangada: *First showcased in Santiniketan. Nivedita Ghosh, who later became Nandalal's daughter-in-law.*

Chitrangada (1936), *Shyama* (1938) and *Chandalika* (1938), to be dilated upon in Chapter 8.

Bhava Nritya—*Mood Dance*

If there were any connecting bonds among Tagore's dances in the experimentation phase, it was the accent placed solely on expressing *bhava*—each song as an item. *Bhava* was the essence in all dances that Tagore himself participated in or encouraged others to accomplish. He explained:

> In human life, luxury and misery, weal and woe, have all a natural playfulness in visual, aural and tactile sense. If all of it could be aural, it would be ethereal music; if, on the other hand, all of it could be only mobile, it would then become dance.

Dance, to Tagore, was the language of body-kinetics providing mobility to his songs. Whenever he directed the Ashram girls in dance, he insisted upon the song's *bhava* to be felt in the dancer's kinaesthetic, so that she would pour her heart and soul into achieving the rhythmic mobility of the song she is depicting. Tagore's dance was, therefore, a mood dance *par excellence*. Like his poems and melodies describing the fleeting clouds in the blue sky, the breeze stirring the tree-leaves, the joy of light glistening in grass, the overflowing radiance of the moon, the blossoming and fading away of flowers, the rustle of dry leaves coupled with human emotions of being sad and glad at the turn of events, the overarching keenness of reaching out to others or withdrawing in utter solitude—could all be made manifest in mood dance through hand gestures, facial expressions and body movements! The range of mood dance—from the furious thunderstorms in the skies and the mighty breakers of the seas to the huge upheavals of human emotions—would be infinite! Tagore's idea was to have *vishuddha nritya,* or pure dance according to rhythm sans feelings, being taught in the Ashram and to combine it with mood dance for expressing the lyrics' inner meaning. Under Tagore's guidance, the dancers gradually became adept in picking up the pure dance based on rhythm and work out its confluence with the feelings and emotions of the lines and stanzas so that the mood of the song would become explicit.

Varsha Mangal *and* Shesh Varshan

Varsha Mangal (1925) was staged at Santiniketan with Tagore's bouquet of fifteen older songs in the form of a pre-Wagnerian opera with dominant music, but without a storyline that celebrated Nature's cascading of incessant rains. It began with an invocation: 'The clouds, gathered under the skies, are beckoning: come, come, come; Responded by cries echoing in the blackberry and mango forests: we're going, going, going' and it ended with the post-farewell adulation: 'Your garland, O *Ashadh*, is woven with the thunder-jewels; Your serene green scenario carries the scorching burns of lightning'. Its dance component comprised a few solos and the rest were group dances: primarily in the Garba folk style.

Unlike *Varsha Mangal, Shesh Varshan*, showcased the month following *Ashadh*, that is *Shravan*, in Kolkata. It was a music drama consisting of twenty songs that were composed around a lyrical dialogue amongst the music-loving king, his alter-ego Nataraj and the courtiers who were varyingly gifted in their appreciation of the muses! It began with the invocation of the late rains during autumn: 'Come to the *neepa* woods under its shady bowers; Come and bathe in the waters of the fresh showers'. It was one of Tagore's significant early poems, one of great style and alliteration—'There comes, in the tumultuous glee, the fury of the rains priding in its plumage of newly acquired youth and drenching earth with its perfumed waters, while wearing its soft, wet countenance of solemnity'—set to a reverberating melody and concluded with a song of wistful nostalgia: 'My song floats away ever and anon, don't call it back but bid it a fond adieu'. Setting the paradigm of a lyrical music drama, *Shesh Varshan* was a success with its elaborate mime-actions and dances in the Garba folk-form.

To set the records straight, *Varsha Mangal* came back in other incarnations in later times, mainly because the rains were Tagore's out-and-out favourite and he was always eager to pay his special obeisance to that turbulent season! In the 1931 event at Santiniketan, it was heralded by a *pas de troix* accompanying the marathon song: 'The universe reverberates with *vina* refrains captivating the world's heart: on earth, in waters, in the firmament, in forests and woods, in rivers and caverns, over expanses of water: with enduring sweetness of music and all-pervasive gestures of dance' and before the final mime-tableau, it concluded with a group dance: 'The torrential rains are over, the airs are redolent with the tune of farewell; Cease all music for the present, you have to travel very far'. The dance pattern was interesting: with a Gujarati Garba interlude, with solo dances by girls performed in Manipuri and group dances composed blending varied styles and keeping the dance rhythms in view. The other features were: a male solo by Santimay—'Is that the pre-summer cyclone that has enveloped the evening sky'—primarily in Kathakali style along with a sprinkling of wild gestures from Manipuri; and a special solo by Srimati Thakur—'Come to the *neepa* woods under its shady bowers'.

The other charity event of *Varsha Mangal* held in Kolkata in the same year (re-named as Geetotsav, Festival of Songs) was a more spectacular one, with all fifteen items accompanied by a wide range of dances, comprising Vasudevan's performance of semi- Bharatanatyam (mentioned earlier); Srimati Thakur's mood dance; Santidev's Kathakali with stress on *kalasam*; the Ashram girls' dances in mixed forms dominated by Manipuri; and liberal inputs in folk forms like Baul and Raybenshe. 'I know you so well, O the foreign lass' was the finale by the Hungarian maiden Elizabeth Sass Brunner (who was mentioned in Chapter 2). A major highlight was the classic poem 'Jhulan' ('I shall play the game of death staking my soul at this nocturnal hour') recited by Tagore and visualised in a vigorous style by Srimati Thakur. 'Who has drenched in colours the girdle round your slender loins and tied round your limbs the colourful garment?' (a children's poem composed by Tagore in 1903 about a mother addressing her child, and set to tune by him later in 1931) was another rivetting dance, executed by three winsome toddlers, with Srimati Thakur enacting the mother. All in all, in 1931, the entire programme was, apart from its wide variety, a copybook presentation of all the dance trends then prevalent in Santiniketan, which were gradually gathering momentum for Tagore's dance-dramas!

Natir Puja

Covered in Chapter 5, this ever-popular music drama of 1926 was the happy augury of Tagore's mood dance. In a sense, its principal danseuse offered her prayer to the Buddha almost as the initiation-rite for the full-blooded mood dance at Santiniketan. Gouri Bose (nee Bhanja)—who was a major sensation as *Nati*, but later got married and discontinued dance—noted about her own mood dance:

> Under Gurudev's (Tagore's) instructions and with the aid of Guru Nabakumar Singha, I embarked on *abhinaya* according to Manipuri style and as taught by the latter, and gave prime space to 'expression' in my dance. I tried to internalise the external parameters and give them my own independent form in order to visualise the varied creativity of Gurudev. I did so for my dance as well. Any dance style, I feel, can be moulded to capture the essential text and mood of Tagore's oeuvre, and used to visualise—in dance—the same in rhythms and expressions unique to Tagore's thought-process.

Nataraj–Riturangashala

Abbreviated as *Nataraj* and *Rituranga*, this 1927 production followed the success of *Natir Puja* in what Tagore called an amalgam of 'dance, music and recitation of poems'. The felicitation of the six principal seasons—in all their nuances and resonances—provided the connecting thread, reminiscent of the previous millennium's *Ritu Samharam* by Kalidasa. But primarily, *Rituranga* was meant for dance. As Tagore visualised (cited by Santidev Ghosh):

> In the *tandava* dance of Nataraj (Shiva), his one footstep spans the outer worlds; the other footstep strikes the inner world of mind: to trigger the domain of *rasa*. If both the inner and outer worlds can join

> in the rhythms of his universal dance, the human mind rids itself of all living bondages of time and space, and goes on to savour the taste of a cosmic playfulness.

The take-off point of the musical, interspersed with narrative in verse, was the four-stanza classic song: 'In the cadences of dance, O Nataraj, break all earthly bondages; Banish the slumber and awaken in the heart the rhythm of your ever-free melody'. The four stanzas came out with four different rhythms (at the suggestion of the dancers themselves) and Tagore urged the two ace dancers, Jamuna Bose and Amita Sen, to dance with duality of gestures and tempi: slow and fast. Vasudevan (see Chapter 2), in the role of Nataraj, sparkled a dark-ebony body—'cast in bronze', as master Nandalal termed it, decorating his bare torso with an artiste's palate—and danced divinely by combining his nominal Bharatanatyam with Manipuri. Jamuna and Amita, too, blended Manipuri with the southern idiom. A new, yet complete, dance form seemed to be finding itself out in Santiniketan.

In the poetic musical, Tagore composed six short 'songs of salutation' before the odes to each of the seasons took off, woven in six different rhythms. They were soft, supple and supplicant like Manipuri *lasya*, in sharp contrast to the southern salutation reflecting Nataraj's contemplative statue: sombre, solemn and serene. Along with both forms of salutations were mingled the earthen-lamp prayers at the *tulsi* platform in the warm evening glow, in an utterly meditative mood.

Mood dance, indeed, was the touchstone of *Rituranga* in most of its twenty-nine recorded songs, apart from the frequent recitatives for the poems. Here are some illustrations:

- 'Who're you to have made the lotus of unsullied light blossom forth, and break the slumber of the blue firmament': the dancer heralds the onset of autumn and in the slowest of motions, helps open the petals of the flower, one by one.

- '*Shiuli* blossom, *shiuli* blossom, under what forgetfulness did the night's wind bring you to be dumped in the forest shade?': the youngest of the dancers for autumn prances to and fro, with her billowy skirt getting puffed up to swirl around.

- 'Alas, Lady Frosts, why are your eyes covered—the deep veil of snow is painted with sombre grey colours': the dancer for *Hemanta* or the frosts enters decorated as the season and looks like a flickering lamp.

- 'Leaving behind the snow-capped mountain, O sage, whatever for did you come down to the plains? Here are the entreaties of *kunda* and *malati* flowers: please do be happy': a very special dance that ushers in not paddy-corns or mango-buds or even clouds above or breeze from the south, but a fireplace around for warmth! The artificial fireplace shaped in a square is brought in and it throws its flickering glow on stage. As regards enjoying the fire's warmth, Tagore would promote his idea: 'It's cold, biting cold and you're all shivering. You'll dance round the fireplace, extending your hands to pick up the fire's warmth, often standing up or sitting down and at times, going round and round the fire'. While saying this, Tagore would stand up himself and would make circles round the fire: with hands spread over the fire in varied postures. Since his heavy robe would be in the way, he would lift its lower ends in one hand and would extend the other hand over the fire. It would be the best mood dance from Tagore himself! Interestingly, the lifting of the robe became a recurring image in Tagore's later dance-paintings (See Chapter 11).

■ 'My lamp got extinguished while traversing my lonely walkway; It was the whiff of the impending storm, which I gained as my new companion': the dancer progresses alone as winter's companion, with the burning lamp in hand that gets repeatedly put off; the dancer is devastated by the howling winds of the thunderstorm and loses her sense of direction. She collapses, yet gets up with renewed vigour and lurches forward in the enveloping darkness—'[Who's to] put colours on the forests and cause waves in the winds', and the lone dancer for spring traipses sweetly in a light rhythm—'Colour up everything with your frenzied brush, before you finally leave: it should be your own splashes, your very secret hues, with the tinge of your youthful laughter, the pathos of your tearful melody'. It is the finale of spring and the entire group of dancers lets itself loose in joyous abandon, in the full-moon festive night.

The entire stage-décor was tastefully done in Javanese style by Surendranath Kar, on the basis of his first-hand knowledge of the area. The costume was also procured from Java, as evident in Tagore's description (cited by Santidev Ghosh):

> With golden tier on coiffeure, golden necklace with a crescent-moon pendant, snake-faced bangles on arms, tightly-draped upper garment from chest to waist, and pleated skirts with colourful *batik* motifs hung down to the feet from the gilded waist-belt—with shoulders and upper arms kept bare, immediately recapitulating an Ajanta fresco...

However, in capitulation to Indian prudery, Pratima Devi draped the dancer's upper torso with a matching golden blouse sans a loose cover. Again, the absence of the latter garment caused some consternation, but the resistance melted after the glittering show—indicating a triumph both for Tagore's aesthetics and for introducing Asia-Pacific décor—in a pioneering sense, keeping the historical period in mind.

Sundar

The 1925 version of *Sundar*, woven with seasonal songs, was initially abandoned due to an untimely thunderstorm, but performed a month later at Santiniketan. Its second version, enacted in Kolkata in 1929, was a vastly different one: changed into a dialogue between two characters—Queen and companion Vasantika (Rama Kar and Amita Thakur, nee Sen, respectively), sitting on stage who would dilate upon the implications of each song and the latter would entail its individual dance. The narrative was a lyrical invocation of spring defying winter: sending intimations of immortality and cloaking its appearance in a highly mystical sense. The portent was as mysterious as in *Raja, Arup Ratan* and *Shap Mochan* and the presentation was as nuanced. Over two nights, the number of dances went up from eleven to twelve and remained an endearing ovation to spring (Tagore's second best favourite season, after the rains).

Naveen

On a full-moon night in the spring of 1930, *Naveen* was conceived as a musical, mixed with textual narrative and, like *Rituranga* and *Sundar*, had dance as its leitmotif. Its lyrically formulated idea came best from Tagore:

> I have been urged to produce something new for the spring festival, but the cognoscenti—with a heightened sense of taste—insists that they want the nascent, not the new. According to them, the *madhavi* tree does not annually change its adornment, while *ashoka* and *palash* are as fresh as ever in their age-old colours every year. This old earth cocks a snook at the familiar novelties and echoes the Vaishnava poet—'Age after age have I surrendered my heart to your heart and they still do not breathe in unison'.

In the one-night and four-night recitals at Santiniketan and Kolkata, respectively, there were a score of songs (sung by a dozen singers): almost all interpreted in dance by a dozen dancers. Most dances had a prevalence of Manipuri rhythm and, in particular, the group dances were based on pure rhythm. Three leitmotifs are certainly worth noting:

- Folk idiom was copiously used. 'To where have my calls reached at this part of day' alongside the last melody from the tired hours of *Fagun*, earlier a Baul dance by Santidev with *ektara* in hand, was now transformed into a *pas de deux* using Raybenshe and Jari forms. Another mixed duet dance was: 'O my heart, there comes probably your surge of spring waves and the *joie de vivre* to break all barriers'. In fact, the success of *Naveen* was the set-off point to search for a virile masculine dance form, which culminated into identifying Kathakali as the best-suited style for this purpose.

- Mood dance came into its own strength, since the solos were rhythm-based dances that could express all: mood, spirit and joy. For instance, 'In the nascent joy of *Fagun*, I've woven this song of mine; The forest bowers have added to it the sparkle of the cuckoo's melody and filled it with the aroma of *bakul* blooms' was a fluent solo in rapid-fire rhythm, playing on small cymbals in hand, that went so well with the spirit of the lyric. Again: 'O the householders, throw ajar your doors, for, the colour fest has come: on earth, in waters, pervading the forest-places; do open your gates' was another solo, depicted in vigorous jumps and leaps in Manipuri, with a powerful body and its virile gestures.

As regards arhythmic mood dance—without the constant support of percussion—there was but one supreme request from Tagore to the dancer, as revealed in the following extract:

> Do you get such rhythmic footsteps when you're tired? The tedium must be brought out by your worn-out body and its gait. When you sing: 'When the mango-buds have tired out well-past their prime', then your entire body and torso must reflect that weariness.

Once the dancer picked up the idea and slumped down with the *ektara* in hand, Tagore came forward again and picked up the *ektara*, urging her:

> Bend further, still further down for your dance, as though you're biting the dust in tiredness. But, when you sing: 'O the sal tree, you oblige the spring in its solar world with your ramrod presence', then you would stand up straight and raise both your hands, as high as possible, above everything. You must remember you're now talking to the sal tree!

These were Tagore's own inspiring words for his mood dance!

Shravan Gatha

The 1934 version of *Varsha Mangal,* which was a regular ritual for welcoming the rains at Santiniketan, was named *Shravan Gatha* in 1934 and was a two-evening programme. Much similar to *Naveen* and *Vasanta* (see Chapter 4), it was a musical with a lyrical text, comprising three characters: Nataraj (Tagore himself), the king and the court-poet who sat at the wing-side during performance and described the contents of the songs and dances in their dramatised dialogue. There were in all twenty-two songs out of which one was depicted through mime-action and fourteen through dances: solos, three duets and two as groups. On *khol* was an especially versatile drummer: Nitaibenode Goswamy. Although Santiniketan in Tagore's time had not many talented instrumentalists, the versatility of a few was a fortunate support for the concomitant dancers and an asset to Tagore.

First Kindred Soul: Isadora Duncan

Tagore's repertory of the above musicals, based on his total assimilation of the spirit of nature, was much akin to Isadora Duncan, the poet-danseuse across the seven seas. Like Tagore, Isadora imbibed

Isadora Duncan: Dancing legend from the West.

the flow of dance into her psyche from stirring of tree-leaves, the breaking of billowy sea-waves, the vibration of birds' wings and the blue pigment of the wide firmament.

While any links between Tagore and his contemporary Isadora are not known, many of the prominent Ashram dancers felt an instinctive affinity with Isadora in composing their mood dance for Tagore songs as was evident in Dame Margot Fonteyn's observation on Isadora in the 1979 centenary tribute which was quoted by Amita Sen later:

> Isadora Duncan was a poet of motion. A poet uses the words we all know and, following his own inspiration, creates a movement... She wanted to become nature itself, to be the sky, the language personal only to him. That is what Isadora did with human waves, the breeze, not to transmute them by any known formula or art.

Fonteyn clarifies how Isadora invented her own formula.

> She had to find how she herself would run or skip if joy motivated that reaction, how she herself would bow down if someone crushed her, then she used those movements and gestures as her dance steps.

How intimate was the spiritual communion between the two great minds has yet not been firmly established.

Second Kindred Soul: Ruth St. Denis

Tagore's links with Ruth St. Denis, the American contemporary dancer, was much closer and perhaps less esoteric. Ruth had danced to a Tagore poem in New York in 1929 and known to have begun investigating Asian dance having seen an image of the Egyptian goddess Isis. She used to wear a flowing veiled costume that must have been seen by Tagore, for, the likeness of the mysterious veil became a recursive motif in Tagore's later paintings (see Chapter 11).

An outcome of their acquaintance during Tagore's visit to America was an informal conversation that took place between Tagore and Ruth in 1931. The subject of conversation was their combined poetry-and-dance recital which they were to stage at the Broadway Theatre on a Sunday night: for the benefit of Tagore's 'international university', as reported in the *New York Morning Telegraph* in 1930.

Conclusion

In Tagore's dance persona, 1926 and 1927 were the two watershed years, with *Natir Puja* (1926) and *Rituranga* (1927) as the two milestone events. Earlier, use of dance on stage was of little consequence to Tagore and was juxtaposed within his well-structured plays; dance—coming along with other mime-actions—was a minor event any way. It was in *Natir Puja*, where the play itself hinged on the cathartic event of a single dance, which inexorably changed the scenario. Tagore now proclaimed in public that he was the poet-disciple of Nataraj and would adopt the mantra of liberation from the Lord of Dance. The song-and-dance: *'Nrityero tale tale, hey Nataraj'* (In the cadence of dance, O Nataraj, break all earthly bondages) became his preamble for *Rituranga*, the six-season ode to seasons, where all the poems, songs and dances professed Tagore's unequivocal pronouncement that he considered Nataraj as his guru, precisely because he saw dance as a noble part of education, without any qualm of conscience. This opened the floodgates of various structured and semi-structured forms of dance—classical and folk—going through the sieving process of 'natural selection' and being incorporated in his many-splendoured celebrations of nature, as mentioned earlier. It was only a matter of time—as will be seen in Chapter 8—that dance became the mainstay of Tagore's drama, carrying the play's theme on its shoulders!

Biographical Notes

Isadora Duncan (1878–1927)

Born in San Francisco, Isadora Duncan spent many happy hours of her childhood playing and dancing upon the beach and even teaching dance to younger children in her teenage years. Isadora travelled to Chicago and New York, working and performing in various productions of Shaw and Shakespeare. But it was not until she reached London, however, that Isadora began to find acceptance for her dancing. Throughout her career, Isadora had a driving vision—like Tagore—the education of young children, grounding their learning in art, culture, movement and spirituality as well as academic lessons.

By 1900, she settled in Paris, moving to two large apartments: living on the ground floor and using the first floor for her dance school. Barefoot, dressed in clinging scarves and faux-Grecian tunics, she created a primitive style of improvisational dance: to counter the rigid styles of the time. She was inspired by the classics, especially Greek myth. She rejected traditional ballet steps to stress improvisation, emotion and human form. Isadora believed that classical ballet, with its strict rules of posture and formation, was 'ugly and against nature', and gained a wide following. She became so famous that she inspired artists and authors to create sculpture, jewellery, poetry, novels and photographs, water colours, prints and paintings.

Throughout her career, Isadora did not really like the commercial aspects of public performance and distractions from what was her real mission: the creation of beauty. A gifted pedagogue, she was the founder of three schools for young girls. The first in Germany gave rise to her most celebrated group of pupils called 'Isadorables'. The second had a short pre-War existence as a chateau outside Paris. The third was part of Isadora's tumultuous experience in Moscow in the wake of the Russian Revolution.

Ruth St. Denis (1879–1968)

Ruth Denis, born in New Jersey, was encouraged to study dance from an early age. Her early training included ballet lessons, as well as learning social dance forms and skirt dancing. In 1892, Ruth began her professional career in New York City and by 1898 she began performing as a featured dancer, under the stage-name of 'Ruth St. Denis'. Her artistic imagination was ignited by the dance-dramas of Japan, India and Egypt, apart from the influence of Sarah Bernhardt's acting style, in which the tragic fate of her characters loomed centrestage. After 1900, she formulated her own theory of dance-drama, based on her readings into philosophy and the history of ancient cultures. The image of the Goddess Isis of Egypt sparked her imagination and she began relating to Egypt and India.

By 1905, she was a solo artist and designed an elaborate costume and a series of steps: telling the story of 'Radha', a mortal maid who was loved by Lord Krishna. Entitled 'Radha', this solo dance—with three extras—was an attempt by Ruth to 'translate' her understanding of Indian culture and mythology to the American dance-stage. She surrounded her Indian maiden image with the symbols for five senses: bells for hearing; flowers for smelling; wine for tasting; jewels for seeing; and kissing of the palm for touching. Like Isadora Duncan, Ruth felt attracted towards Europe and arrived in London, travelling in the continent and performing her 'translations' until 1909. During the next five years of her tour on both sides of the Atlantic, her reputation as a 'classic dancer' put her in the same category as Isadora Duncan. But while Isadora sought the 'Self in the Universe', Ruth sought the 'Universe in the Self', intending to interpret the exotic worlds from the vantage-point of her body. In 1914 she hired Ted Shawn and became dance-partners everywhere. Ruth's solo 'translations' were unique *mise en scene* as also the contemporary dance-steps that combined theatrical and concert dance traditions.

The growing tempo of well-defined choreography had finally 'arrived' and was going to be almost explosive in the decade prior to the Poet's demise

Final Fruits

The phenomenal success of *Natir Puja* (1926), where the theme of the entire play veered on a single solo dance and that too performed by a female dancer— breaking out of the 'invisibility' of segregated women spectators—following Tagore's burst of creativity and under his benign guidance, signified the occurrence of three things all at once:

First, the Lord of Dance could be given a high pedestal at the front-stage—both physically and metaphorically—and fragmented dance items with individual songs could be made far more cohesive. They could, for instance, now bear the burden of an entire theme. Thus came gradually *Tasher Desh* (1933) and the illustrious quartet of its compatriots: *Shap Mochan* (1934), *Chitrangada* (1936), *Shyama* (1938) and *Chandalika* (1940), besides an incomplete *Mayar Khela* (1939), all of which used dance, carrying forward the theme of the drama: not perfunctorily but with full respectability.

Second, and actually flowing from the first, the growing tempo of well-defined choreography had finally 'arrived' and was going to be almost explosive in the decade prior to the Poet's demise. This was because Santiniketan was already the cradle of Manipuri dance—the only space outside Manipur—lustily suited to the women dancers, to which was added Kathakali for the vigour of male dancers, thanks to the untiring efforts of Santidev and the subcontinental gurus.

These forms undertook another veneer with both grace and mobility brought in from the Asia-Pacific region—particularly with mutually-aided flowering of Sripalli in Sri Lanka and Tamanshishya in Java—that came immensely handy to the growing orb of dance kinaesthetics at Santiniketan.

Third, and finally, structured choreography using individual dance elements—ranging from classical to folk, from solo to group—in Tagore's later oeuvre could now be incorporated not only by 'natural selection' but also by 'modification' and 'co-adaptation'. The seeds of this evolutionary process were already sown in the 1920s with the structuring of the method of teaching dance. Thus, the co-existence of *abhinaya*-based classical dances and *abhinaya*-less collective folk dances came about, often emphasising one or the other. For instance, the tree-planting ceremony for: 'Wave the flag for conquering the deserts' and the spring-celebration with: 'Throw your doors ajar, O the householders' would emphasise on group dance in folk-idiom. In sharp contrast to this, in the dance-drama *Chitrangada*, Arjuna offered unrequited love to the princess and in resentful agitation, broke into a scorching dance: 'What's the burning sensation that this turmoil has set on me; it's piercing my heart with its cruel arrows mercilessly' instead of trying to interpret each line of this song with hand gestures and footsteps set to vigorous rhymes; hence, a composite virile form was evolved mixing a few Indian classical styles with certain folk forms: for expressing wild hand and leg movements.

Even aspects of questions–answers within a dance-drama (as within an individual song) received attention: initially structured through the Manipuri *raas*, but later adapting itself to the Kathakali style. The latter confined itself to the hand and feet movement according to its pure dance forms like *kalasam*, but discarded verbatim copying of the intricate *mudras* of Kathakali. Indeed, the classical dance styles—like Kathak and Bharatanatyam, other than Manipuri and Kathakali—were sequentially arranged, warranted by the *bhava* of the characters of the dance-drama. After a lot of experimentation and analyses, Kandyan dance of Sri Lanka, Serimpi and Legong dances of Indonesia, Ram Poye dance of Myanmar (then Burma), dance of Thailand (then Siam) and dance of Japan (see Chapter 6) were suitably used in Tagore's dance-dramas—*Chitrangada, Shyama* and *Chandalika* (as well as in individual songs)—to achieve the best 'adaptation' results. And, all the while, Tagore's oeuvre was entirely consistent with the main culture of the land where music, drama and dance—since ancient times—have always been an integral part of its cultural manifestation: expressing myriad moods and spirits!

Dartington Methodology

As briefly mentioned in Chapter 2, Pratima Devi, in 1931, learnt from Dartington School of Devonshire, UK, the methodology of planning a new dance-drama, as developed by Kurt Joos (disciple of Rudolf von Laban) in his workshop.

The essential steps were:

- building up of each scene of the dance-drama as an independent 'chapter';

Tasher Desh: *Santidev and others.*

- amalgamating the part-dances gradually into a complete reference manual;

- using all the available student efforts to help contribute to the creation of an integrated choreography.

Akin to the concept of 'harmony' of many notes in Western music, the European dance too uses the concept of co-existence of manifold gestures and movements in the same scene. An instance could be the 'road-scene' in Joos's particular dance-drama, where a group of people was merrymaking; a lover-duo enjoying their sweet privacy; and a gaggle of unknown women throwing banters around. Display of different feelings and emotions in the same scene did not bring ennui, as they kept changing their expressions of feelings to keep the viewers' curiosity alive.

Joos's process of 'constructing' a dance-drama—alongside its inherent interplay of freedom of expression—was considered very useful by Pratima in Tagore's dance-drama. She also observed the need for liberating the rhythms in order to express different feelings. The European system allows for this freedom, which left a lasting impression in Pratima's mind. On return, Pratima used the methodology to the hilt, contributing a great deal of the required discipline in support of the new oeuvre of Tagore's music drama and dance-drama. It was perhaps near providential that Pratima was there in the right time at the right places to contribute her mite!

Phases of Dance Evolution

Tagore's dance-related dramatic oeuvre could be briefly summarised as follows:

Phase 0—dance nil: This was the phase of the recently Europe-returned Tagore penning his post-Wagnerian 'music drama': *Valmiki Pratibha* (1881) and *Kal Mrigaya* (1882) both of which had strong themes. He named them: 'drama set in melody'. Later, the song-studded *Mayar Khela* (1888) was a clear pre-Wagner opera, without a storyline. They all had rudiments of mime-action, but had no dance, as none was prevalent then.

Phase I—dance incidental: This phase was entirely of well-structured plays where dance played only an informal role—to supplement actors' mime-action and comprised Raja (1911), *Sharodotsav* (1911), *Achalayatan* (1911–12), *Falguni* (1915) and *Arup Ratan* (1920). Out of them, *Falguni* did not have defined characters and *Arup Ratan* tackled the same Buddhist legend from the *Kush Jataka* as in *Raja*, but keeping the male protagonist strictly in the background. While it saw Tagore as the dancing Grandfather—his last stage-role in life— Santidev was the singing and dancing *baul*, injecting the latter folk form into a full play for the first time.

Phase II—dance formal: This was the phase when Tagore introduced dance as a pre-requisite component for most of the songs which were lyrically conceived and were inspired odes to nature (barring the monumental work of theme-based *Natir Puja*, 1926, which brought for the first time the solo female dancer on Indian public stage under the garb of a legendary Buddhist courtesan). The repertoire consisted of *Vasanta* (1923), *Shesh Varshan* (1925), the phenomenally successful *Nataraj–Riturangashala* (1927), *Sundar* (1929), *Naveen* (1930), *Varsha Mangal* (1931, plus two later versions) and *Shravan Gatha* (1934). They were primarily musicals with lyrical dialogues providing links as in a drama. In *Nataraj* this was done by a narrator in pure verse, and in *Sundar*, there were two narrators who provided a running commentary.

Phase III—dance partially integral: Dance was related to the theme and used to mirror the dramatic conflicts—to quite an extent—in *Tasher Desh* (1933, as well as with an enhanced print version with new characters, new words and new songs in 1938) and *Shap Mochan* (1936). These two were in the nature of music dramas: with engrossing story-line, poetic dialogue, mime-action with songs—solo and chorus—and bringing in several dances, according to the situation,

Shyama: *The courtesan with Vajrasen. Nandita and another dancer.*

especially conceived to take the dramatic action forward.

Phase IV—dance fully integral: This was the acme of Tagore's dance vision: the entire theme told through dance completely integrated to the storyline—certainly music drama *par excellence*. The format was entirely recitative, with all dialogues expressed melodiously. As will be seen, *Chitrangada* (1936), *Shyama* (1938) and *Chandalika* (1938) brought in an absolutely new genre, named 'dance-drama', that was neither like Western ballet nor like Indian folk-form traditions.

Trendsetters—Jhulan *and* Shishu Tirtha

Complete assimilation of dance in a play was attempted in *Shishu Tirtha* (1931), a playlet inspired by the Passion play on Jesus Christ (see Chapter 3). *Jhulan*, staged in the same year, was a precursor of this form. The latter, written in 1892, was a rousing 'art poem' of Tagore starting with: 'I shall stake my soul today, to play the game of death at nocturnal hours', and ending with: 'The dream has vanished and the two madcaps have come out, Swing, push the swing'—much like the German *lieder* of Goethe, set to tune by Schubert. In 1931, Tagore, instead of using melody, recited the poem *Jhulan* in his sonorous voice and Srimati Thakur danced to his recitation, using the new Impressionistic choreography of Europe. Srimati's production style was the first of its kind at Santiniketan and thus much applauded by the cognoscenti. The repeat performance in 1936—with a similar recitation in Tagore's voice—was, however, enacted by Santidev in Sri Lanka's Kandyan style, with a touch of Indian Manipuri and Kathakali forms. The main idea was to make it completely a mood dance, where dance would reflect the feeling and emotion of the poem.

Shishu Tirtha was a much more elaborate art song in the manner of the German *lieder* (detailed in Chapter 3). The prose portions of each of the ten stanzas were read out by Tagore, and the dance troupe attempted mime-action for the narrative, followed by mood dance—solo or group —to express the inherent feeling of the accompanying song. Some special features were Srimati Thakur's dances in her own style for the opening and two feature-dances in between; two of Vasudevan's mood dances with elements of Bharatanatyam; and elaborate mood-entries and sitting down of all dancers with: 'The night has dawned, the road has ended—hark to the melodies of light in ethereal spheres' and their stylised getting-up with: 'Open the gateway of darkness, enter silent-footedly; O my mother, arise amid these new crimson rays'.

Music Drama with Prose Dialogue—Tasher Desh

Tagore described *Tasher Desh* as: 'romance and realism put side by side'. Arising out of a short story *Ekta Ashade Galpa* (A Cock-and-Bull Story), at the suggestion of Pratima Devi, it took the form of a full prose-drama in a very short time. The Poet even created three songs for the Prince out of his poem *Vanijye Vasate Lakshmi* (The Goddess Lakshmi Dwells in Commerce). Created in 1933, the play was hugely successful, enacted in six years on nine occasions—in Kolkata, Mumbai and Santiniketan—till 1939, within Tagore's own lifetime, and underwent many changes on each occasion except for the last one.

In essence, *Tasher Desh* is an out-and-out fantasy, with two sets of characters: the Prince and his travel companions (reduced to one in the last version) on one side and the minions of the Card Kingdom—club, spade, heart and diamond, culled from the card-game—masquerading in mobile human forms, on the other side. The setting is the Card Kingdom itself, where the Prince lands after a shipwreck and takes the humanoid Cards by surprise. The rousing conflict is between the wayward, happy-go-lucky Prince with his group and the stodgy, rule-bound Cards: their two worlds being poles apart. The plot thickens when the Card-women begin breaking rules and the precipice of the Card Kingdom—with its age-old pinnacles of ossified rituals and built-in prejudices—falls by the wayside. The play is from the point of view of the freedom-loving Prince who eventually 'contaminates' the whole Kingdom, even the King, and the tone throughout remains one of biting irony. The mood, therefore, is entirely iconoclastic!

Pratima wanted the play to begin with its shipwreck scene with frantic gestures for survival and irregular dancing, but it was not found feasible. The movements of the Card characters, according to Tagore's own participation-style, were to be listless and idle, moving around like zombies, falling down when they tried to march, and having, in general, no semblance of intelligence, thereby bringing out the sour humour of the Prince in his caustic remark: 'These people are neither dead nor alive'.

With successive changes of the script and introduction of new songs, the female Card characters (depending on the availability of Ashram girls who could dance) would dance according to the spirit of the song: sung by the supporting group of musicians.

Tasher Desh: *Romance and realism side-by-side. Uma Roy, wife of Kshitish Roy, as queen.*

The Prince and his cohorts, in contrast, were lively and their dances were energetic, even boisterous, with an abiding effort to instill a sprit of discontent—eventually leading to rebellion—in the still life of the Card Kingdom. In order to reflect this fully, inspiration was taken from a French dancer who had come to Santiniketan and demonstrated modern dance. Another source of idea was Srimati Thakur's modern dance of the Impressionist kind learnt in Germany. The final adoption was to use entirely an Indian idiom, keeping the European ballet's virility in mind. The 'natural selection' of Eastern idiom followed two paths. In the early phase, the base was mainly Manipuri, mixed with a few folk forms. In the later phase, opportunity was taken to utilise Manipuri, Kathakali and Kandyan dances with Indian folk tradition. This was possible mainly for the solo dances while group choreography had an abiding touch of folk.

One particular dance, among others, which was introduced during the play's performance in Mumbai—at the suggestion of the fiery patriot-poet Sarojini Naidu—stood out for the song: 'The crouching back in hesitancy is humiliating the self; don't get distressed at the sheer thought of an impending disaster'. This song, which was composed in 1938, included elements of Japanese wrestling and the primary exercises associated with judo. As a group dance it was performed by the Ashram girls, who had been earlier initiated into judo training. Tagore particularly appreciated the judo touch and the encores that it received from the viewers!

A special word needs to be mentioned about the jewellery and costumes of the Card Kingdom which had a unique relevance to its dance. Some of the female characters had learnt Javanese dance and had put their best foot forward, under Santidev. The master-painter Nandalal Bose, then quite aged, ordered the Javanese jewellery— preserved in the Kala Bhavan archives—to be replicated on leather base and used to a spectacular effect, since, according to Nandalal, 'the Javanese dance can only go well with Javanese dress and make-up'. Nandalal also elaborately planned costumes: with the primary goal of achieving a colour harmony. He worked out use of multi-coloured papers and clothes on pasteboard and drew on them *alpana* (folk figuration with votive and decorative motifs) to bring out adornments of individual Card characters. These were used as dress-material so that each actor could reveal a successful artistic façade. It was also important to keep in view the fact that there should be a harmonious colour unity—and no sense of jarring contrasts—when the actors appeared together on stage. On the whole, a universe of colour and rhythm opened up before the spectators' eyes, perceived as a many-splendoured, fairy-tale world!

Tasher Desh was, on balance, an emphatic statement of Tagore that no social system could carry on indefinitely by basing itself on a web of soulless, meaningless set of regulations. And no such superstructure of rules and rituals, imposed on society by the powers-that-be, could be everlasting;

it is bound to crumble down one day at the flimsiest of resistance. The Prince was able to remove the cobwebs of the Cards Kingdom not through war or through muscle-power or even through craftiness, but simply through the open force of youth, through an abounding message of joy and infectious fearlessness that touched one and all, even the Card King!

Music Drama with Narrator—Shap Mochan

Shap Mochan (1931), rightly speaking, is a musical narrative where the powerful storyline, which is recited by a narrator, is interspersed with songs and mime-action, most of which are integrally interwoven with dance. The occasion was the observation of the Poet's seventieth birthday when, at the request of the students of Calcutta University, Pratima Devi suggested to the Poet an adaptation of *Arup Ratan* (1920) in a song-and-dance narrative, somewhat resembling *Shishu Tirtha* (1931). Accepting the idea, Tagore wrote out the narrative in running prose, based on *Raja* (1911) and *Arup Ratan*, for enactment on 'Students Day' in Kolkata. After Kolkata, it was successfully performed in Lucknow in 1933—for the first time outside Bengal—and then many times in Delhi, Chennai, Mumbai and Sri Lanka, by the time it reached maturity.

Thematically, Tagore ascribed the genesis of *Shap Mochan* to the Buddhist *Kush Jataka* where the legend has a Bodhisattva born as an utterly ugly-looking king, Kush, who is married at his mother's behest to the beauteous princess of Madra Desh. The marriage, consummated only in total darkness to hide the king's ugly visage, falls apart and the dissatisfied princess then returns home. After many dramatic vicissitudes, Kush becomes a handsome prince, blessed by the jewel *Virochan* (name of another Bodhisattva) and the couple re-unites in happiness. Neither *Raja* nor *Arup Ratan* explains the genesis of the king's ugly countenance, but in *Shap Mochan's* overture, Tagore does mention an incident of the king's previous life in paradise when he was a singing *gandharva* in the royal court of Indra where, having made a serious mistake in his music concert, he was cursed by the latter to be born on earth.

Characters in *Shap Mochan* are few and far between. After the overture in Indra's court—with king Indra, queen Sachi, *gandharva* Sourasen and *gandharvi* Madhushri—leading to the curse as *cause celebre*, the rest of the narrative features only the utterly lonely earthling-queen Kamalika (besides her occasional maids) and her pining lover-king Aruneshvar (with companion). The latter remains hidden from her presence throughout the play. The setting is a fantasy-space purported to be the boudoir of the queen. The conflict is entirely in Kamalika's domain, who is constantly beseeching Aruneshvar's visible presence as well as lamenting the unfairness of his 'willful' invisibility. The narrator switches the points of view from one protagonist to the other. The tone is quite lyrical and the mood verges on the spiritual: between the ardent devotee and her besought godhead. Indeed, the burning passion of the queen for her desired 'vision' could be rubbed off on the Sufiana *kalam* of the distant Persian shores.

Dance was used to follow the flow of the lyrical narration by the story-teller and was especially used to express the mood of dramatic conflicts: aided by mime-action. While it did not possess the nature of dance-drama all through, it did blend dance very well with music and mime-action. The competent band of trained dance pupils—including, among females, Amita, Jamuna, Nivedita, Nandita and, not the least, Srimati Thakur whose dance training had begun in Santiniketan, and Santidev among the male dancers—was an asset for such creative work. Interestingly, due to the sudden indisposition of Santidev, Dr Harry Timbers danced and used mime-action as Aruneshvar opposite Amita as Kamalika and Jamuna as the principal maid. Timbers, well-acquainted with Russian folk dance and a few other European dances, was initiated into the spirit of the narrative in English by Tagore who explained to him the meaning of each of Aruneshvar's songs. To Kamalika, Tagore demonstrated personally the finale: her meeting with Aruneshvar—'How profoundly moved am I by witnessing you, wherefrom having you appeared in my heart of hearts'—how, in her mood dance, a heavenly glow should light up her whole visage!

The play's overture with the curse-scene began with the protagonists doing consistent mime-action along with the verbal narration and performing rhythm-based dance with the songs otherwise. The setting of the dramatic mood was interesting: with *gandharva* Saurasen (later Aruneshvar) playing on the *mridanga* alongside the solo dance of Urvashi, the celestial nymph: 'I'm scared lest I forget the melody and lest the snapped chord wins over', and committing the error in rhythm count, having remained preoccupied as he was thinking about his absent wife. This was followed by another solo by his repentant wife Madhushri (later Kamalika), a *gandharvi*, who sought thousand apologies from everyone and danced her departing number: 'Let the farewell pot brim with the nectar of remembrance; do bring it back when we hold our re-union festival'. Pratima's instructions for Madhushri's mood dance were clear: she should approach every companion of hers to bid goodbye and should complete her *abhinaya* accordingly, not just execute a solo and move away. For the rest of the narrative, the pattern followed was of mime-action with the verbal narration and dance with the songs—sung in the background—in dialogues between Aruneshvar and Kamalika. The resources available and used were the Manipuri dance form, folk forms of Bengal and the ones recently acquired from Kerala (see Chapter 5).

What Tagore wrote about *Arup Ratan* as its introduction could also, *mutatis mutandis,* express the very essence of *Shap Mochan*:

> Sudarshana (Kamalika) sought the King (Aruneshvar) outside. She sent her garland of acceptance to where things are visible in one's own eyes, collected in the closed chest, and touched by men, money and fame. Using her own reasoning power, she had resolved that she would achieve success in life in the externalities. Her companion had told her that when the Lord appears within the innermost chamber of mind, one should recognise him so that recognising him outwardly can no longer be mistaken—otherwise, those who use illusion to deceive the vision, would be mistaken for the King. Sudarshana did not listen. She saw the beauty of Suvarna and mentally surrendered herself to him...How her self-indulgence ebbed away being struck by sorrow and how, at the end, she gained the companionship of her Lord who could be realised within one's innermost joyous heart in all lands, at all times, in every form, has been narrated in this play...

This was perhaps nearest to Sufism from another ethos—moving from mundane love of *ishq majazi* (where both lovers endure normal earthly feelings of joy and pain, agony and ecstasy) to ethereal love of *ishq haqqiqi* (where the lover is a human being and the beloved is God)!

Basic Tenets of Dance-drama

It was only in the last half decade of Tagore's life that his dance consciousness reached its zenith and he could offer the best of his lifetime passion for dance in the form of three dance-dramas, namely, *Chitrangada, Shyama* and *Chandalika*, beside the incomplete *Mayar Khela*. The major features of Tagore's dance-dramas have been summarised below.

All these three dance-dramas were akin to *Valmiki Pratibha* and *Kal Mrigaya*, predominantly 'recitative' music dramas.

The clear storyline was piggybacked mainly on the 'recitative' pattern of the melodiously articulated dialogues (barring the occasional poetry in *Chitrangada*), which was interlaced with songs.

Dance finally found its mooring and was completely integral to the theme from beginning to end: providing the play's *leitmotif* in myriad moods.

The beats of the songs, now unlike the earlier music dramas of *Valmiki Pratibha* and *Kal Mrigaya*, were deliberately structured in order to facilitate the footsteps of the dancers.

The songs were not put together in a bunch. Instead, they changed their tempo and rhythm every now and then, keeping in view the question-and-answer mode of the intervening 'recitative' dialogue.

The Indian rhythms (see Chapter 10) like *Chautal* (sixteen beats), *Dhamar* (fourteen beats), *Surphanktal* (ten beats) and so on, have different capacity of expressing *rasa* and Tagore—as a consummate artist—kept in mind the inherent strength of rhythms in order to amalgamate the texts of the song's lyrics with their rhythms.

Harking back to the tenets of Herbert Spencer who inspired him in his early youth (see Chapter 3), the Poet used one rhythm for an angry mood, another for a solemn mood and yet a third rhythm to denote a joyous mood. The same rhythm was never used in any dance-drama of his to express all of anger, pain and happiness. The melodies, too, changed their colours in favour of the rhythms of the songs. The same *raga* would express different flavours for different songs, keeping with the variety of their rhythms.

The compatibility of *raga* and rhythm with the mood and emotion of the song was achieved to the highest order, possible only because of Tagore's deep knowledge of Indian classical and Bengal's folk music (see Chapter 10).

Although Indian dance is primarily based on music and its expression, Tagore did not adopt the instrumental orchestra to provide the backbone of his dance-drama, a la Western ballet.

And even though Tagore's dance-dramas were meant to be enacted in the form of dance, the main *rasa* of the play was kept uppermost in mind. The dancers were vehicles of conveying that spirit to the viewers, dwarfing their individual skills and dexterity all the while.

The male and female dancers often came from the background of different styles and techniques. But the aim defined for them by Tagore was to convey correctly the nuances of the song they were meant to dance with.

Above all, no dance technique was considered anathema to his dance-drama as long as the technique was capable of conveying the essential mood and spirit.

Facing page: Chandalika: *mother duo—Nandita and Mrinalini Swaminathan.*

First Dance-drama— Chitrangada

Tagore wrote his major poetic work *Chitrangada* in 1892, as a verse-play taking the original characters from the epic Mahabharata. Written in blank verse and divided into eleven sections, the verse-play recounts, in flashback, how Princess Chitrangada—brought up in the garb of a boy by her father, the king of Manipur—was rejected by the Pandava-hero Arjuna and how she seeks from the God of Love supreme feminine beauty to conquer Arjuna. The boon is granted and the new Chitrangada is able to lure Arjuna, notwithstanding his vows as a hermit, and spends a year in conjugal bliss. Every good thing has to come to an end, for Arjuna wakes up to reclaim his masculine prowess and counter bandits in Manipur, an act accomplished earlier by Princess Chitrangada. The veil falls and the princess meets her lover now: as an equal and without any pretence. The play's slightly abridged nine-act version,

Chitra, appeared in 1914, in Tagore's own English translation.

The play's transformation into a dance-drama went through four defined stages. In January 1936, Pratima Devi first planned to convert the verse-play into a dance-and-mime version and prepared a five-act skit, a la Dartington schema. During rehearsals, she introduced more dances to replace the mime-action. By the third stage, Tagore warmed up to the idea and added a few songs, and eventually took up full charge and composed many more songs to replace the previously planned ones. The complete dance-drama took shape in February 1936: within just a month of frenetic activity!

Already well structured as verse-play, *Chitrangada* as a dance-drama is still tauter in its six-act depiction: with dramatic events played out without flashback and with the character Vasanta dropped altogether. There are only three major characters: Chitrangada (with female companions), Arjuna and Madana (God of Love). The setting is mainly the Manipur forests and the hermitage of the recluse Arjuna. The see-saw conflict is very real: 'early' Chitrangada's overture to Arjuna and the latter's stern rejection; 'new' Chitrangada's reluctant offer of the self and Arjuna's instant surrender of male machismo; Chitrangada's constant self-introspection and Arjuna's conjugal fervour; and so on, till the resolution of conflict takes place on equal terms. The point of view is mainly Chitrangada's, with Arjuna's egotistic self-opinion playing only a second fiddle. The tone is of self-examination throughout for Chitrangada whose mood is wildly variant spanning: utter dejection; earnest devotion; veiled jubilation; conjugal elation; jaded satiation; and final self-revelation on equal terms.

Facing page: Chitrangada: *The Choral Group; Sujata and others.*

Between 1936 and 1940, *Chitrangada* was showcased nearly forty times: first in Kolkata, and then all over West India. As the leader of the troupe, Tagore would sit front-stage and recite the poetic dialogues of Arjuna, Chitrangada and the female companions as well as the finale of Sanskrit hymns: to be interpreted in the actors' dance gestures. Mahatma Gandhi arranged a donation of Rs 60,000 to help Visva-Bharati and considering the Poet's advanced age, urged him not to undertake such fund-raising tours any more. Tagore abided by his request till death.

As seen above, the poetic and academic *Chitrangada* was re-composed as musical and terpsichorean *Chitrangada*, with the latter's dignity and valour taking new shape in variegated rhymes and melody. This brings up the issue of 'natural selection' of different dance forms, referred to earlier as 'modification' and 'co-adaptation'. For *Chitrangada*, this often became a question of 'juxtaposition' of different classical dances of the land. The 1936 performance was entirely done in Manipuri form, with a mix of some folk movements and touches of Asia-Pacific styles. By 1937, and with regular Kathakali training, that form was juxtaposed in Arjuna's dance in 1939–40 with Kelu Nair performing as Arjuna, but he, too, had to be 'broken in' to adopt only broad hand gestures of Kathakali in consonance with the song's mood and avoid grammatically correct Kathakali *mudras*, as delineated in *Hasta Lakshana Deepika* (see Chapter 9).

Although different forms of dance were used together, their 'juxtaposition' was made so skilfully that the same *tala* would have many ingenious variation patterns and thus avoid boring repetitions. This is *sine qua non* in European dances where the tempo of the dance starts slow, gradually reaches a crescendo and finally comes down to a standstill. As a matter of fact, even in Indian dances, especially from the South, such variations in the *tala* are introduced for the dancer by the percussionist on *mridangam* by virtue of five *jaatis* and their arithmetic sum is built up to a multiple of the given *tala* so that the *sam*, that is, the culmination of the rhythm-cycle, is duly maintained (see Chapter 10). Perhaps in Tagore's time, such competent instrument players were not available in Santiniketan.

Some instances of dance 'juxtaposition' have been cited below. These clearly depict the excellent effect of mood dance in *Chitrangada*.

■ 'Arjuna, so you're Arjuna' is the first highly emotional adulation by Chitrangada that rises to a peak of jubilation and then comes down slowly, upon Arjuna's sharp rejection, to a pathos: 'Alas, the wretched girl, what's this reception from the exulted who came like a god and went away deceiving you?' and descends to the depth of despair. This impact is achieved by using a variety of melodies and rhythms, which comes at the end of a *tala's* time cycle and admirably fulfils the need of dramatic conflicts;

■ In the bath-scene, the dance combines the Manipuri *Pancham* (eighteen beats) and *Charitali* (eight beats) rhythms with the Hindustani *Teevra* (fourteen beats) and *Dadra* (six beats). Hence, in the song: 'I listen to the beckoning of the bottomless oceans every moment and ever in my heart; my listless mind is unable to remain standstill at home', two dance forms come together to express the mood of new jubilation after the depression is over. Interestingly, Manipuri normally does not register feelings on the face or eyes, but expresses them through *tala*; here an exception was made to use facial expressions in Manipuri.

■ In the dramatic scenes when the God of Love is worshipped, where Chitrangada commands her companions to bring flowers, Arjuna sets forth for hunting and where Chitrangada asks her companions to leave the woods, only *tala* is used to express the feelings. Similarly, conventional dance style is discarded in Chitrangada's introspective solos, after the heartless refusal of Arjuna: 'What's this radiance of yours, *Mon Amour*, that has lit up my eyes, perhaps you were concealed in the dazzle of the solar orb' and later, 'Such a tear-besmirched spring, my dear companion, had never assailed us before'.

■ When Arjuna, after many nights of indulgence, wakes up to reclaim his masculine ego: 'If I could meet her, I would rush out with her to relieve the distressed', his countenance would wear a distant look, reflected in the lyric and the melody. The hero's face is not caught by the viewers' gaze, but the music and rhythm conveys that Arjuna has received the call of duty and is straining at the reins to go out, after regretting and repenting for the passage of time in luxuriant indolence. Arjuna's body is taut and erect, and no feeling or mood is registered on his countenance because none is needed!

■ A speciality of *Chitrangada* is the occurrence of small poems—as in a few exclamations of female companions and once the lament of Chitrangada—which connect with the main storyline and permit the spectators' mind to have a break from the song-and-dance. In the real sense, these poems, in the play, resuscitate the corporeal dance and allow to rejuvenate the viewers' mind to the forthcoming dance.

Chitrangada, on balance, was a culmination of the 'modification' and 'co-adaptation' process of dance that was going on in Santiniketan and kept the same ideal in view. The norm of choreography was not to add rhythmic dance gestures to a song found suitable for enactment. On the contrary, the main force of emotion in a song was kept into focus and favourable rhythms and dance gestures from different Indian dance forms were culled together to bring out that force. Besides, for songs suitable for enactment, mnemonic-based dance was interlaced in the same *tala* so as to bring out the variety of rhythms. As a rule, Bharatanatyam and Kathakali were used to express the firm thinking spirit of Chitrangada, whereas the Manipuri style was adapted towards the soft, emotion-laden demeanour of the 'beautiful' Chitrangada.

The main aim was, steadfastly, to express the mood of the song. No Indian or Asia-Pacific dance style was left out of choreography to achieve this propose, backed by continual training in Indian classical styles, folk forms and Asia-Pacific dances. Even the non-resident dancers, who joined from abroad, had to be 'broken in' for this purpose. While Kandyan dance was somewhat 'sanitised' for this purpose to shed its extra virility, on the other hand, four Ashram boys were selected and trained for the fourth scene, to perform in the Kandyan style with the vigorous song of villagers: 'Lo, there appears the gang of bandits, coming down fiercely like the torrential flood-waters', with wooden swords wrapped in silver foils held in one hand and shields, decorated in colourful patterns, held in the other hand, executing a martial dance to everybody's appreciation.

This process of combination by which different *talas* and melodies became one to express a specific feeling in *Chitrangada* could be termed an 'aggregation' and is a common phenomenon in European ballet, but is relatively unknown in the Indian dance tradition. While almost all the dances in *Chitrangada* were classical-based, a few 'rhythmic' dances were created to instil a variety in *nritta*, as otherwise only music would not sustain *nritya*. Another point about *Chitrangada* was that its artistic excellence was not dependent on the oral text of written words, but on the performance text of melody and rhythm, and the mood mirrored by the dancers' body language. The dancers needed strong body-lines which, in turn, were accentuated by the background colours and lighting, without which the dance-drama would remain insipid!

In *Chitrangada*, Tagore wrote:

> The expression of truth is apparently in the exteriors of accoutrement and the variants of colours—its ostensible attraction envelopes our mind. Once the externalities are removed, the enlightened mind realises the complete manifestation...The play's theme is that the initial bondage of love is pure infatuation; later, when it is freed from that illusion, the plain truth shines in its unadorned glory.

But, beyond the riddance of individual infatuation at the tortuous end, there is a higher dimension: about femininity. The earlier verse-play began on the note of an abject offer of surrendering of womanhood to the altar of man, to be his companion, charioteer, follower in hunting, night-guard, devotee, servant and subject—while the dance-drama catapults the image to a transcendental level, again in Tagore's own words: 'I am Chitra. No goddess to be worshipped, nor yet the object of common pity to be brushed aside like a moth with indifference. If you deign to keep me by your side in the path of danger and daring, if you allow me to share the great duties of your life, then you will know my true self'. This is the triumphant voice of universal femininity! Indeed, Tagore was very particular about the stentorian proclamation of the princess in the finale: 'I'm Chitrangada, the daughter of the king of kings; I'm neither a goddess nor an ordinary female'. He urged the protagonist: 'Never forget your exalted status; express it to the hilt in all your feelings and gestures'. This was mood dance rejoicing womanhood!

Second Dance-drama— Shyama

Like *Chitrangada*, *Shyama* underwent many versions. Inspired originally by the Buddhist story from *Mahavastu Avadan*, the first version was *Parishodh*, a long episodic poem written in 1899, about the royal courtesan Shyama and her sudden passion for the handsome stranger Vajrasen—caught on a false charge of theft—for whom she does not hesitate to sacrifice her young lover Uttiyo at the gallows. On the felony being known, she is summarily discarded by her 'new' lover Vajrasen. In the rhymed poem, the rich resonance of Nature—to the variegated course of raw passion and its retribution—is unparalleled, a role taken up by Shyama's female companions as the 'voice of conscience', in what Tagore called 'dramatised musical' version of *Parishodh* in 1938. The musical was set entirely in melody and, unlike *Chitrangada*; no portion was left for simple oral narration. *Shyama* was the final version, substantially enlarged and enriched, enacted as dance-drama at Santiniketan and Kolkata, in 1938 and 1939.

The two main protagonists are Shyama and Vajrasen, besides the king's minions as well as the youth Uttiyo, with the courtesan's companions acting as a 'voice of conscience' and serving the same purpose as they did for Princess Chitrangada in the eponymous play—a well-known ploy used in Bengali folk-drama *Jatra* essayed by *Vivek*, literally meaning conscience. The setting varies from a public avenue, to Shyama's chambers, to the prison-cell, to the luxury-yacht carrying the fleeing lover-duo, to the forests on the riverbank, to the final separation. The plot is playing out of *amour propre* between the lovers: now infatuated, now quarrelling and desperately estranged. The point of view is entirely Shyama's: besotted with passion and eager to elope, to the admission of her felony and her eventual desertion. The mood is of the urgency of the lovers' union: only to fall apart. The tone is, for both lovers, psychologically nuanced—unlike the deep intelligence and understanding of Chitrangada, countered by a strident Arjuna, deliberately vaunting bravado of male ego. The primary beauty of *Shyama* is the heaving rise and fall of its conflicts and their Spencerian tempo: almost like the Western music's overture with *allegro*, leading on to *adagio* and *rondo*, and then to the denouement in *adagio*: on the waxing and waning of the passage of arduous passion between the two principal contenders.

Shyama, coming after *Chitrangada*, reached another hallmark of both 'modification' and 'co-adaptation' of dances. In the 'natural selection' process that was going on in Santiniketan, efforts were made to experiment with all the five classical styles that had reached the Ashram: Manipuri, Bharatanatyam, Kathakali, Kathak from India and Kandyan dance from Sri Lanka: in the following roles:

- Shyama by Nandita Thakur (nee Kripalani), Tagore's grand-niece, who had learnt Manipuri at Santiniketan;

- Vajrasen by Mrinalini Swaminathan (nee Sarabhai), a student at Santiniketan, who knew Bharatanatyam well;

- The watchman (which is a cameo role) by Kelu Nair, an alumnus of Kerala Kalamanadalam, who had come as a Kathakali teacher at Santiniketan;

- Uttiyo by Asha Ojha, a relatively new arrival at Santiniketan, who had learnt Kathak well from the Jaipur *gharana*, with emphasis on movement and footwork;

- *Kotal* (royal guard, another cameo role) by Ananga Lal, a student from Sri Lanka, who knew Kandyan dance well; and

- The female companions by the Ashram girls who had learnt Manipuri from the teachers at Santiniketan.

As seen in Chapter 5, Tagore took care, for instance, to make a personal check of Asha's skills with different *talas* as well as *abhinaya*. Thereafter, for Uttiyo's songs, the mood and *tala* of each line was expressed through Kathak style and then *bol* and *tehai* were executed for the same *tala*—carrying forward intact the mood of the previous line in the facial expression, hand gestures and body postures, before embarking on the following line or a new song. This involved substantial effort, which was considered worthwhile for bringing in Kathak. Similarly, for Kotal, Ananga performed valorous Kandyan dance before Uttiyo's tragic end, and before jumping on him—in a *tehai* stance—with open sword in hand, with the whole stage turning instantly dark, to achieve maximum effect.

For Kathakali, Kathak and Kandyan dance styles—in both *Chitrangada* and *Shyama*—the excessive play on *drishti bhed* and *griba bhed* was avoided. These movements might have come to India under outside influence, a surmise which did not apply to Manipuri style that never overplayed the face or waist perhaps due to its insulated existence in the Northeast.

Some senior dancers themselves, it must be admitted, did not take kindly to the 'juxtaposition' of styles. Srimati Thakur, for instance, recorded later, 'In *Chitrangada*, the Manipuri technique appeared the best'. For *Shyama*, she observed,

> Apart from the group dances which are generally in the Manipuri style, we find Vajrasen dancing in Bharatanatyam and Kathakali (in a later version) styles, the watchman rendering his part in the Kathakali technique, while Uttiyo exhibited his proficiency in the Kathak style. To some, this exhibition of the three techniques in one play is a great achievement. For me,

Shyama: *A performance by Nandita.*

> however, they seem to be artificially pushed in, disturbing the atmosphere of Tagore's play...To me, Tagore's dramas and characters—[including] the whole atmosphere of his plays—have an aesthetic appear[ance] and cannot form a platform for exhibition of various techniques.

The main point that Srimati might have missed was Tagore's real intent. While the Poet's dance-dramas were meant to be performed through dance, each play had its own mood or set of moods—that constituted its essence. The dancer was a tool to enact that mood and make it as express as possible to the audience. The aim was, as stated before, not to show off how great the dancer was or how sublime her technique could be, but how much of the mood and spirit of the play the dancers, all put together, were able to convey to the viewers. This viewpoint has been uniformly true for all his music dramas as well as dance-dramas.

The import of *Shyama* is in the overwhelming guilt that Shyama carries that makes her unacceptable to Vajrasen. The heinous depth of Shyama's guilt for making the innocent Uttiyo a victim of her 'lust' for Vajrasen—all the more galling because Uttiyo is far too young and still willingly offers his life—makes it comparable to the Christian Guilt: with Shyama as the sinning *femme fatale* and Vajrasen as the condemning Lord, and with the same overtones of temptation and manipulation. Vajrasen seems to be both cursing and be cursed: first at his outburst of love and then at the wretchedness of his situation of having been saved from sure death at such an enormous cost. The other and more material messages are equally relevant, such as the foreigner being duped, the need to keep the administration well-oiled at any expense, the power of money to the minions of the establishment, the reach of wealth ('royal ring') even into the dungeons and the fatal attraction of sexual favours apparent everywhere. These messages are valid to this day.

Third Dance-drama—Chandalika

Chandalika, like the other two dance-dramas, had a chequered history. It was written first, in 1933, as a two-act prose-play and adapted from *Shardula-Karna Avadana*, a part of the Nepali Buddhist lore, and confined virtually to a dialogue between Prakriti and her mother. The story, as encapsulated by Tagore, takes place at Shravasti where the Buddha is residing temporarily. His favourite disciple Ananda, once after a meal with a householder, feels thirsty while returning and asks for drinking water from Prakriti, a *chandali*, who was fetching water from the well-side. Prakriti gets infatuated with the handsome monk and, in the absence of any other alternative, seeks help from her mother who knew magic. The mother, initially reluctant, performs her elaborate magic rites and throws one hundred and eight *arka* flowers, one by one, into the sacrificial fire. Ananda is unable to resist the magical force and arrives at her place in the night. While Prakriti is preparing the nuptial bed, Ananda feels severe compunction and prays fervently with tears to the Buddha for redemption. The distant savant realises the condition of his devotee and rescues him from the mantras of the *chandali*.

In 1938, the draft of a new version was prepared by Pratima Devi to convert the prose-play into a dance-dominated musical and introduced dramatic action. In this version, there is initially a village fair where the boys and girls are generally enjoying themselves, and the *santhal* tribals are busy dancing. Prakriti's mother enters and there is consternation all around as she orders her daughter to stop dance, fetch water and return home. When Prakriti is dancing and lifting her bucket of well-water, the Buddhist Shamans pass her way, with the last one asking for water to drink. On Prakriti's initial hesitations, he assures her of her essential humanity and blesses her after the drink. Prakriti is almost mesmerised.

Tagore at that point was acutely aware of the countrywide spread of communal disharmony and was deeply pained about its evil consequences. Pratima's proposal came in handy and the Poet resolved to transform the prose-play into a full-fledged dance-drama, turn it entirely into a 'recitative' form and after adding a few songs from his available repertoire, innovate with a number of brand new prose lyrics and set them to music. Lyrical prose, incidentally, did not occur in any other dance-drama earlier. The play was staged in Kolkata and at Santiniketan in 1938 and 1939. The 1940 performance at Santiniketan was witnessed by Mahatma Gandhi and was highly appreciated by him for its theme of untouchability. It was last produced in Asansol in 1940 while Tagore was alive.

A dramatic scene from Chandalika.

The much enlarged three-act *Chandalika* has many characters, besides Prakriti and her mother, such as the upper-caste village-belles who take quite a dim view of Prakriti's efforts to hobnob with the flower-vendors, curd-seller and bangle-supplier. There are also chanting Shamans and their leader Ananda. The setting is the milieu by the well-side and the secluded hamlet. The plot is virtually the same as the Buddhist episode, barring that the latter's innuendos of physical union are wonderfully sublimated into deeply divisive psychological conflicts—starting with the mother's mind—from simplistic caste reservations to a fiendish proclivity to wield witchcraft—and ending with Ananda's transcendental purity torn asunder under the spell of magic and the unbearable pain of potential perdition.

But the utmost conflict is within Prakriti: between her passionate love and carnal desire for Ananda on one hand, and the convulsions in her mind on the other—by realising the monk's anguish, not merely to let him free but also to fall into his footsteps: a substantial departure from the original ending. The point of view is primarily that of Prakriti: a mindset that changes from muted acceptance of social rejection to an awakening into 'spiritual freedom' in this birth itself (enunciated remarkably well in the Buddhist *Lotus Sutra*), from her fiercely possessive passion for Ananda to an enlightenment to follow him, which is normally much above her station of life. The mood is largely of desperation to achieve a self-defined goal and the tone varies from a stentorian call to her mother to get to the desired object fast up to the shearing self-flagellation that tears her into total submissiveness.

Conflicts in *Chandalika*—both inter-character as well as intra-character—are on an extraordinarily large scale. Also, each conflict spans a wide range: rising to a precipice and diving down to a deep gorge: almost staccato in nature. If Tagore took liberty in using prose-librettos to express a gritty, earthy texture in his text, he did justice to their variety and range by using an incredible diversity of tunes. Appropriately termed the 'solar universe of melody' by Pratima Devi, the play had both 'recitative' dialogues and actual songs, creating together a musical panoply *ad extensor*. The filigree of tunes filled the oral–aural space: starting with *keertan* and *baul*, followed with the *ragas* of Purabi, Sahan and Paraj, and ending with the mystic sounds of Bhairavi and Bageshri, when the conflicts were finally resolved. An orchestration of contrasting melodies to create a total 'unity of action' was perhaps the first of its kind in India, barring the *Natya Sangeeta* in Maharashtra.

In keeping with the wide range of melodies used to resonate the burning passions and their fractured expression in the play, Tagore also used a different 'juxtaposition' of dance. Since the dramatic mood was less given to the graceful, gliding flow of Manipuri and more to structured body-lines and vigorous footsteps, he looked to the South: Kathakali and folk forms of Kerala (like *Swaram, Kaikuttikali* and *Kalammuli* already taught at Santiniketan), the then-existent Bharatanatyam (after its recognition and christening in 1935) and the virile Kandyan dance from Sri Lanka. Kathakali, for one, contributed less with facial expressions and complex hand gestures, but more with rhythmic footsteps that ended the rhythm-cycles with *kalasam* (see Chapter 9). Kandyan, for another, was retained with shapely masculinity in body movements but denuded of its aggressive postures for the dance of the curd-seller. Kandyan mnemonics, for another, were also used for the self-assertive dance of Prakriti: 'Whoever is the divinity that has sent me to this dungeon of ignominy, I won't, I won't, and I won't worship that unwholesome deity'. On the whole, the 'natural selection' of the southern forms was made into what has been christened a 'chemical solution' and not individually identifiable elements. On the other hand, there is only mime action when Prakriti is lifting water from the well, sans any dance.

Together, *mishra sur*—blended melodies, *mishra bhangi*—harmonised body movements as well as *mishra tala*—synchronised rhythmic steps achieved a new innovative height of 'dramatic unity'. This could best be illustrated from a single character like Chandalika. In the evolution of her own mindset, the entire evolutionary pattern of the human mind was mirrored, proving truly that 'ontogeny is the recapitulation of phylogeny'. What is the real, primal passion of a female for her male provided the motif of her opening dance. That the body had its fatal attraction which could set in turmoil even heavenly calm was the adage proved by her clawing vigour and the tensions of the man–woman confrontation that gave her a raw force—in melody and rhythm—that utterly consumed her. While *raga* Purabi brought out the pathos of her exhaustion, the refrain of *baul* introduced the right note of resuscitation with renewed energy. The dances with the changing melodic mode etched out almost an entire canvas of human emotions!

A dramatic moment in Chandalika.

The song-and-dance stream carried her forward endlessly: now wild and boisterous, now down-and-out in agonised ennui, now resurrected into renewed restlessness. The flow of passion ultimately reached its confluence in sea: the lust lost itself in love, the storm subsided and there was serenity of peace. The physical desire reached the end of its quest in a transcendental plane and was satiated. As visualised by Tagore, the culmination point, although deviating from the original theme, was dramatically more potent and psychologically more fulfilling: in its chiaroscuro of choreography.

The play bears three clear messages. At the very outset, it is a low-caste struggle for survival, humiliating and infra-dig at every moment of its existence, from which the symbolic act of offering water to the monk provides a redemption, a birth into new human dignity: never experienced before, something that appealed to the Mahatma and attracted generations of dancers ever since (see Chapter 12). At another level, it is a primordial tussle between lust and love, between passion and its resolution, beginning in the warp and weft of Prakriti's humdrum life and ending in her devout surrender to the profundity of new values that Ananda revealed to her. But if that is true for Prakriti, it is also an upheaval within Ananda's mind, as seen in the magic mirror and in the shadow play. He is torn between the protection of his wisdom as well as the attraction of the mortal world to its carnal desires. It is eventually a triumph of the higher values that allow the power of his spirit to rise above the sensuality of the flesh. But at a spiritual level, it is a metaphor of the eternal duel between *Purusha* and *Prakriti*, the dormant force and the driving power—the confrontation between the *Yin* and the *Yang*—that drives the entire material universe.

Fourth (Incomplete) Dance-drama—Mayar Khela

Written within a decade of Tagore's return from England, his *Mayar Khela* (1888, see Chapter 3) was similar to a pre-Wagner opera of the West: dominated by songs with very little dramatic outline. Tagore himself termed it: 'a musical outpouring when the mind was entirely drenched with melody'. What was later called 'dance-drama' came from Tagore as a script, at the behest of Pratima Devi and proposed by her for dance *abhinaya*, in 1938–39. The script was tightened to two-third of its earlier length and as many as sixteen new songs were added, although male and female characters were not really altered. Tagore explained the alterations thus:

> I had only attempted to express mental feelings at my early age, which I hope I have undone now. The feelings at a mature age are not to be merely verbalised in songs, but are to be viewed essentially for their beauty.

Out of the sixteen, for instance, the song: 'The maiden who was a wayfarer in my dreams had always eluded me and I had spent days in her quest' was perhaps a better rendering than its earlier form: 'I don't understand anybody, but I've only understood you and obtained you through light and doubt of darkness' as a foray in aesthetics.

Both these versions are fantasy games of both love and separation, not materially different from each other. Each has two female protagonists—Pramada and Shanta—besides the illusive maidens or *maya kumaris* and the trio of male characters, out of whom Amar is sought after, Kumar is the roaming casanova and Ashok is the eternal lover. The setting is an illusive forest. The conflicts are forever effervescent: now uniting, now separating and now consummating again, to all of which the maidens are alternately stoking fires of desire and despair. There are no specific points of view, except that of passion: unquenched or satiated. The tone and the mood are vaguely reminiscent of Shakespeare's *A Midsummer Night's Dream*: both set in fantasy woods like a dreamland; with shades of Shakespeare's Titania, Queen of the Fairies, evident in Tagore's Pramada and Shanta; Fairies and their repetitive solos and choruses resembling the recursive musical refrains of the illusive maidens; the love-potion in sleep akin to Amar's sudden drowsiness; and the attitude of the Fairies to mortals much similar to the illusive maidens' mindset for the three hapless males. Only Puck and his Puckish humour, if anything, is missing in the later poet's work!

While the conception and composition of the dance-drama was followed by rehearsals in 1939, only a fragment was staged at Santiniketan during that year's colour festival, but the entire play was never showcased. So the evolution of the dance form for the re-written dance-drama was not really known and is not taken into account hereafter.

Conclusion

Interestingly, in Tagore's last sextet of dance-borne dramas: *Natir Puja, Tasher Desh, Shap Mochan, Chitrangada, Shyama* and *Chandalika*: as many as four belong inspirationally to the ancient Buddhist legends, other than two—the epic-based *Chitrangada* and the 'cock-and-bull' theme of *Tasher Desh*. Again, just as many of Shakespeare's classics had their original muses elsewhere, Tagore's transmutation and often transcendence of the original sources were so complete and so very contemporary that their originality of treatment, brilliance of texture as well as the grand idea of making dance increasingly central to the dramatic action was certainly unique: in both dramaturgy as well as dance choreography. While *Natir Puja* ushered in 1926 a new era for women coming out of the cocoon of veiled orthodoxy and conduct dance in public, *Tasher Desh* was a whiplash attack against the rigidity, frigidity and futility of dry dogma; *Shap Mochan* was the harbinger of higher spirituality; *Shyama* upheld clear ethical values against reprehensible lust; and *Chitrangada* and *Chandalika* were complete de-mystification of femininity and demythified their original themes, while using a 'chemical solution' of dance forms evolved till then.

From the choreography angle, *Chitrangada, Shyama* and *Chandalika* had several distinctive rhythmic sections and even a few purely verbal narratives, yet both these elements required dance to encapsulate dramatic action.

But this did not mean that the dancer discarded *tala* for the sake of drama. *Tala* was neither dispensed with nor given undue prominence, but occupied its specified space. Indeed, these dance-dramas had music and dance so intimately interwoven that it would be difficult to say which of the two had a more dominating influence. For, it was through dance mood, melody and meaning became one organic whole.

Chandalika: *Mrinalini and another performer in an intense scene.*

From the aesthetic viewpoint, it was ensured that the dance—howsoever 'modified' and 'co-adapted'—would have the body-line absolutely perfect. Any redundant body movement would make it difficult to harmonise rhythm-cycle with overall gestures. It was the question of convergence of body-line and rhythm cycle, without which the dance would not achieve its completeness. What the difference was between prose and poetry was, in a sense, the distinction between dance-drama and pure drama. Dance provided the semiotic art whose contribution to drama remained ineffable. Dance, unlike pure drama, was not overt and tangible in providing inspiration. Its gesture action and rhythmic play worked, on the contrary, through signs and images that left a deep impression on human psyche: inexpressible through language, but visualised in the domain of mood and emotions. It was not easy to comprehend the significance of the art of such dance by the ordinary mind, but its attraction for the cognoscenti was surely everlasting.

Nandita in a scene from Shyama.

Quotes on 'Spirit of Dance'

Rabindranath Tagore on *Chandalika*:

Long ago in 1912, when I saw a Russian dance-drama in London, it was an unforgettable experience. The luscious body of the danseuse surged up with the emotion of courtship and the gestural expression created a world of illusion with the successive notes of melody. It was a wonderful creation of the artistes who could transform the trivia into something extraordinary. The subject matter was the normal scene of Russian marriage, which was an ordinary event, but still could be made into something sublime, thanks to the power of the artistes.

The role of *Chandalika* [the downtrodden girl] has true literary merits, based on the perspective of mental evolution of man. Whatever constitutes the primitive attraction in men is reflected in *Chandalika* dance style, capturing the physical attraction that could disturb even the meditation of Shiva. That eternal, inner conflict between the masculine and the feminine touched *Chandalika's* soul, and its impact on the vibrant mind expressed itself in the languor and melancholy, and an abundant compassion.

The maidens draw artistic filigree with their bodily gestures resounding to the musical melody. I wonder about its meaning, its relevance to the complexities of our beleaguered everyday existence. If the daily deficiencies were the last word of truth, this dance would have no appeal. Yet the complete cadenza of its beauty confirms its ultimate verity, much more deeply and intimately than whatever is apparent to our gaze at the torn-down, unclear realities.

Pratima Devi on aesthetics of dance-drama:

What we did not accept from the age-old traditions in our dance-dramas was the play of eyes and shoulders from the northern and southern styles. Although this has been the continuing legacy from the ancient times, I think there is a foreign trend in it. When the Arabic and Persian influences came into our music, the movements of eyes and neck percolated in our dance. Perhaps that is why we do not perceive such movements in our folk dances. Only the Manipuri dance has retained its purity precisely because it did not get any foreign influence, having maintained its Indian ideals.

The extra-sensory emotions that pervade Indian dance transcend the barriers of time, space and objects. That is why the *tandava* dance of Shiva, which once charmed the land, still manifests its power in hundreds of icons. These neck-and-eye movements seem so irrelevant in that powerful dance. But in North India, where the Persian influence blended with music, these gestures may seem to go well with *Krishna Lila* or *ghazal*; for, they do seem consistent with themes of love. The purity of aesthetics is, however, poised on such a delicate balance that any burden of grossness would make it slide downwards. This very apprehension made us leave out many prevalent dance styles.

The dance training [at Santiniketan] progressed with great aplomb among the students. Among those who shaped up well within a few years—Jamuna, Nivedita and Nandita were particularly praiseworthy. Among the men was Santidev. We could count Srimati among our students as well, since her first training in dance was under Manipuri teachers in Santiniketan. Although she acquired considerable experience in dance forms later by travelling in many European countries, there was little doubt that the foundations of her dance were based on Gurudev's [Tagore's] music.

Pratima Devi on *Chitrangada*:

Chitrangada reveals many alterations, but the sheer poise of her might is caught in manifold rhythms and melodies. This dance-drama combined many *talas*, such as Manipuri Kawali, which was Keharba in Hindi; Manipuri Chartaal that is Ada Chautaal in Hindi; and Teora and Dadra from Southern dances. Again, Jhanptaal came from Gurudev's songs. In Arjuna's dance while breaking his meditation, have been added skills of Tehai-Toda-Parhant. Hearing this, some might wonder if our students are practising the dance styles of North India. We, however, got it from Manipuri dance.

Santidev Ghosh on *Tasher Desh*:

For the first-time staging of *Tasher Desh*, the responsibility of planning costumes and stage decorations was handled by Nandalal Bose and Pratima Devi. While Nandalal looked after the dress of the male characters, Pratima did so for the female roles. Pratima Devi's design was based on the many pictures of Javanese dance-dramas. But, due to the severe inconvenience felt by the *dramatis personae* during the inaugural night performance in Kolkata, Nandalal and Pratima joined hands to drastically alter the female costume by the very next morning!

Veils and billowy skirts for females as in Manipuri and elaborate body painting as in Kathakali were rejected outright by Tagore

Canons *of* Choreography

The only thing constant in the evolution of choreography in Tagore's dance—spread over a quarter century—was change! The dynamic, dazzling chiaroscuro in Tagore's dance filigree was founded in his words:

> Dance is the language of the non-verbal...ranging from the quivering grass-blades to the garland of rhythms grafted in the stars...Verbal expressions can only convey the universal resonance, as known to every dancing atom...The flow of rhythm from such cosmic genesis into the body and limbs of the human being can make the creation process manifest.

Looking back, once teaching of dance was started in the early 1920s in Santiniketan—much before Rukmini Devi Arundale's Kalakshetra and Uday Shankar's Almora Dance Centre—learning included *abhinaya* of the classical traditions as well as group dances of folk tradition without *abhinaya*. What mainly came into vogue was classical *nritya* supported by *abhinaya* in solo roles and non-classical *nritya*, mostly among group dances, sans *abhinaya*: both to support Tagore's music with occasional *bol* intervals. Group dances followed, in the late twenties, mostly the Manipuri approach of *cholams*—group dance with accompaniments such as drum, cymbals or simple clapping—and *Jagoui*—collective dance without any other accompaniment: these were mainly from the *Ras Lila* and *Sankeertan* styles.

Through the 'Looking Glass' of Western Ballet

The above was in remarkable contrast to the concept of Western choreography (from where the word 'choreography' came in the first place), especially in ballet. Both classical

Chandalika: *'Give me water'*. *Nandita and Kelu Nair.*

and modern ballets in the West follow some distinctive patterns, as generalised below.

■ Group choreography executes countless patterns in still and moving forms, unlike, for example, the limited Manipuri patterns mentioned above.

■ Ballet groups on stage can be very large, whereas even Kathakali groups seldom exceed four.

■ The tenets of entry and exit, sitting, standing, beckoning, instructing and so on, for Tagore's dance are clearly stylised, although ballet dancers can mix stylisation with natural movements at will.

■ In modern ballet, body movements as well as movements in space are usually not re-traced. This is contrary to the Indian classical approach and also against the grain of Indian dance where the 'mirroring' of each body movement and space movement is usually sacrosanct.

■ Tagore's dance-dramas, in particular, tell stories in full, which may or may not be the case for Western ballet presentations.

■ Tagore's choreography follows *sahitya* as an immutable prerequisite, completely in tune with the Indian classical traditions for *abhinaya*. For Tagore, this comes from the treasure-trove of his verbalised music and 'music drama', in contrast to Western ballet going in tandem entirely with the orchestration of instrumental music.

■ To a considerable extent, Western ballet is distinguished for its techniques of movements and expressions. This is unlike

Tagore's dance, which was created mainly through inspirations, derived from feelings as well as emotions.

There are a few fundamental differences between Indian dance tradition and Western ballet that includes Tagore's dance. First, Western ballet does not follow in its movements rhythmic time cycles, sacrosanct to Indian music and dance as *tala*.

Second, in ballet there is a tendency to deny gravity in its leaps and pirouettes, whereas Indian dance is deeply earth-bound, hugging the surface of the ground with footsteps almost reverentially.

Third, the facial expressions are played down in Western ballet, keeping in view the distance factor between the stage and the audience. In India, on the contrary, facial *abhinaya* is a key ingredient of dance, perhaps because of their *mehfil* origin. Finally, the development in modern ballet since Martha Graham has been to use the 'solar plexus' for originating body extensions, particularly leaps, arabesques, pirouettes and, in general, energy release. This is not true in Indian dance.

Through the 'Looking Glass' of Uday Shankar

Uday Shankar, the doyen of contemporary choreography in India—striding the scene between the 1930s and the 1970s—differed from Tagore in many vital respects. These differences arose primarily because Shankar was, first and foremost, an intuitive dancer, in the best sense of the term. The story goes that when he first saw in London the bronze statue of Nataraj, he could not sleep the whole night, lost in creative contemplation. By early dawn, dance started to descend into his whole being, with the dynamics of body movements and hand gestures beginning to emerge: diverging from and converging into the statue. This was the genesis of Shankar's famous solo *Nataraj*.

In his career path—from Rothenstein's fine arts studio in London to the American stage in dance partnership with Anna Pavlov, to the solo dancing in French salons and elsewhere, to the formation of his famous dance troupe conquering the world, to the formation of the Almora Dance Centre with Manipuri and Kathakali gurus, to the making of the film *Kalpana*, to the famous solos, duets and his excellent group choreography—his individual dances, with a superb body display, were masterly showpieces. For Tagore, his musicals, music drama and dance-drama were creations that would exist for posterity without the Poet. Shankar discarded verbal songs for all his dances, his musical support being entirely instrumental: not with orchestrated Western musical ensembles creating harmony but with the Indian instruments playing a blend of Indian melody and rhythm—under master composers such as Baba Allauddin Khan and Timir Baran—taking the cue from his choreographic oeuvre that came first and could have passages of virtuoso improvisation. For Tagore, instrumental support was minimal, while verbalised songs were supreme and written texts sacrosanct, with dance following, interpreting and visualising his songs and carrying the text forward. Only in the Almora phase did Shankar go for formalising his techniques into clearly followed exercises—a corpus still waiting to be codified.

Tagore felt that choreography was predominantly for emoting the 'mood' of his brilliantly crafted songs. Dance would be a process of 'natural selection' from the available genres with the needed 'modifications' and 'co-adaptations', with certain dos and don'ts. And, finally, having been reared in the West, Shankar nurtured the presentation values and also believed in classy showmanship. For Tagore, both dance and drama could go even with the bare accessories—with costumes and stagecraft desirable but not mandatory or diversionary. Incidentally, like Nataraj, Shankar did create other solos with traditional gods such as Kartikeya and Indra in his initial phase, but Tagore's dance—despite the best provocations from the Indian classical traditions—did not go in for creating icons on stage and, if anything, did away with all kinds of myths and mythification. The dancing Nataraj was, for him, a highly endearing metaphor: for the resonance of universal dance.

Basic Tenets of Choreography

The essential features of Tagore's dance has been summarised below:

- It is mainly an expression of the flavour of his poetry in a balanced harmony, with its staple of poetic melodies.
- More than grammar of dance, it is the 'mood' and 'spirit' that have dominated in his dance.
- Any overarching role of both physical gestures as well as body flexing has been carefully discarded.
- His dance has been a 'chemical solution' of diverse genres of dance.
- There is simplicity, transparency and avoidance of heavy props for his dance.
- Both stagecraft and presentation pattern are distinctive and original.
- It avoids an undue concentration on instrumental music for rhythm cycles, as done in *nritta* of Manipuri, Kathakali and Bharatanatyam styles.
- It has not accepted preponderance of *mudras* or hand gestures as prevalent in Kathakali and other styles.
- Both music dramas and dance-dramas use dance primarily focussed on the 'mood' of songs.

Since the above is not too far from the fundamental ethos of Indian traditions, one can delve, at this stage, into the sources of choreography in this land. Interestingly, while there are clear-cut grammars—in Tamil and Sanskrit—which give the codification rules of the *margi* or classical forms, virtually all of them have drawn sustenance from the *desi* or the regionally prevalent genres by way of extensive re-construction.

Grammar of Classical Dances

The Tamil grammar *Tolkapiyam* (first-second century AD) was prevalent in the days of *Silappdikaram*, the great Tamil epic, for the character of its ace danseuse Madhavi. The grammar was meticulously written and provided with *sarai*, equivalent to *rasa* of Bharata's *Natya Shastra* (first-second century AD). The latter was India's indisputable *magnum opus* of virtually all classical traditions. It was unique in the annals of world literature, being the first ever compendium of all performing arts—dance, music and drama, embracing both *margi* and *desi* forms.

In particular, the *Natya Shastra* and Nandikeshvara's *Abhinaya Darpana* (ninth–eleventh century) are followed for Bharatanatyam and Kuchipudi. *Natya Shastra* and *Ramayana Samkshepam* are followed by Koodiyattam, India's oldest Sanskrit-based dance theatre from Kerala and the *Natya Shastra* is used by Kathak

Stage décor in Santiniketan. Stage set for *Natir Puja* by Suren Kar in Javanese style.

dance in the North. *Hasta Lakshana Deepika* is followed by Kathakali and Mohiniyattam dances in Kerala. *Atta Prakaram* is used in another old female form of dance, *Nangiyar Koothu,* in Kerala. In the North, *Govinda Sangeeta Vilasa* and *Sangeeta Damodara* are followed by Manipuri dance, *Abhinaya Chandrika* by Odissi dance and Shubhankara's *Srihasta Muktavali* by Sattriya dance.

Interestingly, the corresponding canons for classical music, after the *Natya Shastra*, were defined by Matanga's *Brihadesshi* (fifth–seventh century), which enumerated the various Indian *ragas* in detail. From Sharangadeva's *Sangeeta Ratankara* (twelfth century), the bifurcation began into the Carnatic and Hindustani music systems and is still prevalent.

Re-construction of Classical Dances

A classical dance has not always been a single cohesive whole, but it evolved in time through give-and-take with local forms and was codified under proper grammars thereafter, as illustrated below:

- Manipuri—from the pre-Vaishnava Lai Haraoba, Sankeertan, Ras Lila and village forms;

- Kathakali—from Koodiyattam, Krishna Attam, Ramanattam, Ashtapadi Attam and village forms;

- Bharatanatyam—from Sadir (or Dasi Attam), Bhagavad Mela, Kurubhanji, and village forms such as Therukuthu and Chinnamaelam;

- Mohiniyattam—from Ashtapadi Attam, Nangiyar Kuthu, Theradicchi Attam and village forms like Kummi, Sari;

- Kathak—from Vraja Ras Lila, Dang Lila, Parsee dance and village forms like Panihari, Nautanki and Ghumar;

- Kuchipudi—from Yakshagana, Bhagavad Mela, Brahmana Mela, Nattavu Mela and village forms;

- Odissi—from Mahari, Gotipua, Bandha, Mayurbhanj Chhau and village forms; and

- Sattriya—from Ankiya Nat, Bhaona and ritual forms practised at the religious *sattras*.

Body Language in Classical Dances

The body language used in classical dances are summarised below:

- There are three fundamental variants: *tandava, lasya* and *pratibandha*.

- There are in all one hundred and eight dance poses called *karanas*, enshrined in the *Natya Shastra*.

- Dance expression is four-fold: *vachika, sattvika, angika* and *aharya*.

- *Angikas* have three forms: *mukhaja, sharira* and *chaste*.

- There are six *angas*: head, hand, hip, chest, sides and feet.

- There are six *upangas*: eyes, brows, nose, lips, cheeks and chin.

- There are also neck, shoulder, arms, wrists, belly, thighs, shanks and knees that take part in dance.

- In *Nritya*, there are two kinds of *hasta mudras: asamayukta* with twenty-eight gestures and *samayukta* with twenty-four.

- In *Nritta* there are in total thirty hand movements.

- There are four kinds of *bhangi bhanga*—serene like Shiva; *samabhanga*—equipoise like the Buddha; *tribhanga*—bent in three segments like Parvati; and *atibhanga*—bent in four segments like Nataraj.

- Movements of feet are of four kinds: *mandala, utplabana* and *bhramari*.

- There are ten kinds of *chari* on stage and seven kinds of *padachari* in support.

These apart, there can be several kinds of glances and movements of the brow, eyeball, cheek, lips, neck, head, chest, sides, hips, thighs, shanks, feet and hands.

Abhinaya *in Choreography*

Abhinaya is the art of aesthetic communication, comprising the creation of *bhava* by the performer and consequent transcription of *rasa* in the minds of the viewer, referred to as *rasika*. In Tagore's choreography, this would be achieved by music—predominantly verbal with some instrumental melodic support—known as *vachika abhinaya*, along with instrumental rhythmic assistance. This is enlivened by facial aesthetics termed as *sattvika abhinaya*—with only the barest necessary emotive histrionics, called *rasa abhinaya*, as it means to create rapture in the *rasika*. Such rapport also requires physical aesthetics through *angika abhinaya*—body kinetics—and auxiliary aesthetics through *aharya abhinaya*—adornment as well as costumes. *Abhinaya* is, thus, everything in a choreographic presentation: the very body and soul, conveying one or more messages in a form that is enjoyable to the connoisseur.

Vachika Abhinaya

As stated earlier, the literary potential of *sahitya* by Tagore is fully utilised in *nritta* for folk-based (and occasionally Manipuri) group formations as well as interpretative *nritya* in classical repertoire. With the enormously rich treasure-trove of his music (see Chapter 10), his *vachika* aspects of choreography can be endlessly exploited. This is in keeping with the Indian dance traditions, except that the practice in classical dances (other than Manipuri) is that each line of the lyric is expressed in *sthayee bhava* and additionally adorned in *sanchari bhava*.

Instead, Tagore's *vachika abhinaya* could be either of the following, as has been explained below:

■ The entire lyric is treated as an organic whole. Melody and rhythms are viewed as integral to the central *sthayee bhava* and expressed in a *natyadharmi* form by the dancers. This is mood dance *par excellence* where *abhinaya* has ample scope to express the 'mood' of the whole song through *sthayee bhava*. The large corpus of Tagore songs is *bhava-pradhan* and should fall in this category for purposes of dance.

■ The other approach, apparently akin to the classical practice, is where each line is interpreted either through *alankara* or ornamentation. The dance is allowed to follow a *lokadharmi*—explicit to the public—approach: more used with group-formations, with little or no *mudras* of hand, and playing down elaborate facial expressions and expressive hand gestures. Two instances could be:

- *'Aji dhaner khete roudra chhayay'* (It'll be the game of hide-and-seek in the paddy fields today);

- *'Madhu gandhe bhara mridu snigdha chhaya'* (Under the *neepa* groves full of heady aroma and casting gentle, soothing shadows).

Sattvika Abhinaya

This was deemed essential for categories like solo, *pas de deux* and *pas de trois*. It was imperative for Tagore's choreography that singers—who would sit behind—and the dancers—who would occupy forestage—got together and analysed the lines of the lyrics. They would keep in mind the meanings and nuances of the libretti and the dialogue of dramatic characters, appreciate the song's *bhava* and decide on the song's interpretation.

Virtually following Spencer on *rasa*, Tagore used solemn and serene *ragas* (and their variations) and rendered them in *vilambit laya* for articulating prayers, devotion and paying tributes, and in *drut laya* and rapid-fire rhythms to embody happiness and wondrous joy; and based melodies on *meend* and *komal* flat notes in *madhya laya* and broken rhythms to express sorrow, disappointment and downright despair—suitably altering the timbre of voice in consonance with the prevailing *rasa*. In other words, different musical 'moods' need precise comprehension and they are then rendered in favourable *talas*. An outburst of anger and its cool, measured response—as between two characters in a dance-drama like *Chitrangada*—would take the guise of a special song with tempo and rhythm of one kind, while its calm reply would have a song, tempo and rhythm of the opposite kind to make the contrary *bhavas* compensate each other.

A highpoint of classical traditions is the evocation of *nava rasa* through facial and physical aesthetics. Going directly back to the *Natya Shastra*, there are eight sentiments of the dramatic arts: *shringara, hasya, karuna, raudra, vira, bhayanaka, bibhatsa, adbhuta,* and the later ninth: *shanta*. These principal emotions are evoked in the *rasika* by nine *sthayee bhavas* which are: *rati*—love; *hasya*—merriment; *shoka*—sorrow; *krodha*—fury; *utsaha*—enthusiasm; *bhaya*—terror; *jugupsa*—disgust; *vismaya*—astonishment; and *shanti*—serenity. Now, a depiction of these evoked emotions in isolation cannot be meaningful, since each *rasa* could itself have various degrees of intensity depending on the character, situation and cause—leading to that particular expression of emotion.

On the other hand, many colourful bouquets of mood dances can be constructed from Tagore songs for *Nava Rasa*, as identified by the cognoscenti, which satisfy the above criteria in their triadic combination of lyrics, melody and rhythms. Two selections, presentable as individual items, are mentioned here for illustration:

- *Shringara—'Dhora diyechhi go ami'* (Though a bird from the open sky, I've allowed myself to be caught); *'Premera joyare bhasabo donhare'* (We shall allow each other to be floated away in the tide of love);

- *Hasya—'Ah, benchechhi ekhon'* (O dear, I've just saved myself, never again will I turn to that side for my life); *'Ichchhe,— ichchhe'* (It's my wish, my wish that makes and breaks, gives and takes);

- *Karuna—'Aji kanna kara oi shuna jai'* (Whom do we listen to crying today, where the deprived ones are lamenting); *'Jeevan jokhan shukaye jai'* (When the life dries up, drench us with your compassion);

- *Raudra—'Sarba kharbatare dahe'* (All the inanities get burnt by the flames of

Chitrangada:
Villagers performing.

your angst); *'Jago hey Rudra'* (Awake, O the furious one, awake);

■ *Veera—'Tomar ason shunya aji'* (Your throne is vacant today; we beseech you, O hero, to possess it); *'Baje rey baje rey oi rudratale vajrabheri'* (The trumpets have sounded their thunderous call—the human waves are surging out in heroic outfits);

■ *Bhayanaka—'Jage ni ekhono jage ni'* (The hideous female-serpents from the nether worlds haven't woken up yet); *'Baje guru guru shankara danka'* (The drums of trepidations are beating, the storm gathers afar in deadly silence);

■ *Vibhatsa—'Eto ranga shikhechho kotha mundamalini'* (Where did you learn your playfulness, O the fiery one garlanded with severed human-heads, the heart trembles witnessing your dreaded dance); *'O rakshusi ki korli tui'* (O the vile demoness, what evil have you done;

■ *Adbhuta—'Ae ki ae, ae ki ae, sthir chapala'* (What's this, what's this: a frozen lightning; the brilliant radiance makes every direction look bright); *'Ae ki swapna! ae ki maya'* (What's this—a dream or an illusion?);

■ *Shanta—'Ailo shanta sandhya'* (The peaceful evening has descended, the tired sun has set in the western horizon); *'Samukhe shanti parabar'* (The ocean of peace is spread ahead; do float your boat, O boatswain).

In Indian classical dances, the *Nava Rasa* choreography is often created around a single epic character like Rama. It is remarkable that Tagore left enough trails in a single dance-drama like *Chandalika* where a mood dance repertoire of *Nava Rasa* could be built up as items or a sequence, against the contemporary scourge of untouchability—illustrated through songs and narrative—as follows:

■ *Shringara—'Ami chai tanre'* (I desire him who gave me the honour of serving him...);

■ *Hasya—'Sat deshete khunje khunje'* (After scouting in seven lands, we got you finally here, you've really saved our fate);

■ *Karuna—'Prabhu esechho uddharite amay'* (My lord, you've come to rescue me, having paid such a price, having suffered so much sorrow);

■ *Raudra—'Je amare pathalo ei apamaner andhakare'* (Whichever god sent me in this dungeon of ignominy, I deny him any worship, I deny, I deny);

■ *Veera—'Ki asim sahas tor—aamar sahas!'* (What an indomitable courage you have—My Courage! His courage has no parallel);

■ *Bhayanaka—'Ore sarbanashi, ki katha tui balis'* (O my dreadful girl, what languages are you using, it's playing with fire);

■ *Vibhatsa—'O ke chhuon na, chhuon na, chhi'*...(Don't you touch her, she is the despicable untouchable lass);

■ *Adbhuta—'Tui abak kore dili amay meye'* (You've totally surprised me, my girl, I've heard in the ancient treatises that Uma had meditated under the fiery sun—Is that your case);

■ *Shanta—'Kalyana hok taba kalyani'* (Blessed be you, my blissful girl).

Angika Abhinaya

In classical dances, *angika abhinaya* comprises the movements of the face and limbs of the body, with support from the body as a whole. While the face is principally used for a reflective expression of emotion, as discussed earlier, the hand is the principal organ which uses gestures for interpretative ideas and objects. In all dances, the gestures, whether of the face or hands and legs, are spontaneously linked with rhythm, giving a symbolic, indicative and visible manifestation of ideas and objects. These stylised gestures—especially in Tagore's mood dance items or sequences—lend greater power to *natyadharmi* expressions than to the realistic *lokadharmi* forms, lending credence to Tagore's large literary oeuvre.

An amalgam of dance styles as well as their *angika abhinaya*—built upon the foundation of Tagore's lyrics, melodies and rhythms—gives rise to the edifice of the Poet's distinctive choreography in his later dance-dramas. Indeed, their damascened filigree is more successfully designed and executed than ever before, welding and grafting many approaches together according to the dance forms, the nature of characters and the textual underpinning. Thus, the gentle Manipuri goes hand-in-hand with virile Kathakali; Bengal's Baul side-by-side with Sri Lanka's Kandyan dance; and South India's Bharatanatyam with North India's Kathak—achieving an overall organic harmony, a 'chemical solution', as it were.

Aharya Abhinaya

In Tagore's dance, *aharya abhinaya* does not attempt any radical transformation of the human face as well as figure (as in Kathakali) using elaborate facial make-up and costume, intended to transport one to the distant realm of the imagination. On the contrary, *aharya abhinaya* is used in a naturalistic setting: to let the mood dance convey the deeper meaning and aesthetics. In order to create the necessary milieu of *abhinaya* in a music drama or a dance-drama, stage décor, accoutrements, jewellery and make-up were all blended together. In fact, special attention was given in these dramas to evolve a commensurate art of stagecraft. Both Kathakali and Bharatanatyam tenets of decorative donning of a character were dispensed with, as was the Manipuri custom of wearing veil on face and can-can skirts below waist. Instead, a distinctive variety was instilled in the costumes of *Chitrangada* and *Chandalika* with the former blending with a bright and gorgeous white stage and the latter having a rural décor with rustic costumes.

The *Natya Shastra* norms of *aharya abhinaya*, as relevant here, are: *pusta, alankara* and *anga rachana*. Used as support material, *pusta* in drama include: *sandhima, vyajima* and *vestima*. These apart, artificial objects like hills, vehicles, chariots, armours, flagstaff, trees and so on are *pustas* for production of drama. *Alankaras* are embellishments like floral wreaths, jewellery, garments and so on, as well as various inquests that are applied over the body and limbs. The details about *abharanas* cover: *abhedya*—limbs pierced and worn, *bandhaniya*—tied up on limbs, *prakshepya*—worn over limbs and *aropya*—put around limbs. *Anga rachana* is decorative painting and make-up to indicate a character in any drama or even a community such as the female soldiers in *Chitrangada* or the witchcraft-companions in *Chandalika*.

Realistic imitations, implied in *aharya abhinaya* above, are surprisingly modern and were taken care of at Santiniketan in Tagore's time in natural body decorations, costumes and garments, stage properties as well as supportive lighting and sound. These underwent many experiments and innovations helped by Tagore himself and others like Nandalal Bose, Pratima Devi and Surendranath Kar.

A few examples of the type of stagecraft that was adopted then to give a feel of reality are illustrated below:

■ For *Valmiki Pratibha*, two cotton storks, painted curtains with boars concealed in groves, and trees and plants hanging with ropes on stage—to be lowered when needed—were used. Drop curtains were made of velvet clothes, with lighting through gas lamps and dumbbells were rolled to create the sound of a thunderstorm. Tagore later termed these as 'a little childish'.

■ By the time dances had entered into Tagore's dramas, the approach evolved from a domestic milieu into less *pustas* and *alamkaras* so that the spectators' gaze did not get diverted, with Nandalal creating simple decorative colours like yellow, red and blue. Tagore emphasised stage sans painted backdrops and elimination of distance from the viewers, an idea that prevailed later.

■ For *Natir Puja* held at Santiniketan's 'Konarka', a few big earthen pots were kept inverted backstage, with Nandalal and Surendranath painting over, to make them resemble Buddhist stupas. The fights among the Hindus and Buddhists, with sticks and lighted torches, were discarded in later performances.

■ Nandalal, while taking over as head of Kala Bhavan, introduced the use of different colours like indigo, yellow, blue and red for costumes. The stage lighting used to illumine the performers was red. As dances grew in number and intensity, exuberance of colours to create symbolic illumination on a bare stage became the norm approved by Tagore. This approach of Nandalal replaced completely the earlier realistic mindset.

Facing page: Chitrangada: *Nandita dressed as Surupa.*

■ The principal stage design was done through thick clothes—of indigo, yellow, blue and red hues—as back curtain, side-wings and 'skies'. The back curtain was indigo; preceded by two deep yellow wings four feet in front; with two equidistant blue wings placed further front; the third set of indigo-blue wings five feet further upfront; and the fourth set of red wings kept nearest to the audience. A few cubits wide each, these four wings were mounted on wooden frames and stuck up on two sides of the stage, with vertical lengths as per the stage height. Matching these colours, four equally wide 'skies' were spread from one set of wings to the other—stretched across the stage's entire length. The back curtain and the side-wings were often enlivened with small square or rhomboid cloth pieces of multi-coloured design;

■ During performance, there could be white lights, converted into a matching colour-quartet: keeping in view a scene, part-scene or even a song's essence. The *bhava* and the evoked *rasa*—as per the *Natya Shastra*—allowed for the blending of two or more colours, as might be considered necessary.

■ Alternatively, blue lights were hidden under the first 'sky', mellowed yellow lights were under the second and third 'skies', and red under the fourth 'sky'. Instead of using footlights at the front stage, standing spotlights from behind the side-wings were projected on stage. This was the specific lighting arrangement for *Chitrangada*, exclusively under Surendranath.

■ In the first production of *Chitrangada* in Kolkata, an ornamental middle door backstage: made sculpturesquely with designed cloth pieces: was created by Surendranath. This was in the form of a temple gate kept in parallel with the back-wings and used for exit and entry by the *dramatis personae*. Such an ornamental gate was not experimented with later.

■ For the presentation of Tagore's music drama or his dance-drama, the team of singers and instrumentalists sat together at the backstage, separated from the dancers and actors upfront by a low, tastefully erected curtain.

The bulk of the above ideas, as promoted by Tagore, have become an all-India norm today, influencing deeply the presentation ideas of musicals and dance-dramas. The same is also the case for Tagore's concepts of individual décor and costuming, as can be illustrated below from Tagore's time:

■ The musical *Valmiki Pratibha* had costumes that were almost in European style: red cloaks looking like embossed mantles of the British royalty. The goddesses Lakshmi and Saraswati wore traditional white saris with red *zari* handiwork. The *vanadevis* wore coloured saris, tree-leaves and plants, and open-hair coiffure with flowers stuck in. The dacoits' costumes underwent some change later on, with *dhotis*, vests, and headbands replacing turbans.

■ The music drama *Tasher Desh* was costumed, on the first occasion, entirely

Mayar Khela: In the presence of Tagore.

by Nandadal for the male actors and by Pratima Devi for the female characters. Nandalal's designs for Card characters with paper cuttings and cloth pieces—tailor-made for each role yet creating a harmonious whole—were a riot of colours and all of them looked having come out of a fairytale world, captivating the spectators. Pratima initially went for Javanese models for female dress—copied out of pictures—but after the premiere show, they proved inconvenient for the dancers and were replaced overnight.

As stated in the beginning, veils and billowy skirts for females as in Manipuri and elaborate body painting as in Kathakali were rejected outright by Tagore, while adopting a lot of Manipuri group dances, body movements and rhythm cycles, as well as Kathakali rhythms and pure dance of *kalasam*.

More important were the revealing features of the characters: to be highlighted in their dress and stage illumination. For this venture, the role of painters and artists of Santiniketan was of great help. But Tagore's own eye as a painter (see Chapter 11) was of equally conspicuous importance. As will be seen, he drew on canvas his imagery of 'dancing women'—which had no precedent anywhere—in the 1930s, when in the same decade he was also creating his dance-dramas on the proscenium stage. This was a singular coincidence not to be missed!

Group Choreography

Contrary to common beliefs and indeed in contrast to the predilections of classical artists to concentrate on solos (barring the recent spurt of dance-dramas), the *Natya Shastra* does dilate upon *pindi bandha* or female group dance, which it says resembles a lump. Among the three variations stated, *shrinkhala* holds the dancers together as in a cluster (in loosely or tightly-knit circles); *latabandha* resembles the cluster of creepers (spirally bound chains criss-cross each other); and *bhedyaka* is the dance by a single danseuse isolated from the group (typically Chitrangada dancing separately from the cluster of her companions or Chandalika dancing as segregated from the village-maidens). What lovely concepts!

Among the few seminal influences that came in Santiniketan's way, the main was from Manipuri. Here group dance could be either in the form of *cholam* along with *sankeertana* performed any time with some accompaniment like *pung, kartal* or *tali* in the temple or outside on any ceremonial or social occasion, or group dance without any accompaniment, which could be *jagoi* of either *Ras Lila* or *Goshtha Lila* kind. *Ras Lila* would be a love-play between Krishna and *gopis* only at night (as the women had to return home before dawn!), in the form of *Maha Ras, Vasnata Ras, Kunja Ras, Nitya Ras* and *Diva Ras*, with there being a principal *gopi*, usually Radha. This *jagoi* would be in *lasya*, with only Krishna doing *tandava*. *Goshtha Lila*, in contrast, would be a *jagoi* performed in daytime—moving from temples to open meadows—depicting young Krishna's pranks with cowherd boys and his killing of Kaliya, the snake and sundry other demons enacted in *tandava*. All rhythm cycles would be simple and traditional like *Chali, Tanchep, Mendhup* and so on.

The second influence from the outside was Kerala's folk forms such as *Kaikutti Kali* performed predominantly by women accompanied with the clapping of hands. The items that fell into its repertoire were: *Kalammuli* (eight beats); *Kummi* (six beats); *Saari* (eight beats, as in Kathakali) and *Swaram* (eight beats).

Bengal's own influence at Santiniketan group dance was through its virile folk forms like Baul, Raybenshe and Jari. They did not have defined body movements and certainly not structured as such, like, say, Japka of Chhau. Rhythm patterns for Baul dance were *Khemta* (twelve beats) and *Keharba* (eight beats). Raybenshe did not have a specified *tala*, moving off-beat all through, with Solfa syllables like *jhaur gijar gija ghini dha*. Jari dance followed a seven-beat pattern, somewhat unusual for folk forms and a departure from the more common six beats.

Margam *in Choreography*

After all the *abhinaya*, body movements and rhythm cycles are taken care of, most classical choreographers lay out a pattern, a sequence in which the individual items are to be presented by dancers, without causing undue ennui of the audience! This is known as *margam*. For Bharatanatyam (of course, in its previous incarnation), *margam* was set forth by the Thanjavur quartet in the nineteenth century as *Alarippu, Jatiswaram, Shabdam, Varnam* (the major *Nritya-Nritta* item), *Padam, Javali* and *Tillana*—which is followed till today. For Odissi, it had to wait until the middle of the twentieth century when a few gurus and redoubtable scholars formed the 'Jayantika' group and together reformed Odissi with *margam* as *Mangalacharan, Batu Nritya, Pallavi,*

Savinaya Pallavi (*Nritya-Nritta* item), one or more *Ashtapadi* (from Jayadeva's *Gita Govinda*), Oriya song (from, say, the old poet Banamali Dasa or Kavi Samrat Upendra Bhanja) and *Moksha*.

In a similar manner, keeping in view the enormous variety and quality of Tagore songs, it may not be entirely out of place to suggest a possible *margam* for Tagore's mood dances. (*Margam* is indeed being attempted by Alpana Roy of 'Saptak', Santiniketan and Valmiki Banerjee of the 'Delhi Ballet Group', the latter with support-vocabulary, basic grammar and training syllabus—among some others.) The first suggestion here would be to follow Tagore's own major themes as arranged in *Geeta Bitan*: *puja*—prayers, *swadesh*—patriotism, *prem*—love, *prakriti*—nature, *vichitra*—miscellaneous and *anushthanik*—ceremonial, or a micro-sequencing from out of any of these six themes.

A second suggestion would be to devise a few *margam* headings for Tagore's mood dance and indicate illustrative song choices that follow a fairly balanced pattern and does only a modicum of justice to his mind-boggling range:

- Invocation—*'Prathama adi taba shakti'* (Yours was the genesis of forces, the primordial effulgence that is pervading all firmaments); *'Agunerb parashmani chhonyao prane'* (Touch my soul with the talisman of Your fire, sanctify this life with that scorching torch of Yours);

- Affinity to nature—*'Aay aay, aay amader angane...'* (Tree planting) (Come, come, come to our courtyard, O our guests: the little saplings, come in our affectionate company and come to our home...); *'Maru vijayer ketan udaao shunye'*(Afforestation) (Fly aloft the banner of conquering the desert, O mighty spirit, sanctify the dust with your compassion, O soft soul...); *'Phire chal, phire chal, phire chal matir taane...'* (Rural farming) (Let's go back, go back, go back to the earth, earthy, the soil which has spread its cloth-end for us and looking at us expectantly...); *'Hey akashbihari-neeradbahan jal...'* (Digging for underground water) (O water, wandering in the sky and carried by the clouds, your abode was the snows at hilltops where you originally resided...); *'Aay rey mora phasal kati...'* (Harvesting) (Come one, come all, let's reap the crops, and let's reap the crops...);

- Tagore's Baul—*'Amar kantha hotey gan ke nilo bhlaye...'* (Whoever has stolen away melody from my throat; perhaps he has made his nest within the silent mind...); *'Ei to bhalo legechilo...'* (It's this joyous feeling, this dance of the light on the tree-leaves; It's this wild breeze in the Sal forest that captivates my mind);

- Tagore's *keertan*—*'Amar praner majhey sudha achhey, chao ki...'* (There's nectar deep within my soul, Do you want to share; Alas, perhaps you're not even aware of It...); *'Tomra ja balo tai balo...'* (Whatever you wish you may say, it does not appeal to my mind; Time ebbs away, just ebbs away without any rhyme or reason...);

■ Environment—*'Akashbhara surya-tara...'* (The sky displays the sun as well as the moon; the universe throbs with life; I've gained my place in this cosmic carnival...); *'Aamar mukti aaloy aaloy ei aakashe...'* (My freedom pervades this sky, my liberation touches every speck of dust, every blade of grass...);

■ Seasons of nature—*'Vishva veena rabey vishvajana mohichhey...'* (spring, rains and autumn) (Denizens of the universe are enchanted at the sweet melody of the cosmic *veena*: on earth and waters, under the skies, in woods and forests...);

■ Ode to seasons—Any seasonal song/s apt for the specific season, chosen out of seventeen for the summer; one hundred and fourteen for the rains; thirty for autumn; five for the frosts; twelve for the winter; and ninety-six for the spring;

■ Feel of beauty—*'Phule phule dhole dhole...'* (The gentle breeze moves from flower to flower, swaying them to and fro...); *'Phul bale, dhanya ami...'* (The flower declares: I'm blessed having been born on this soil, O my god, I'm here to serve you at my own home...);

■ Pure dance (*nritta*), flow of rhythm—*'Mamo chitte niti nritye...'* (Who's the one who dances in my heart now and evermore, *Ta Ta Thai Thai, Ta Ta Thai, Thai...*); *'Dui hatey—kaler mandira jey sadai bajey...'* (The cymbals of eternal time plays in your two hands, on left and on right, the slumber breaks and the dance arises, with their every novel strike...); *'Nupura beje jaye rini rini...'* (The anklets play on a sweet cadenza, my mind gets alert, saying: I recognise her...);

■ Flow of melody—*'Nrityer taley taley, Nataraj...'* (O Nataraj, remove all shackles with the cadences of your cosmic dance, banish slumber, and awake in the heart rhythms of free spirit...); *'Pralay nachan nachle jakhan aapan bhuley...'* (When you danced your dance of dissolution, forgetful of yourself, O Nataraj, your matted hair got unlocked...);

■ Love of Man—*'Bhalobasi, bhalobasi'* (I love you, I love you,—this melody resonates in my flute, on waters and earth, near and far...); *'Aamaar paran jaha chaye tumi...'* (You're the one, you're the one whom my heart yearns for, and I've none besides you in this wide open world, no one at all, nothing...); *'Premer joyare bhasabey donhare...'* (The full tide of passion will carry away the duo—snap open the bonds, snap them open...);

■ Love of God—*'Aamar hiyar manjhey lukiye chhile...'* (You were hiding in my heart of hearts, I never noticed, I never noticed, I had been keeping my eyes open to the outside, but never looked at my heart inwards...); *'Dhay jeno mor sakal bhalobasa...'* (Let my entire love surge towards you, my Lord, only towards you, only towards you...); *'Mari lo mari, amay*

Chandalika: *The debating mother and daughter, Mrinalini as Maa.*

banshite dekechhe key...' (Bless my soul, who has beckoned me by his flute? I thought I'll stay home and won't stir out, but now that the flute has played its tune outside, what shall I do?);

- *Tarana* or *telena*, mnemonic-based song—*'Sukhahin nishidin paradhin hai...'* (You're wandering in poor spirits, bereft of all happiness, day and night, under colonial bondage; always, alas, full of worries; continually scared and sick...);

- Finale—*'Bhengchho duar, esechho jyotirmay...'* (You've broken asunder the doors and arrived, O the radiant one, it's an apocalyptic appearance tearing out darkness,—let glory be yours...); *'Jaya hok, jaya hok nava arunodaya...'* (Let victory is, let victorious be the nascent dawn, let the eastern horizons be radiant in light...); *'Oi mahamanava asey...'* (There comes the Supreme Soul, the horizons all around are frenzied with excitement, affecting the earth's grass and trees...).

Pancha Bhuta *in Choreography*

Another category that suggests itself on the lines of classical choreography—to have a cosmic perception—is to use culled poems and songs, and interpret them for *pancha bhuta*. Tagore's literature is so rich that such an effort to select his gems can bring out absolutely new illumination. What follows is an illustrative list of five such categories that may do just enough justice to the traditional *pancha bhuta* concept using Tagore:

- *Kshiti* or earth—*'Mati toder dak diyechhe'* (The earth has called you—come one, come all; its basket is full to the brim with its ripe yield, what a lovely sight);

- *Ap* or water—*'Hey akashbihari niradbahan jal'* (O the waters those are laden in the clouds and freely float in the sky; you were frozen in the mountain tops as your favourite abiding place);

- *Tej* or fire—*'Alo amar, alo ogo, alo bhuvan bhara'* (The dazzle of light, my dear, permeates the whole universe; its radiance fills up my eyes and all the pores of my heart);

- *Marut* or wind—*'Khara vayu boye bege, chari dik chhay meghe'* (Tempestuous winds are blowing, all directions are darkened with clouds; O my boatswain, sail your boat mighty carefully);

- *Vyom* or wide universe—*'Mahavishve mahakashe mahakala majhey'* (In the wide open universe, in its vast firmament, in the timeless horizon of time—I'm the solitary mortal wandering alone in endless wonder).

It is possible that had Tagore been alive a little longer, he would have worked on a tome: giving directions and final touches to his concepts of dance choreography. That this is not such a wild surmise is established by the fact that he was always systematic about whatever he created in terms of documentation, like his corpus of music notations documented in *Swara Bitan*, with

Chitrangada:
Tagore watching a pioneering performance.

the first four volumes out in 1935, 1936, 1938 and 1939 (paving the way for the publication of successive volumes; sixty-four volumes been published after his death till today). There is also the fact that his dance-related thinking reached a zenith in the late 1920s and the entire 1930s, making him create the oeuvre of dance-dramas only in those late years while drawing pictures of 'dancing women' on canvas alongside. In many ways, Tagore's creative faculties were sharper with the advancing years, his poetry touching new heights, his music becoming unmistakably many-splendoured and even his political views becoming more radical. It is unfortunate that he did not live a little longer and produce one, or more, codified *Nritya Bitans* for his dance, comparable to the treatises for the other established styles, on the lines of the notated *Swara Bitans* for his music!

Angika Abhinaya for Classical Styles Relevant to Tagore's Dance

Manipuri: Body Movements

Main body movements are structured into *bhangis—abhangs, samabhangs, tribhang* and so on at specific rhythms and time cycles. There are five *bhangi parengs:* three *lasya* for females and two *tandava* for males.

Lasya bhangi parengs for females are:

- *Achouba bhangi pareng* (seven plus seven beats, starting with *Rajmel Tala*): Dhun Taa Dhin O / Dhun Taa O / Dhun O Then O / Dhun Taa O / Ten O Taa O / Ten Taa O / Taa O O O /Khit Ghima Ghar; etc.
- *Vrindavani bhangi pareng* (eight beats, starting with *Teental*) Khit Gingar / Dhin O / Dhai Ginagar / Dhan Taa / O Dhantaa / Taa Khit / Ten Taa / O O
- *Khumumba bhangi pareng* (seven plus seven beats, *Rajmel Tala*) Dhin O Thai O / Dhin Thai O / Dhin O Thai O / Dhin Ghin O / Tan O Tan O / O O O / O O O O / Khit Gina Gar, etc.

Tandava bhangi parengs for males are:

- *Goshtha bhangi pareng* (seven plus seven beats, *Rajmel Tala*) Ten O Taa O / Ten Tao O / Ten O Taa O / O O O / Ten O Ten O / Ten Tao O / Ten O Taa Tren / Ghit Ghin Ghar, etc.
- *Goshtha Vrindavani Pareng* (eight beats, *Teental*) Dhan Dhin / Dhai Ginaghar / Dhrenkhit Taa Ginaghar Dhenta / Taa Khit / Ten Taa / Taa O Khit Ginagha, etc.

Manipuri: Simple Rhythm Cycles

These are indicated below with drum-mnemonics:

- Four-beat, *Tanchep* (1, 2, 3, 4)
  Dhanten—Ta Ta Dhai Ghinadhai
- Three-beat, *Mankup* (1, 2, 3)
  Dhin-Dhan-Ta-
- Seven-beat, *Tintalmacha* (2, 2, 3)
  Ta -Dhen / Ta Dhar Dhai Gragrx / Dhin- Thun- Tenta
- Seven-beat, *Tevda* (3, 2, 2)
  Dhen-Ten-Tag- / Ta Ta Khit Ta / Dhinta Dhentu
- Seven-beat, *Dashkosh* (2, 1, 2, 1, 1)
  Then- Ta- / Ta- / Then- Ta- / Ta- Tata
- Eight-beat, *Tintalmel* (4, 2, 2)
  Then- Ta- Tha- Ta- / Ta- Then- / Takhi Tata
- Eight-beat, *Chali* (4, 2, 2) [Basic form for beginners, c.f., *Adavu* in Bharatanatyam]
  Dhin- Ten- O Ta- / Dhin- Ta- / Ghan- Ta
- Ten-beat, *Mayang Surfak* (4, 2, 4)
  Dhin- Ten- Ta- Gragra / Dhin- Gragra / Dhin- Ten- Ta- Gragra
- Ten-beat, *Jhaptal* (2, 3, 2, 3)
  Tat- Ta- / Dhen- Ten- Ta / Dhen- Ten- / Dhen- Ten- Ta
- Twelve-beat, *Cahutal-Tanjao* (4, 4, 2, 2)
  Dhe- O Ten- Ten- / Tag- -Ta Ten- Tag- / Khita Gradhi / -Ta Khita
- Twelve-beat, *Kattavali* (3, 9)
  Dhin- Gragra Dhin- / Ta- Dhin- Ten- Ta- Ta- Ten- Ta- Khit- Ten
- Twelve-beat, *Duital Macha* (3, 9)
  Dhin- Dhina- Dhai- / Dhin- Ten- Ta- Ta- O Ta- Ta- Then- Ta-
- Fourteen-beat, *Jayatak* (2, 4, 4, 4)
  Dhin- Gragra / Dhin- Dhenta Then- Tadhin- / Dhentag Tadhin Ta Then- / Ta- Thenta Then- Tadhin
- Sixteen-beat, *Khenji Tala* (1, 3, 1, 3, 2, 2, 4)
  Dhin- / Dhen-Ta-Gragr / Den- / Dhen- Ta Gragra / Dhentag Tathin / Tata Thenta / Dhenta Gragra Dhaidhin - Dhai
- Eighteen-beat, Pancham (4, 4, 4, 2, 4) [Mentioned by Pratima Devi] Ten- Ten- Ten- Den- / Ten Dhen- Ten- Ten- / Ta- Ten- Ten- Ten- / Dhen- Ten- / Dhen- Dhenta Ten- Ta

N.B.: There are also twenty-eight-beat Brahmatal *(4, 2, 4, 2, 2, 4, 2, 2, 2, 4) and thirty-six-beat* Kokilapriya Tala *(4, 8, 8, 4, 4, 4, 8), commonly taught, but not mentioned here, being too long in beat-count.*

Kathakali: Body Movements

These are pure dances called *kalasam*, normally as unit of body and feet movement which comes as finale for every *todayam* and *purappad*—dance sequences—as a culmination of the section, resembling *teermanam* in Bharatanatyam or *tehai* in Kathak. When, however, *kalasams* form part of the enactments of the text, they are danced to sustain the emotion of characters. As observed by Santidev Ghosh, these are then danced slowly and softly to tender scenes of love and compassion, and violently and fast in rough and aggressive situations. There are nine *kalasams* in Kathakali:

- *Vattom Vechu kalasam*— performed by master artists in slow tempo in *Chempada Tala* in normal course;
- *Iratti kalasam*—executed in slow tempo in *Chempada Tala* in slow motion at the end of a section, ending in the fast tempo in *Adanta* and *Champa Tala*;
- *Ida kalasam*—included in the quatrain at the beginning;
- *Ata kalasam*—employed for heroic situations;
- *Thoon kalasam*—an offshoot of *Iratti*;
- *Eduttu kalasam*—used maninly for aggressive characters as well as mean and vulgar situations;
- *Muri kalasam*—taken at the end of a quatrain portraying valorous action;

- *Valia kalasam*—used at the commencement of a fight and resembles *Vattom Vechu* in fast tempo;
- *Ashta kalasam*—a beautiful long *kalasam* resembling *Valia*. Most of the *kalasams* are in *Chempada Tala*.

Kathakali: Simple Rhythm Cycles

The rhythm cycles are performed at four tempos: *vilambit, madhyam, drut, ati drut,* in the ascending order.

- Eight-beat, *Chempada Tala*
  Thi - Thi - Tayya - Tatta
- Ten-beat, *Champa Tala* (4, 1, 2, 1, 1, 1)
  Tha - Thi - Tha - Tha / O / Thi - Thi - / O / Tun / O
- Fourteen-beat, *Adanta Tala* (4, 1, 2, 3) Tha - Tha - Tha - Thin / O / Tha - Tha / Tha - Thin / O / Thin / O /Thin / O 1/-1
- Six-beat, *Panjari Tala* (5, 1)
  Tha - Thin - Thi - Tom / O
- Seven-beat, *Triputa Tala* (3, 4)
  Ta - Ki - Ta / Ta - Ka - Dhi - Mi
- Six-beat, *Mudi Adanta Tala* (3, 2, 1)
  Thi - Thi -Teyy / O Teyy / O

Bharatanatyam: Body Movements

These are *adavus*, given at the basic tempo, recited by *Nattuvana* and peformed in three different tempos.

- *Tatta Adavu* (body in *araimandi* position, knees half-bent, facing front) Ta Ya Tai
- *Nada Adavu* (all limbs involved—hands, feet, neck, eye)
  Teyyam Tat Ta, Tey Hip Ta Hai
- *Natta Adavu* (very simple time-space coordination)
  Tey Tey Taam
- *Tatta Kuditta Metta Adavu* (complex movement)
  Tat Thai Taa Haa
- *Teermanam Adavu* (three rounds of pure dance, before resuming basic position) Gi Na Tam, Ta Dhin Ga Na Tam, Ta Dhike Ta Dhin Gina Tam
- *Kuditta Metta Adavu* (no movement below torso; toes and heels held static)
  Tai Hat Tai Hi
- *Vishnu Adavu* (space coverage—front, back, sides)
  Taa Tai Tai Taa
- *Shikhara Adavu* (hands only as *shikhara*, use of space with *utplabana*, jump)
  Tat Tai Taa, Dhit Tai Tom
- *Saraikkal Adavu* (same treatment as above)
  Tai Hi Tai Hi
- Advanced *Teermanam Adavu*
  Tari Kita Tom
- *Mandi Adavu* (in *urumandi*, sitting position)
  Tat Tai Tom
- *Pari Adavu* (only stances, sliding to the left and right some body bending)
  Tai Hat Tai Hi
- *Tatti Matta Adavu* (difficult stances in five different *jaatis*, each four times; full use of *hasta mudras*—*asmyukta hasta* and *samyukta hasta*)
  Taa Ka Dhimi—4, *Chaturasram Jaati*
  Taa Ki Taa—3, *Teesram Jaati*
  Taa Ka Dhi Mi Taa Ki Taa—7, *Mishram Jaati*
  Taa Ka Taa Ki Taa—5, *Khandam Jaati*
  Taa Ka Dhi Mi Taa Ki Taa Ki Taa—9, *Sankeernam Jaati*

N.B. After these thirteen adavus *are mastered, choreographic composition can begin.*

Bharatanatyam: Simple Rhythm Cycles

Jaatis, as mentioned above, were the backbone of enumerating *ragas* in the earlier days and are very much used till today to instill variations in the *tala* system of *pancha nadai* (five rhythmic sound-variables), by arithmetic combinations to reach the *sam* (end of the rhythm cycle).

- Seven-beat, *Mishra Chapu Talam* (3, 4)
  Taa Ki Taa / Taa Ka Dhi Mi
- Eight-beat, *Adi Talam* (4, 4)
  Taa Ka Dhi Mi / Taa Ka Dhi Mi
- Six-beat, *Rupaka Talam* (1, 2, 3)
  Taa / Ka Taa / Ka Dhi Mi
- Fourteen-beat, *Ada Talam* (5, 5, 4)
  Taa Ka Taa Ki Ta / Taa Ka Taa Ki Taa / Taa Ka Dhi Mi—*Khanda Jaati*
- Ten-beat, *Jhampa Talam* (7, 3)
  Tta Ka Dhi Mi Taa Ki Taa / Taa Ki Taa
- Seven-beat, *Triputa Talam* (3, 4)
  Taa Ki Ta / Taa Ka Dhi Mi—*Samkirna Jaati*

Mohiniyattam: Body Movements

These are called *adavus*, the same as in Bharatanatyam and are recited by the *natttuvanar:*

- *Jaganam Adavu*
  Jaga Jaga Jam Ti Ti
- *Thaganam Adavu*
  Tey Tey Tit Taa
- *Daganam Adavu*
  Dhanu Dhanum Tam
- *Samishram Adavu*
  Taagitaa Tat Ti

Mohiniyattam: Simple Rhythm Cycles

Same as in Kathakali.

Though formal music lessons were not to Tagore's liking, he had an innate ability to learn by listening

Midas Touch of Music

All Indian classical dances as well as folk forms have an inalienable relationship with music: vocal or instrumental. In classical styles, while *nritya* interprets the literary content of the song, *nritta* is pure dance, abstract in nature, using gestures from temple sculptures without any literary links. In spirit, Tagore followed these precepts—with the richest possible *sahitya* at his creative disposal—with the exception that even where *bols* were involved, he added musical lines as much as possible. Obviously, music was the supreme concern for him, something that he related to *bhuma* as he observes, 'Our music connects to the melody of *Bhuma*; resonating its spirit of renunciation, its peace, its solemnity belying all narrow excitements.'

So the Poet named this cosmic feeling—'bliss of renunciation'—founded on his life-long experience.

Musical Upbringing

The ancestral home at Jorasanko, Kolkata, was a hub of musical activities where the climate was entirely Catholic, with the highest stress unmistakably on Hindustani classical music, with Tagore's father as the chief patron. The accomplished musician Shrikantha Singha was his chief companion and the two would sing and dance—oblivious of the surroundings—to the tune of a religious song. Debendranath was also known to have danced in Amritsar in a flowery orchard to the tune of a *ghazal*. Shrikantha was very affectionate to young Tagore and had spent with him many sessions at dawn, singing together: *'Banshi hamari rey'* (O, this flute of mine).

Though formal music lessons were not to Tagore's liking, he had an innate ability to learn by listening, and more by escaping hard practice than by sitting down for a proper *guru-shishya talim*. For Tagore, absorption of music—and mostly of the highest quality—was entirely an 'osmosis process': including the stalwarts of the day—like the greatest of *dhrupadiyas* like Vishnu Chaktravarty and Jadu Bhatta. They were followed by musicians of the Vishnupur *gharana*—Radhikaprasad Goswamy and Surendranath Bandyopadhyay. After Debendranath's death, his scions got scattered and the ancient custom of attracting musicians to the ancestral abode of Jorasanko was discontinued.

But all the siblings, in the descending order of age—Dwijendranath, Satyendranath, Hemendranath, Jyotirindranath and Somendranath—were immensely fond of Hindustani classical music and learnt Hindi songs. Dwijendranath played on flute and piano; Hemendranath was a vocalist with the *tanpura* in hand; Satyendranath composed Bengali 'Brahmo Sangeet' based on Hindi melodies; Jyotirindranath learnt 'Dillibaz' sitar; and Somendranath was particularly good in singing *tappa* style: indeed, a veritable conglomerate of musicians under the same roof! Especially, Jyotirindranath would compose tunes on piano and, young Tagore, along with a mate, would compose lyrics forthwith set to those tunes.

In 1875, Tagore's famous 'Keep burning, the funeral pyre, the widowed woman would immolate herself' and 'We've tied a thousand hearts in one single strand and dedicated our whole life to one single end' came out of such an early wellspring.

Passing Wind of the West

For the England-returned Tagore in 1879, a few adaptations got from his exposure to English, Irish and Scotch songs came perhaps naturally for his operatic plays. These songs, which proved of no great consequence to his subsequent evolution of music, are quoted below for reference, with Tagore's own composition stated first:

Valmiki Pratibha (1881)

- *'Tabe aay sabe aay, tabe aay sabe aay—*
  Tabe dhal sura, tabe dhal sura, dhal dhal dhal'
  (Western source unknown)

- *'Kali Kali balo re aaj—*
  Balo ho, ho ho, balo ho, ho ho, balo ho'
  ('Nancy Lee')

- *'Mori, o kahar bachha, orey kothay niye jaye;*
  Aaha, oi karun chokhey o kahar paney chaye'
  ('Go where glory awaits thee')

Kal Mrigaya (1882)

- *'O dekhbi rey bhai, aay rey chhute,*
  Moder bakul gachhey'
  ('The Vicar of Bray')

- *'(Tui) Aay rey kachhey aay,*
  (Ami) Tore sajiye di'
  ('The British Grenadiers')

■ *'Phuley phuley phuley dholey dholey bahey kiba mridu baye,*
Tatini hillol tuley kalloley chaliya jaye'
('Ye banks and braes')

■ *'Mana ma manili, tabuo chalili*
Ki jaani ki ghatey'
('Go where glory waits thee')

■ *'Sakali phuralo swapanapraye;*
Kotha se lukalo, kotha se haye'
('Robin Adair')

Mayar Khela (1888)

■ *'(AAha,) Aji ey basantey eto phula photey,*
Eto banshi bajey, eto pakhi gaye'
('Go where glory awaits thee')

The rest of the songs of the above three operas harked back to classical music styles, including *tappa* and *thumri*. Indeed, most of his music during this period had a strong tinge of Hindustani classical system and one had to wait for the following decades for the major advent of *desi* vocabulary into Tagore's phenomenal melodic treasure-trove.

Affinity to Classical Ragas

Ragas in Indian classical styles—both Hindustani and Carnatic—have specific notes, *pakad* in an octave (including flat and sharp notes, and skilful glides over microtones), the ascent and descent within the scale and a characteristic *chalan*. These *ragas* provide the body and soul of the classical music repertoire and Tagore, indeed, had a strong attachment to the *ragas*—their mood and spirit—as would be seen from his notes on different occasions as cited below:

■ When the *sehnai* was playing Bhairavi, it...made the empty sky and even winds before my eyes ring out an anguished cry, wailing deep within, melancholy, yet very beautiful.

■ When the sallies of Bhairavi are perceived aurally, it does seem to wrest out an anguished *raga* from within the very heart of the universe.

■ The morning elaborations in Bhairavi notes, still ringing in my ears, make me highly distracted.

■ Bhairavi is like the inner restlessness of the entire Creation for separation from the dear One.

■ Bhairavi is the eternal, ineffable pain of the companionless cosmos, as it were.

■ The governing deity of our festival wakes us up, on this day of festivity, by singing his melody in Bhairav at our doorsteps.

■ Bhairav is the first stirring of a woken-up morning sky.

■ The very touch of Ramkali and other morning *ragas* immediately arouses a feeling of a worldwide meltdown of piety pervading the horizons and make this *raga* appear to be the Planet's own song.

■ Amidst this raging storm, the shady clouds, the incessant sounds of the downpours, the fury of the thunderbolts—one feels like singing in Kanada or Malhar and have the time well spent!

■ In the evening sky of our hearts, the rains of Shravan are pouring heavily without the bother of any formal dress, it's as though its appearance is entirely to grace a musical soiree, at the behest of its poet. Hence the resonance of a melancholy Megh Malhar.

■ Megh Malhar is, as though, the gurgling of the released stream from the bondage of the Gangotri of the flowing tears.

■ When Megh Malhar sings the melody of the rains, it neither imitates the downpours nor mimics the furious thunders, yet no practical man can hold it to ransom for not being the real thing.

■ Megh Malhar heralds the rains for the entire universe.

■ Whenever I've sung songs on the rains, Megh Malhar has poured forth all the world's texts of tears and filled up my melodies.

■ The rainy clouds, it seemed, had a desire to sing its *kajari* to me so that I could respond later with my own songs.

■ I was so delighted to see the rainy clouds after a long time. Had I been a Hindustani maiden of Varanasi, I'd have sung *kajari* and gone to swing under the *shirish* tree.

A Tasher Desh *performance.*

■ They're playing Multan again and strayed my mind into sadness. It has put a veil of tears on everything green on this earth.

■ Sometimes a bell tolls not too far and it seems to ring silently in the sky, to tell in Multani that time is passing away.

■ Multan, it seems, is the tired whisper of the sunburnt day's end.

■ Purabi, it appears, is the tear of the lonely widow at her empty home.

■ I heard from the boat the violin playing Purabi first and Yaman Kalyan later; the calm river and the still sky were wholly filled up in melody. When the sallies of Purabi flowed out, I instantly realised it was an incredibly deep and profoundly beautiful affair, an outstanding creation—the *raga* mingled so well with the magic of the evening that nothing seemed to be lost —my heart welled up.

■ Everything exits, goes away, we too depart, this depressing thought spread its shadow of melancholia everywhere—the flat notes of Purabi have made our hearts sad.

■ Although I'm going to the Western seas, my mind is busy exploring another shore, where that unmindful boy must end his playfulness in Purabi or this evening will go in vain.

■ This day is one of those kinds that are and yet aren't there. It is an elaboration in Gaud Sarang that, when it's over, does not leave any mark.

■ The Bhupali melody is in the air, there's a call: do stop, do return, Paraj is seemingly the drowsiness of the tired night.

■ Sahana's tune is still and solemn, it has no excesses of frivolous merriments, hence it's the *raga* of our wedding ceremony.

■ Kanada, it seems, is the forgetfulness of a waylaid maiden trysting in the darkest of nights.

■ Khamaj's melancholy sallies spread its cloth's end on the entire township.

Tagore did follow certain ideals of the Hindustani *ragas*. For instance, he followed the ancient practice of using Todi, Asabari, Bhairav, Bhairavi, Ramkali and Kalengra for his songs that referred to morning, light, waking up and so on. For evenings, he went instinctively for Yaman or Purabi, and for nights, the prescribed night-melodies of Behag, Khamaj and Kanada came handy to him. Bahar and Vasant are age-old *ragas* for spring and Tagore made no exception. For autumn, he used morning *ragas*, for, the mornings are the season's best façade. For the rains, Tagore was usually in favour of Mian Malhar and Des Malhar for his countless songs, although he occasionally used Yaman for that season. His music career began in 1880 when songs were needed for the household prayer-meets and festivals, and he followed the criteria of morning and evening *ragas* as would be appropriate. The habit lasted life-long.

The 1938 songs for the *Magha* festival were duly composed in evening *ragas*. And his music drew to a close in 1941 when both of his two swansongs: 'O the ever-new, let another instant of your momentous birth occur again' and 'There comes the Supreme Soul' were composed in the morning *raga* Bhairavi.

Affinity to Desi *Music*

The major streak in the *desi* forms is an equally distributed stress on words and melody, unlike the Hindustani classical system where words in lyrics play generally a minor role. Still, *desi* music occupied a lower platform compared to *dhrupad, khayal, tappa, thumri* and *bhajan*. Tagore's exposure to *desi* was at its grassroots in Dashubabu's *Panchali* (musically-recited religious rhymes) in his household.

Between 1863 and 1878, Tagore became acquainted with *keertan* and *Ramprasadi* as prevalent in urban Kolkata. He composed half-a-dozen songs of these two genres. The major exposure to *desi* forms happened when Tagore, at thirty (1891), became responsible for looking after the family zamindari in the riverine countryside of Rajshahi and Kushthia in East Bengal, and came to know the real indigenous music, for the next decade or so, till he was forty.

Tagore also heard *padabali keertan* in rural Bengal where the lead singer elaborated the words of the main text through melody and rhythm. Called *aakhar*, which Tagore re-named *kathar taan*—sallies in words—this was followed by its lesser cousin *dhap keertan*—easy-rhythm *keertan* for the masses. Another major exposure of Tagore was to the *baul* music, drawling its lineage from such 'simple-living and high-thinking' spiritual savants as Gagan Harkara (the postman), the illustrious Lalan Fakir (the man looking after betel-leaf barrage) as well as his guru (an ordinary palanquin-bearer). The *baul* element was prominently evident in Tagore's patriotic songs which were composed in the wake of the Bengal Partition in 1905. Tagore was then at the vanguard of the movement and wrote such soul-stirring songs—using the *baul* form of East Bengal as:

- *Aamar sonar Bangla'* (I love you, O golden Bengal of mine; your sky, your winds play their flute ecstatically in my soul)—the national song of Bangladesh;

- *'O aamar desher mati'* (O the earth of my motherland, I bow down my head on your sacred soil);

- *'Ore tora nai ba katha balli'* (It doesn't matter even if you don't talk; or wake up the neighbourhood by shouting amidst the fair's congregation);

- *'Ghare mukh malin keno'* (Don't get mellowed down, my brother, at the sight of the sad face home; don't get swayed, my brother, by the dark countenance that is staring outside);

- *'Chhi chhi, chokher jaley bhejas ney aar'* (It'll be an utter shame if your helpless tears moisten the soil under you; Do pull yourself up and close your heart's doors against all inanities);

- *'Je tomaye chhare chharuk'* (Whoever deserts you, my mother, I won't leave you; I'll take firm refuge at your feet, my mother, and won't care for anybody else);

■ *'Je torey pagal bale'* (Don't you hit back to whoever calls you crazy; They might throw dust on you thinking you're mad today, but will turn round to follow you with garlands in hand tomorrow morning);

■ *'Jadi tor dak shune keu na ashey'* (If no one cares to listen to your call and come to you, do step out alone—proceed alone, move alone, go alone; all by yourself)—Mahatma Gandhi's favourite song.

On other occasions, Tagore used the undulating folk form of *sari* from East Bengal and used it in both patriotic and seasonal songs, but these were comparatively rare.

Basic Tenets of Tagore's Music

Before attempting to delve into the enormous complexity of Tagore music, one should note that both the lyrics and melody of Tagore's music—numbering over twenty-two hundred— were very largely Tagore's original creation; much unlike the Western tradition of Schubert composing immortal music to Goethe's rousing libretti (see Chapter 3). The few exceptions were adaptations of some traditional tunes; some melodies of a few classical songs from different states including North, West and South India; a handful of Western tunes; and a few songs of his early youth to which Jyotirindra set the tune on piano.

In terms of content, Tagore's music is extraordinarily wide-ranging and, in almost every genre, has been a success. In the *Puja*—worship—section of *Geeta Bitan*, the songs are in the nature of prayer and meditation touching on lofty ideals such as meditation and resolution, sorrow, assurance, inwardness, self-realisation, awakening, the removal of doubt, contemplation, termination, union, relating to the *baul* and mendicant, the universe and even festivals. In the *Swadesh* part are his famous patriotic songs. In the *Prem*—love—segment, there is an infinite variety of amour and in the *Prakriti*—nature—portion, all six seasons are extolled rivalling in number Kalidasa's *Ritu Samharam* of the same genre! In the *Vichitra*—multiple varieties—segment, there are songs which defy categorisation under any of the above. As sheer lyrical poems, these songs are a value-addition to Bengali poetry. These apart, there are six complete music dramas and dance-dramas (see below) that added a new dimension to Bengal's annals of music and would remain as a permanent asset to Bengali literature.

There were many other themes, not generally tackled in established musical genre, on which Tagore composed quality songs. They included sports songs, wayfarer's songs, songs on roads, birthday songs, marriage songs, songs to offer solace after death, songs on ploughing, songs on harvesting, songs on *Grihapravesh*, songs on the tea-ceremony, songs on banter and humour, songs on thirst for water and songs of empathy for the lowliest of men, besides songs for a multitude of ceremonies at Santiniketan. Thus, his music came close to man's struggle in real life in a way in which no other songster had ever attempted in India.

Form-wise, Hindustani classical music comprises broadly *dhrupad, khayal, thumri* and *tappa*: with fairly well-defined stanzas, all of which forms were used by Tagore. The bulk of Tagore songs followed a *dhrupad*-like structure: with four stanzas of *sthayee, antara, sanchari* and *abhog*—where *sthayee* is repeated after *antara* is sung, and again so, after *abhog* is over. While *sthayee* can start on any note, *antara* usually may foray from the middle octave to the higher octave, while *sanchari* may go down from the middle to the lower and *abhog* often repeats *antara*. Alternatively, they may journey within the lower notes and the higher notes of the middle octave. Thus, the span of notes in the middle octave and, wherever musically warranted, the fringes of the other two octaves are touched systematically and aesthetically, creating musical filigree.

Khayal has usually only two stanzas: *sthayee* and *antara*. *Tappa* and *thumri,* too, have generally two stanzas each. In villages, there are *desi* songs varying from two-liners to multi-liners, but repetition of the first line (or first stanza) at given intervals is a usual feature. As stated earlier, Tagore wrote more four-stanza songs varying between eight lines and sixteen lines, than two-stanza songs ranging between three and seven lines, with some songs going up to twenty-four or even twenty-nine lines.

While Tagore's affinity to classical *ragas* was intimate and far-reaching—often mingling *desi* with *ragas* or transmuting *ragas* themselves in the spirit of his songs, he was very different from an orthodox classical composer-musician from several standpoints. One, the Hindustani classical tradition plays up the melody and attaches comparatively low importance to the lyric while for Tagore, it was lyric which had to be organically interwoven with melody. This interdependence was a supreme consideration for him. Two, *taan kartabya*—vocal display of sallies—was a positive taboo, as much as were other classical ornamentations like *gamakas, gitkiris* and *khatkas*—unless they like *meend* were integrally built into the song with various nuances. Three, Hindustani classical compositions allow a reasonable degree of improvisation by the singer on the concert platform, but Tagore's songs were strictly notated and what he called 'verbal gymnastics' was not permitted during performance. Four, Tagore put the intended *bhava* of the song—combining notation with *gayaki*—above everything else and would not allow it to be compromised during public performance.

Midas Touch in Music Drama

To summarise what has been discussed in Chapters 7 and 8, Tagore wrote some six varieties of music-oriented drama where songs played a relatively important role in the drama. From the music point of view, they could be re-grouped as follows:

Shyama: *Mrinalini as Vajrasen.*

■ First Group (*Valmiki Pratibha, Kal Mrigaya, Mayar Khela*)

All three were modelled on the popular European operas, where only songs and recitatives—musically narrated dialogues—dominate the entire performance. The Indian analogue of such operas is still found in Kerala ('Thullal' and 'Ottam Thullal') and Tamil Nadu ('Vidhi Natakam' and 'Villu Pattu') in the South.

While Tagore's first two operas were post-Wagner 'music dramas' with substantial dramatic content, the third was a pre-Wagner opera, which had dominant songs and was with virtually no storyline. *Ragas* were predominant in all three, with a sprinkling of European melodies.

■ Second Group (*Sharodotsav, Falguni, Achalayatan, Tasher Desh*)

It is a large categorisation of four regular plays, with songs (and some dances) interspersed among the prose-dialogues of the characters—modelled on the older folk form of *jatra* prevalent in Bengal and akin to *Yakshagana* of Karnataka.

Although the dramatic narrative came first, one could realise from the songs in these plays that the songs were not just melodic decorations of the drama, but meant to carry forward what could not be expressed in ordinary dialogue. The method of dramatic action, of course, changed considerably from before. The process did resemble the *Natya Sangeeta* tradition of Maharashtra with songs serving the same purpose for carrying forward the narrative force of the play.

■ Third and Fourth Groups (*Vasanta, Naveen, Nataraj–Riturangashala, Shravan Gatha, Sundar*)

In these music dramas, the dramatic milieu was created only to present several pre-composed songs together. The intention was to weave these songs into a core idea and present them to the viewers in the form of a play. A sketchy storyline was there: only to present the bouquet of the songs, and the dramatic content was only incidental.

Though *Vasanta* and *Shravan Gatha* in the third group were full-fledged music dramas, they were different from other categories. The main aim was to weave together lyrical songs on spring or on the rains, and to visualise these songs through ordinary play-acting or through dances.

In order to keep intact the link of one song with the next one, the dramatic milieu was created through a royal court, where the king, the courtiers and all other *dramatis personae* appeared to have congregated to celebrate the seasonal festival. The links among the songs were maintained through dialogues of the king, the royal poet, Nataraj and the rest who were engaged in mutual conversation to build up these links.

For *Nataraj–Riturangashala* and *Naveen,* belonging to the fourth group, the ploy was a little different. Although they too were celebrations of seasons, the royal court was absent in them. Tagore himself appeared on stage—like the story-tellers of olden times—and created links from one song to the next through singing, reciting poems and dramatic reading. No storyline was made out for them.

For *Sundar* in the same fourth group, two characters within the play acted as story-tellers and allowed a running commentary on the flow of songs and dances.

■ Fifth Group (*Shishu Tirtha, Shap Mochan*)

This was yet another form of music drama where the *sutradhar* narrated verbally the entire events of the play, allowing the characters to enact their roles only during the songs. This has been a widely prevalent form in India and, once upon a time, only the story-teller would talk, sing and dance to carry forward the entire play almost by himself, with occasional marginal support from a group of choral singers. This form would find a familiar echo with the drama of *Ojha Pali* and *Ankiya Nat* from Assam, East Bengal's *Pala Gan* and Bengal's *Kaliya Daman Jatra* (not found any more) and the *Bhagabat Mela* form of enactments by Brahmin Bhagavatars from Andhra. *Shishu Tirtha* and *Shap Mochan* broadly followed this pattern. For both these plays, unlike the earlier format, the storyline was fixed beforehand and quite a few songs were selected that would go well with the spirit of the theme. Most of these songs had been composed earlier and their inclusion here was based on their consistency with the storyline and keeping the flow unabated.

■ Sixth Group (*Chitrangada, Shyama* and *Chandalika*)

Tagore had begun writing operatic plays in his post-teenage era and came back to this form, with dominant, thematically-

A scene from Chitrangada.

linked dance, in the last phase of his life, where all the music dramas were again sung, including the dialogue elements of the drama. The only difference was that in the first group the characters sang their own songs on stage, whereas in the sixth group, they play-acted on stage only through dance, with songs being taken care of by the group of backstage singers. In *Chitrangada* alone, there were snatches of recitations that connected the earlier part of the story with the next.

As has been observed by the literati, many art forms in Tagore's life—such as poetry, stories, songs as well as paintings—were spontaneous creations. The muses came almost on their own—and also disappeared when they wanted to—from some wellspring deep within the Poet, treating him as a surrogate self, as it were! The music dramas and dance-dramas were not of this kind; virtually all of them had been created from external demands, catering to others' enthusiasm. Here is a brief summary of how they evolved.

■ In the initial era, Tagore wrote *Valmiki Pratibha* and *Kal Mrigaya* to meet the need of Viddatjan Samagam Sabha (The Assemblage of Scholars), while *Mayar Khela* was penned for Sakhi-Samiti (Union of Female Companions). There was no dance prevalent in that era nor was it attempted. Normal play-acting was the customary thing and this was done in music with gusto!

■ Music dramas, from *Sharadotsav* up to *Falguni*, came from him to fulfil the need of providing aid to integrated education for the Santiniketan students who were mostly boys and were, hence, without female characters. The music was accompanied by easy body movements, not to be called proper dance.

■ When girls joined as students and started learning dance, it was time to introduce dance with music during play-acting. As dance evolved further through 'natural selection', the full-fledged dramas of music acquired the veneer of dance-dramas. The experience that Tagore had gathered in writing the operatic plays in his first life found expression to become dance-drama in that age of dance. Full-blooded music dramas were undoubtedly inspired by operatic music and acquired their own unique form and content at Santiniketan.

Both, music drama as well as dance-drama, as complete creative entities, were an unparalleled expression of Tagore's genius in music: providing a virtual Midas touch! He was, no doubt, a pioneer in the genre and indeed not much effort by others seemed to have followed in his time in the same direction.

Innovation in Rhythm Cycles

By instinct and upbringing, Tagore used the prevalent common *talas* of the Hindustani (and rarely some Carnatic) classical system for his music, but this did not prevent him from innovating rhythmic variations of his own. They added an illuminating dimension to his music and are illustrated below (with drum-mnemonics at the first tempo):

■ Five-beat, *Jhampak* (3, 2)
Dhi Dhi Na / Dhi Na

'Aji jharer rate' (In this tempestuous night, my companion, my soul mate, you've come over for your tryst with me);

'Bipade more raksha karo' (I don't pray you should save me in trouble—I beseech you to make me fearless in distress).

■ Six-beat, *Shashthi* (2, 4)
Dhi Na / Dhi Dhi Nage Thete

'Amar jadi bela jaye go boye' (Even if my time idly passes by, do know this, my entire mind resonates in your tempo).

■ Eight-beat, *Rupkada* (3, 2, 3)

Dhi Dhi Na / Dhi Na / Dhi Dhi Na

'Gavira rajani namilo hridaye' (The darkest of nights has now descended in my heart, there's no commotion left any more; I only intermittently listen to the sounds of the faraway sea).

■ Nine-beat, *Nabataal* (3, 2, 2, 2)

Dha Den Tha / Thete Katha / Gadi Ghene / Dhage Thete

'Nibida ghana andharey' (In the deepest of darkness, the lodestar shines on; O My mind, don't get listless on the high seas).

■ Eleven-beat, *Ekadashi* (3, 2, 2, 4)

Dha Den Tha / Thete Katha / Gadi Ghene / Dhage Thete Thage Thete

'Duarey dao morey rakhiya' (Keep me occupied at your doors in everyday welfare deeds; I'll wander around listening to calls in your kingdom).

■ Fourteen-beat, Tagore's *Dhamar*, from Vishnupur *gharana* (3, 2, 2, 3, 4)

Ka Khe Te / Dhe Te / Dha O / Ga Di Ne / De Ne Tha O

'Jagey nath jochhana ratey' (The Lord is awake in the moonlit night—Do wake up, my heart, do wake up);

'Veena bajao hey mama antarey' (Do play your lute in my innermost heart, My friend, in company and in solitude, in happiness and in distress).

- Eighteen-beat, *Naba Panchataal* (2, 4, 4, 4, 4)

(Mnemonics not readily available)

'Janani, tomar karuna charana khani' (My mother, I've witnessed your soft footfall in this dawn's nascent rays of the sun).

Tagore's other published, but unnamed, rhythm cycles are illustrated below, but without mnemonics:

- Six-beat cycle (4, 2)

'Hriday amar prakash holo' (My heart finds its expression in the limitless sky; the plaintive flute parlays on in the blowing winds).

- Nine-beat cycle (5, 4)

'Byakul bakuler phuley' (Among the undulating *bakul* blossoms, the honeybee has lost its way).

- Nine-beat cycle (6, 3)

'Jey kandaney hiya kandichhey' (I find the one, whom my heart pines for, is weeping alongside my tearful face; the bondage that binds me tight is tying him up too...).

- Nine-beat cycle (9)

'Duar mor pathapashey' (My doors are by the wayside and I keep them ever open; My eyes are wide ajar, lest I miss the sight of his approaching chariot).

- Eleven-beat cycle (3, 4, 4)

'Kanpichhey dehalata tharathara' (The soft body is trembling; Tears are welling up in the eyes).

- Twelve-beat cycle (6, 6)

'Sakhee, pratidin haye esey phirey jaye ke' (My companion, who's the one that comes every day and returns in futility; Do offer him a flower from my coiffeure).

The fairly popular rhythm cycles such as *Jhampak, Rupkada, Nabataal* and *Ekadashi* were composed in the interregnum between 1903 and 1917. *Shashthi*, the most popular one, was published in 1922 along with the rest. It is to be noted that no section of Tagore's rhythm cycles has *khali* or *phank* unlike the Hindustani form and the stress on beats is equi-distributed; each section has at least two beats; and *jaatis* of the Carnatic form (where each of the common rhythm cycles sports five *jaatis*) are not used at all.

Mnemonics Available within Lyrics

All classical dances use literary songs for interpretation in *nritya* and mnemonics, recited by *nattuvanars*, for presenting *nritta*. Tagore, in general, did not leave much mnemonics in his songs and substituted words; perhaps to present these elements in different rhythm and tempo.

Still, in his multifarious variety, enough scope is discernible to devise pure dance with perhaps repetitive mnemonics, as has been illustratively culled out below from select lyrics:

Rinirini, kimikini and *jhinijhini* from the same lyric—*'Nupura bejey jaye rinirini'* (The anklets keep tinkling and my mind picks the refrain; I know you, I know you);

Ghana ghana jhana jhana jhananana from the lyric—*'Hey mahaduhkha, hey Rudra, hey bhayankara'* (O the high sufferance, O the ferocious, the hideous one);

- *Riniki riniki rinijhini* from the lyric —*'Sey asey dhirey'* (She comes soft-footedly, retraces her steps covered in coyness);

- *Kalakal chhalachhal* from the lyric—*'Eso eso hey trishnar jal'* (Welcome, most welcome, O the waters for the thirsty);

- *Rimiki-jhimiki barishan, jhillijhanaka-jhan-nan* from the lyric—*'Thamao rimiki-jhimiki barishan'* (Stop the drizzle-dazzle downpours, O *Shravan*, with the crickets chirping ceaselessly);

- *Rimijhim rimijhim rimijhim, kkachita kkachita chakita tadita*, and *uchchala chhalo-chalo* from the single lyric —*'Mana mor meghera sangee'* (My mind is the tireless companion of the clouds flying far and anon to the distant horizons);

- *Runu-runu runu-runu* from the lyric—*'More bhavanare kee hawaye matalao'* (How my thoughts have been intoxicated by the wild wind; my mind swings to and fro in unreasoning glee);

- *Tata thai-thai, tata thai-thai, tata thai-thai*, from the lyric—*'Mama chittey niti nrittey key jey nachey'* (In my mind, who's the all-pervasive one, who dances with his enduring cadenza);

- *Tere-kete mere-kete dhan dhan—dhainye* from the lyric—*'Paye padi shono bhai gaiiye'* (Please, my musician-brother, let me touch your feet, but do keep our locality severely alone from your musical prowess);

- *Runu runu jhunu* and *jhini jhini* both from the lyric—*'Nach, shyama, tale tale'* (Do dance, Shyama, in sync with rhythm. The anklets are tinkling on, sweet melody rises aloft, the bangles interplay with each other and clapping sounds echo the rhythms. Do dance, Shyama, dance, dance).

Notations in Music

One reason why the Western classical music has been able to survive over centuries and yet been able to maintain its pristine purity is because of its scrupulous adherence to standard notations in music. For any given composer's music, every pianist and every violinist would play according to their given bars of notation and produce identical music: anywhere, anytime. Indian classical music has, in contrast, blissfully preferred improvisations to any notational system for ages and every singer (or instrumentalist) would be her own composer and would present a *raga* to her heart's content—after adhering only to a minimal set of conventions with regard to its delineation, and every concert would be a unique live event, not repeated by anybody else: anywhere, anytime!

Notations for Hindustani classical music was introduced by Maula Bux of Baroda and used by Krishna Rao Pandit of Gwalior, but standardised notations, as known today, came from Vishnu Digambar Paluskar in the 1910s and Vishnu Narain Bhatkhande in the 1920s. None of these could, however, notate the complete concert of a maestro, for the inherent nature of classical performances mentioned above.

There has also been the parallel genre of pre-composed music in India, such as the South Indian *kritis* (say, by the Sangeeta Pitmaha Purandara Dasa) or Tagore's own music in Bengal. Pioneering contribution to notations for pre-composed music in Bengal came from the Tagore family, initiated by Dwijendranath in the late nineteenth century, modified to *sankhya-matric* by Sarala Devi and *akar-matric*—form-centric—by Jyotirindranath, the latter still in use in Bengal.

Chandalika, *directed by Shanti Bose.*

Tagore was generally very aware of the need of notations for his pre-composed songs: first, to guard against his own creative obliviousness and second, to avoid later distortions. Notations for individual Tagore songs were published in several music periodicals like *Tattvavodhini* and *Bharati* in his time and compiled in *Geeta Panchashika* (1918–19), *Geeta Beethika* (1920) and two volumes each of *Nava Geetika* (1922) and *Geeta Malika* (1926, 1929), besides *Swaralipi Geetimala* (1–4) by Jyotirindranath (1941). Other than Jyotirindranath, it was Dinendranath Tagore, rightly called the *bhandari* of Tagore's music, who meticulously attended to Tagore's music notations! Thanks to the concerted effort of more than a dozen gifted musicians, male and female, documentation of Tagore's songs in notated form began in *Swara Vitan* (so named by Tagore), Volumes 1 to 64 so far, with the first four volumes published between 1935 and 1939 in his own lifetime.

Conclusion

The above is necessarily a very sketchy survey of Tagore's music, starting from

Tasher Desh:
Pranati and others.

his musical upbringing right up to the documentation of his pre-composed music, with special allusions to his music drama and dance-drama. An important point for recapitulation, why his songs could be smoothly shuttled—thematically and chronologically—in and out of many of his dramas, was the strong predilection of the Poet to transcend the narrow limitations of subjects like love or worship or nature, and compose crossover music that could fit in multiple contexts. No wonder, Tagore's music has sublimely stood the test of time!

Desi Music Used by Tagore

Keertan Music

From ancient times, *keertan* has been a customary way of expressing divine qualities in congregations; generally at high pitch and sung with accompanying musical instruments. This has been the practice in the Vaishnava temples of North and West India since the Middle Ages and called *keertan* rather than *bhajan*. In South India, a similar practice is termed as *bhajan sampradaya keertan* like *Radha kalyanam*. In Bengal, the collective singing of Radha-Krishna names since Sri Chaitanya's period in the early sixteenth century is called *naam keertan* and extolling Radha-Krishna's many virtues and life-incidents in musical gatherings is named *padavali keertan* or *leela keertan*.

The latter form was perpetrated by the Vaishnava guru Narottam Goswamy, on return from Vrindavan, starting with elaborate *Gourachandrika*—overture—and followed by *leela keertan*. This form was termed *Garanhati* from where it originated. A later form was *manohar sahi keertan*: with abridged tempo and rhythms, and with high musical quality. Both these formats were confined to the musical cognoscenti. The other prevalent forms included: *reneti, mandarini* and *jharkhandi*. A comparatively popular form was *dhap keertan* with easy melodious structure and widely disseminated through early recording media.

Padavali keertan often used a narrator keeping up the story-telling format in uneven rhymes and melodies, quite independently. *Aakhar* is another format where elaborations of melody are made: not through wordless *taan* but with text-based melodies and in keeping with the framer's rhythms. Tagore used the format in a few songs, calling them 'sallies in words'. The liberty taken by Hindustani classical singers in ornamentation has quite a parallel through compositions of melodious *aakhar*. On the contrary, the *keertan* singers do not attempt to express a *raga* structure like their classical counterparts.

One of the best instances of Tagore's affinity to *keertan* was revealed in his early adolescent composition *Bhanusingher Padavali*, which was based on Radha-Krishna love episodes, followed by some patriotic songs and much later in life, in seasonal, religious and love songs. Normal practice in *keertan*-singing, namely, to start with slow tempo and gradually move towards faster tempo, was not followed by Tagore, maintaining easy three-, four-, five- and seven-beat rhythms.

Baul Music

Tagore freely acknowledged the influence of *baul* narratives on his music, based on his acquaintance with *baul* groups during his Silaidaha stay and acceptance of their forms in his songs: often blending them unconsciously with his *raga*-based songs. These *bauls* were Bengal's freelance musicians yearning for spiritual liberation. Baul music is intimately linked with their lifestyle. They do not follow any religious treaties or any ritual strictures. Following a system called *Sahajiya*, they meditate on love in the abstract, which they long to attain through beauty in the world. The object of abstract love is also called *Moner Manush*—the being residing in the innermost heart—perhaps the divinity. They do not look outside for their object of love. They strictly follow gurus: to initiate them and to show continually the way of worldly meditation.

Their origin is steeped into antiquity, probably dating back to the Vedic times. Later, *natha yogis* resembled them, as did the Buddhist *siddha* poets and the *dohas* they wrote. In the Islamic era, the Sufis profoundly influenced them as did the emerging *tantrik* cult. Their addiction to music and dance has been proverbial and, in particular, gave rise to both Vaishnava *bauls* and *fakirs* in Bengal, equally adhered to by Hindus and Muslims. Almost all *bauls* carry *ektara*, held close to their ears. Another common instrument, which is tied to their waist, is *baaya* (small drum), used for self-regulated rhythm.

Baul music has usually two segments: the first line and the musically separated second line, with the rest of the song following the spirit of the second line in rhythm and tune. The singing takes place in varied rhythms, with accompanied dance-steps executed at will. Expression of joy remains the leitmotif of both singing and dancing, and spontaneity is the last word of *baul* art. While Tagore wholeheartedly adopted the form for use with a variety of contents: seasonal songs, patriotic songs, love songs, prayer music, spiritual ditties and even music drama and dance-drama, his songs with *baul* tunes followed wide variations between *sthayee* (first stanza) and *antara* (second stanza), with *sanchari* (third stanza) set in a new tune altogether. Many of his *baul* songs are blended with *ragas*, retaining both *baul* features and *raga* quality, yet maintaining the easy gait and rhythm of the original *baul* form.

Sari Music

Sari music of East Bengal was another distinctive form that attracted Tagore. A *sari* song, coming from the riverine part of Bengal, is essentially an oarman's song, generating a work rhythm. Like all work-oriented songs, it comprises onomatopoeic syllables, to be voiced together, at the start and the end of the song. Unlike its more popular counterpart *bhatiyali*, *sari* is always a joyous song that is sung in chorus whereas *bhatiyali* is a loner's song full of pathos, sung by the boatman pulling the oars during *bhata*.

In 1905, Tagore first used *sari* to compose a rousing patriotic song: *'Ebar tor mara Gange ban esechhe'* (The floods have broken in now in the dry stream of your Ganga River; bring out your boat and let it float, sail ahoy!). Two seasonal songs followed in the same genre much later in life: *'Basante ki shudhu kebal'* (Is the spring earmarked only for the freshly-bloomed flowers? Haven't you noticed the heap of dry leaves and the play of discarded flowers?) and *'Aji dhaner kshete'* (In the paddy-fields today the sun and shadows are playing hide-and-seek, only hide-and-seek; Whoever has floated the ships of white clouds in the blue firmament). The occasions remained few and far between.

Biographical Notes

Vishnu Chakravarty (1804–1900)

One of the foremost musicians of nineteenth-century Bengal, Vishnu Chakravarty had his talents revealed at an early age and became proficient in *dhrupad* single, along with his brother Krishna. At the age of twenty-four, Vishnu became the lead singer in the Adi Brahmo Samaj under Raja Rammohan Roy and continued for a long time. His specialty was not to give much predominance to ornamentation of *taan* in *ragas*, but to concentrate on their core structure. He mainly sang *dhrupad* and *khayal* and was seminally responsible to take care of Tagore from childhood to teach *desi* forms, besides a thorough (though informal) exposure to *dhrupad*, Vishnu's main forte. Apart from being a highly gifted vocalist, Vishnu was also an innovator in teaching children through musically set nonsense rhymes. He retired from Brahmo Samaj at the age of seventy-four and was warmly felicitated to have motivated a large segment of public to join the community by virtue of his music.

Jadu Bhatta (1843–83)

Possessing extraordinary musical talent, Jadu Bhatta's name is still remembered as a musician, teacher and scholar. Tagore unstintedly acknowledged his musical supremacy in being able to impart 'originality to every song' and expressed gratitude for inspiring him into the mould of *dhrupad*. Belonging to the progeny of Senia *gharana,* he completed his apprenticeship in Kolkata and was heralded as a phenomenal singer who could remember notes by just listening once and could also sing continually for twenty-four hours. Besides being a singer, he was a gifted composer of Hindi lyrics and showed great dexterity in the musical structure. His untimely death was mourned by one and all, including Tagore.

Jyotirindranath Tagore (1849–1925)

The fifth son of Devendranath Tagore, Jyotirindranath was a natural singer and composer, responsible very largely for providing Tagore, the youngest sibling, the earliest directions to channellise his musical creativity. Born artist, he discontinued his studies in Presidency College and concentrated on singing and painting. His initial apprenticeships were under Vishnu Chakravarty, Jadu Bhatta, Shrikantha Singha and the third brother Satyendranath. Apart from being a vocalist, he learnt sitar from Muslim Ustad and, above all, piano from the elder Dwijendranath. He could also play violin and harmonium well. He allowed the little Tagore unlimited time and opportunity to discuss literature and musical studies. In particular, when he composed new melodies on piano, Tagore (with Akshay) was persuaded to write librettos for the newborn tunes nearly simultaneously! Tagore later admitted this to be a very good training ground for creativity in lyrics.

Jyotirindranath was not merely adept in experimenting on *ragas* and blending them in innovative ways; he was also instrumental in helping Tagore to use the Irish melodies from the West in *Valmiki Pratibha* and *Kal Mrigaya*. He mixed Italian tunes with *raga Jhinjhit* to create 'Italian Jhinjhit' and, on similar lines, 'Irish Bilawal', 'Scotch Kedara', 'Scotch Bhopali' and 'Spanish Baul'. Jyotirindranath's seminal contribution to music was to have introduced alphabetic notation scheme; to have started a Bengali music magazine; and to have established Bharat Sangeet Samaj to promote music teaching. Besides, he was a noted lyricist for Brahma Sangeet and a reputed playwright with many prose-plays and musicals to his credit.

Dinendranath Tagore (1882–1935)

Dinendranath, son of Dwipendranath and grandson of Dwijendranath (eldest brother of Tagore), was born in 1882 at Jorasanko, Kolkata.

Dinendranath was an excellent singer and his rich baritone, without being accompanied by any instrument, added a unique dimension to Rabindra Sangeet. Dinendranath will always be remembered as the preserver of the melodies of Rabindra Sangeet, apart from being its meaningful critic. Possessed of enormous energy and phenomenal memory, he could replicate accurately every song in the form of notations and note them down for future generations. He could also write Western staff notations. Dinendranath was the principal of Sangeet Bhavan from its very inception. After a break of four years from 1923–27, he joined as principal again. He was also a drama artist, having acted as dacoit or Valmiki in *Valmiki Pratibha* (1881 onwards), as Pancham in *Achalayatan* (1914, 1917), as Raghupati in *Visarjan* (1923), and as Devdata in *Tapati* (1929). He was an able director of Tagore's plays. He travelled with the Visva-Bharati drama troupe as director on its tour to Mumbai in November 1933 for the staging of *Tasher Desh*.

Hindustani Rhythm-cycles Relevant to Tagore's Music

The common Hindustani rhythm-cycles are indicated below, with drum-mnemonics, for the basic tempo:

- Six-beat, *Dadra Taal* (3, 3)

  Dha Dhin Dha / Na Tin Na

- Seven-beat, *Teevra* or *Teora Taal* (3, 2, 2)

  Dha Den Ta / Thete kataa / Gadi Ghana

- Seven-beat, *Rupak Taal* (3, 2, 2)

  Tin Tin Na / Dhin Dhin / Dhage Terekete

- Eight-beat, *Keharba Taal* (4, 4)

  Dha Ge Na Ti / Na Ka Dhi Na

- Ten-beat, *Jhanptaal* (2, 3, 2, 3)

  Dhi Na / Dhi Dhi Na / Thi Na / Dhi Dhii Na

- Ten-beat, *Surfanktaal* or *Sultaal* (2, 2, 2, 2) or (4, 2, 4)

  Dha Na / Dhin Tha / Kit Dha / Ti Kath / Gadi Ghan

or

  Dhin O Nage Thete / Dhin Na / Dhin Dhin / Dhage Therekete

- Twelve-beat, *Ektaal* (2, 2, 2, 2, 2, 2)

  Dhin Dhin / Dhage Terekete / Dhun Na / Kath Tha /

  Dhage Therekete / Dhin Na

- Eight-beat, *Choutaal* (2, 2, 2, 2, 2, 2)

  Dha Dha / Den Ta / kath tage / Den Ta / Thete Katha / Gadi Ghene / Dha

- Twelve-beat, *Khemta Taal* (3, 3, 3, 3)

  Dha Thete / Na Dhi Na / The Te Dhi / Na Dhi Na

- Twelve-beat, *Aad Khemta Taal* (3, 3, 3, 3)

  Dha Dherekete Dhin / Dha Dha Thin / Tha Terekete Dhin / Dha Dha Dhin

- Fourteen-beat, *Dhamar Taal* (5, 5, 4)

  Ka Dhe Te Dhe Te / Dha O / Ga Di Na / Di Na Ta O

- Fourteen-beat, *Ada Choutal* (2, 2, 2, 2, 2, 2, 2)

  Thin Therekete / Dhin Na / Tu Na / Kath Ta / Terekete Dhin / Na Dhin / Dhin Na

- Sixteen-beat, *Tritaal* or *Teentaal* (4, 4, 4, 4)

  Dha Dhin Dhin Dha / Dha Dhin Dhin Dha / Na Thin Thin Na /

  Thete Dhin Dhin Dha / Dha

- Sixteen-beat, *Yat Taal* (4, 4, 4, 4)

  Dha- -Thete Dhin -Kerr / Dha Dha-Dha Dha Thin –Trete / Na –Trete Thin –Kre / Dha Dha-Dha Dha Dhin Therekete

Among Tagore's oeuvre of some twenty-five hundred paintings on a very wide variety of themes, there would be at least twenty-five paintings, identified so far, that created an entirely novel world of dance by portraying dancing women (and occasional men) that transports one to a mystical world

Panoply of Paintings

The little child Tagore who used to wonder about 'the beauty of the special colour of a cloud' and would get baffled about it but get totally struck by the forms of the multiple branches of a manicured tree—'some rounded, some octagonal and yet some shaped like temple-towers'—eventually became one of the world's most reputed modern painters. And among his oeuvre of some twenty-five hundred paintings on a very wide variety of themes, there would be at least twenty-five paintings, identified so far, that created an entirely novel world of dance by portraying dancing women (and occasional men) that transports one to a mystical world, not yet fully understood in their ramifications. Even to imagine that he was painting these mysterious dance images while creating brilliant music dramas as well as dance-dramas for performance, and yet form-wise distancing himself far away from the humdrum concerns of the proscenium stage on his artistic palette, leaves one with a feeling of awe!

Evolution of an Artist's Eye

As perceived by the cognoscenti such as Sushovan Adhikary, the long journey to the ultimate manifestation of his artistic self perhaps began quite early. As a very young child, he would spend hours looking at the garden tank: 'almost like a picture'. There were, among others, childhood 'masters of drawing', apparently not much revered, and the many vignettes of the Jorasanko palatial home—full of many dark corridors and stairs, and the separation from the interior courtyards—all probably caught as 'a series of paintings' in his mental eye.

Tagore's subsequent artistic views came as observations of nature: for his extended stay at Silaidaha river-land. Much later, Tagore would divide his landscapes into three parts: almost diagonal straight-line hills; dark trees; and the foreground with water or lengthened shadows. Even where there was no elevation, the landscapes would show undulating topography, reminiscent of the rugged Birbhum. The subsequent artistic imagery in his writings was tinged with the memory of the sudden suicide of 'Natun Bauthan' Kadambari Devi, his inveterate adolescent companion, side-by-side with the use of artistic perspectives, emanating out of his youthful view of Turner and Constable, among the British painters, and wall paintings.

Much of his writings in the 1880s and 90s brought in, other than the black-and-white tone, a feel for colours, most of all, for his favourite blue—pale blue, clear blue, tender blue, deep blue, intimate blue, moist blue, soothing blue, soft blue, collieries blue, sky blue, river blue, sea blue, hill blue, forest blue, cloud blue, turquoise blue, marble blue, cup blue—and endless odes to blue. His next favourite hue was the golden one, as a variant of yellow-golden light, golden wine, golden dusk, deep golden light, golden like the sunshine, the soft plea gold, evening gold, golden canvas of sky, golden lines, golden end of clothes and the yellow of the sandbank, yellow cummerbund of a honeybee, yellow mustard and paddy fields and so on. Then followed green in his colour scheme—deep green, moist green, intimate green, tree green, grass green, meadows green, the undulating green and so on. Next came saffron—clothes, waters, grey sands and grey earth. Even his white and black had many different shades: the expanse of white sands, anaemic white of death, emptiness of the moonlit meadows and the cosmic sufferings from separation, beside the category of sheer *rang*—colour—on innumerable occasions. In contrast, red was not very much evident in his works: ascribed by some to his being a little colour-blind towards the red-end of the spectrum.

During the second decade of the twentieth century, Tagore took his artist friends to Silaidaha for sketching, as a token of his increasing interest in the fine arts. His sojourn to Japan in this decade was an eye-opener where he observed their sense of measured strength and calligraphic quality in their art, far removed from the European arts. The growing dichotomy between 'line' and 'colour' that seemingly bothered Tagore was pithily observed by his nephew Abanindranath, an eminently gifted painter-scholar.

Another era had started already in the 1900s: of evolving designs out of crossed-out portions of his manuscripts, first seen and preserved for his nationalist song: *'Vidhir vandhan katbe tumi emni shaktiman'* (You deem yourself to be as mighty as the Almighty in undoing His strictures). By the 1920s, there began to emerge deliberate shapes and forms, as in the manuscript of *Rakta Karabi* (Red Oleander, 1923) and the typed copy of his speech collection *Talks in China* (1924), the latter with animal motifs and forms of China bronze. The spate of cross-cancellations in his poetry manuscripts and corresponding emergence of fanciful figures gathered momentum in 1925. For the poem *Aparichita* (The Unknown Woman), for instance, there was a page-wide sculpture and an animal with a sharp beak, radiating rays through geometric gaps. The following poem *Anmana* (The Distracted Lass) had page-wide black cobwebs of thick lines in dark pigment and revealing the poem's lines in between. The next poem *Vismaran* (The Forgetting) revealed a primitive animal with sharp teeth and a piano-like torso, looking backwards. Another poem *Batas* (The Wind) excelled in this game of decorative cancellations: a giant facial motif with parted lips, aquiline nose and jutted-out chin: a wonderfully-designed sketch.

The poem *Swapna* (The Dream) occasioned a two-page design of a geometrical folk painting, combined with many animal features, collectively looking as though the form is traipsing upwards. The poem *Samudra* (The Sea)—written on board a ship, like many of the above poems, was divided into three parts—a design made of thin lines, that with dense black or with several tiny interstices, reminding one of 'primitive arts'. It did seem that Tagore had left enough space to spare for a laboured figure which proclaimed of 'monumentality': as though carved out in woodcut as in New Zealand's primitive figurines. The poem *Jhor* (The Storm) had two large figures hovering over the verse: a long-beaked bird and a fearsome animal lurking within transluscent darkness as if to jump out. The poem *Prakash* (Manifestation) had the profile of a ferocious face with dreadful teeth, like a decorated mask or a primitive artifact. *Abasan* (The End) had decorative design and a face-profile; and *Atit Kaal* (The Past) displayed an animal figure of an organically alive face admirably filigreed.

Linkage with the West and Latin America

As seen above, Tagore was emerging as a calligraphy-oriented artist in the early 1920s and would soon foray into the painter's world in the late 1920s and early 1930s. To start with, he wielded, as his tool, not an artist's brush but a writer's pen: an implement he was familiar with since childhood. Throughout this novel venture, he had to reckon with two major handicaps. First, he had, like dance choreography, no formalised training in fine arts. Second, he was possibly a born protanopia—colour-blind—so the bright open vistas of colourful panoply was not really for him, thereby having to forsake the world of naturalist painting of both colour and form.

In looking for possible inspiration for Tagore, the cognoscenti like Ratan Parimoo identified the following little-researched sources: handicrafts of the Eastern Islands of the Pacific Ocean; the artistic heritage of the 'Haida' and 'Tlingit' indigenous peoples of the northwestern coasts of North America; and the handicrafts and textiles of Peru in Latin America. Termed 'primitive art' in the history of arts, all of the above are unbelievably rich culturally and aesthetically—with a heightened artistic sensibility revealed in both their articles of everyday life and sacramental vessels of ritual utility: as seen in totem-poles, domestic towers, masks, decorative ornaments, utensils, boats, hats, baskets, storage trunks, clothes and seat-mats. There is a wide prevalence of animal forms, grotesque faces and eye motifs in all their designs. Such primitive art is embedded in life and had profoundly influenced the Western perception of art.

Tagore, of necessity, concentrated on form and not on colours, and used his pen for a long period as his tool in preference to the brush. In what he called an 'epic journey of form', Tagore also looked to the West, especially to German woodcut prints that became another passage for him to enter the world of fine arts. He not merely travelled extensively in Germany but also studied their art forms in depth. At one end, the German artists imparted the quality of painting in their coloured woodcuts. At the other end, these were given geometric angularities, diagonality, sharp contrasts in forms, rough wooden textures and overall angular composition to express their special sensibilities. As a part of the German Expressionist movement, a process had begun in the early twentieth century in the West whereby Henry Matisse substituted the European nudes in favour of Negro sculpture and Pablo Picasso opted for masks, wooden sculpture, and handcrafted artifacts of the primitive art. On the whole, woodcuts, lithograph and dry point offered techniques that played their distinctive role. For Tagore, German Expressionism provided the right inspiration, with black-and-white woodcuts providing for a suitable school to follow and coloured woodcuts also a good model, with limited application of colours.

Outflow of Paintings

When Tagore was in quest of a route to enter the world of fine arts, he had to discard Naturalism, since he was denied the use of all the colours and would have been unable to imitate 'reality' in its entirety. Also, the lack of formal training was another obstacle. And yet, at his station of life, he was aware that the entry had to be different, just apt and even spectacular. With the urge of an artist, the eye of an artist, the finest sensibilities of an artist and with the wealth of calligraphic cross-cancellation designs behind him, he marked out his entry through *Art Nouveau* ornamentation and by turning the key of 'Primitive Art', giving a concrete shape to his calligraphic experimentation.

Alongside Chinese bronze, aboriginal arts of North America's remote coasts, Peru's artifacts and ritual sacraments, and the ancient Malangan heritage of the New Ireland, the use of 'zoomorphic form' and its necessary link with the 'grotesque' found their special place in Tagore's art. What crowded his paintings were: crocodile, dragon, fish, reptile, bird, bird-man, dog, fox, camel and leopard motifs: in highly stylised decorative forms and with little use of colouration. Among the major images that emanated were: animal motifs as above; portraiture (including self-portrait); and landscapes as discussed earlier.

Some other, and equally strong elements —clearly West-influenced and more germane to the theme of this book—were also present, such as clown; ballet dance; ballroom dance or *pas de deux*; Spanish or Gypsy dance; with a good mix of Rajasthani and Iranian dance-motifs. There were also operatic drama-scenes; Santa Claus figures; guitar-players; harlequin-figures with typical costume and cap; Negro women; Christian nun-like figures; Padre figures of the Eastern Orthodox Church; and glimpse of the Crucified Christ. Many of these motifs are still the subjects of contemporary Western art. Tagore also introduced the concept of 'still life' which was new to Indian art in those times, as were his pure landscapes sans human presence, or portraits of common man and woman. Even some of the 'female nudes' seen in Tagore were fresh elements in the Indian art of his time. Use of 'mask' was evident in extending the scope of facial expression or as a surrogate of face, not only for their grotesque quality, but also for their additional dimension of human emotion as, for instance, in masks of dramas. The treatment was often akin to Picasso's stylisation of 'African masks'. Much of these artistic innovations were termed 'energetic spinal cord' for their ramrod-straight form and 'creative circuit' for their artistic expression by the cognoscente such as Jamini Roy and K.G. Subrahmaniam.

When colours appeared on his palette, landscape and naturescape drew the most of his attention, with yellow and yellow-orange emerging as his favourite and the shades of red generally muted. Red was not entirely omitted, but its use followed some definite patterns and formulae, such as burnt red, maroon-red and black tonality in red, but there was no exuberance of red for vibrant emotions as seen in the brilliant red in Expressionist art from which Tagore drew so much inspiration. On the whole, the colour vision of Tagore was decidedly influenced by his use of pen-and-ink and watercolour; his awareness of primitive art and the contemporary art movement raging in his times; and the breaking-up of established norms of form and colouration by the then European artists. His fine arts oeuvre was a combined result of such interactions and interfaces for well over a decade.

Incidentally, Tagore used unconventional colours on the face, a trend that might have originated in the prevalence of masks among his paintings and the indigenous custom, found worldwide, of using colour-designs on human face. In this book's context, a parallel may perhaps be drawn with the use of symbolic painting on the faces of Indian Kathakali actors. For Tagore, a face and a mask could often overlap and one could be traded with the other. Some unusual colours used in mask (or face) were often yellow, peanut grey and deep brown, with the white paper left blank for allowing a mysterious 'paper white' gaze that could be somewhat unnerving. Another unconventional factor was Tagore's scarce use of green, with only some dense woods reflecting deep, dark green. The overall fact that Tagore dared to rub unusual colours on the human face was like taking a revolutionary liberty even with Modernism.

Despite the initial lukewarm response he got in his own country, Tagore received enough encomium in the West and his first-ever exhibition in Germany in 1930 had resulted in many commercial sales of his pictures. The foreign connoisseurs often likened his works to those of Victor Hugo and his landscapes merited pointed comparison with the similar genre of Van Gogh.

On balance, three features were worth noting. One, the action-and-reaction of the 'creative circuit' has always been a worldwide trend and Tagore—with his give-and-take with the West—was not really mmune from it. Two, Tagore was still quite unique in selecting his forms, his imitation of woodcuts and his use of white spare lines, alongside abounding primitivism, masks, clown-motifs, rule-breaking colouration, emotional outbursts and dramatic expressions. Three, while Tagore's paintings were quite a novelty in India in many respects, they were not exceptional in the world context of his own period.

In the turn of life when Tagore entered the mainstream arena of fine arts, he doubtlessly rode on the crest of the Expressionist wave: in form, in landscape colouration, in the marked preference for bright yellow to other tints, in geometric facial expressions, in dramatisation of themes and partly in the composition techniques. Yet many of his faces mirrored deep pathos, sorrow and depression, unuttered words and unfinished work ethos. The medium of painting offered him yet another artistic outlet for joy and melancholy, for aesthetic amalgam of warm solace and withering sarcasm: both emanating from life.

Glimpses of Dancing Figures

Out of the nearly twenty-five hundred paintings of Tagore around the last decade of his eventful life, about twenty-five dancing figures have been culled out by discerning eyes at Kala Bhavan, Santiniketan and titles have been added by them for the sake of convenience, in the absence of any such captions from Tagore. Here is *prima facie*, a few analytical observations on these paintings (shown in the following pages):

- 00.1981.16 Dancing Figure

Drawn around 1929–30, the figure seems probably influenced by the danseuse Ruth St. Denis, whom Tagore saw performing and interacted with in that period.

- 00.2327.16 Dancing Figure

The figure is in Western style, not Indian, and seems influenced by Western ballet.

1.

2.

Here and in the following pages: Twenty-five dancing figures taken from the collection at Kala Bhavan, Santiniketan.

3.

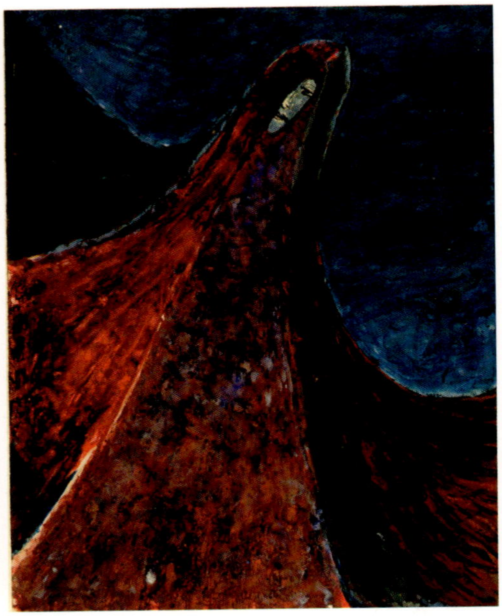

4.

■ 00.2387.16 Two Figures

The dual figures have the lifting of a dancing girl by a male dancer, which is very balletic.

■ 00.2550.16 Dancing Figure

It has a Far Eastern aura, with a long skirt and extended veil, comparable to a Persian dance.

■ 00.2568.16 Two Dancing Figures

These two male and female figures are not again Indian, as per the *angik* as well as the *aharya*.

■ 00.2598.16 Dancing Figure

The dance has come back to India: in its dancing rhythm, balance, the tri-sectrix break-up of the body and the soft stance.

■ 00.2599.16 Dancing Figure

It looks like a flying fairy which has a seemingly Iranian influence. The figure has an Arabian costume with the end of the trailing skirt lifted. This is similar to Tagore's own dance demonstrations by lifting of the skirt-trail.

■ 00.2600.16 Dancing Woman

The figure, in its style of dance and movement rhythm, does appear Indian.

■ 00.2601.16 Dancing Girl with Red Skirt

The figure has a Rajasthani skirt, like those worn by folk dancers, with the leg lifted. Marked below 'Jodhpur', it seems of gypsy origin, with a red handkerchief on head.

■ 00.2602.16 Dancing Figure

This is once again Indian, with a piece of costume held in hand; could it be symbolic of Nati of *Natir Puja*?

■ 00.2603.16 Composition with Three Dancing Figures

The motif is very Indian again. The dancing bodies display the *utariya*—body cover— of the Santiniketan style and with a distinctive Javanese crown on head. It is signed in Bengali in 1933 and mentions *Times of India Press*, Mumbai.

■ 00.2605.16 Dancing Female Figure

This is one of the characteristic most mysterious female figures by Tagore, akin to *abhisarika nayika*—trysting heroine.

■ 00.2631.16 Dual Figures

The figures pertain to the dramatic oeuvre, with a very poignant point of departure.

■ 00.2632.16 Dual Figures

The dual figures again belong to drama, capturing a dramatic moment of strongly bidding farewell.

■ 00.2645.16 Two Figures Like Puppets

The puppet-like figures seem to resemble those from Sri Lanka.

5.

6.

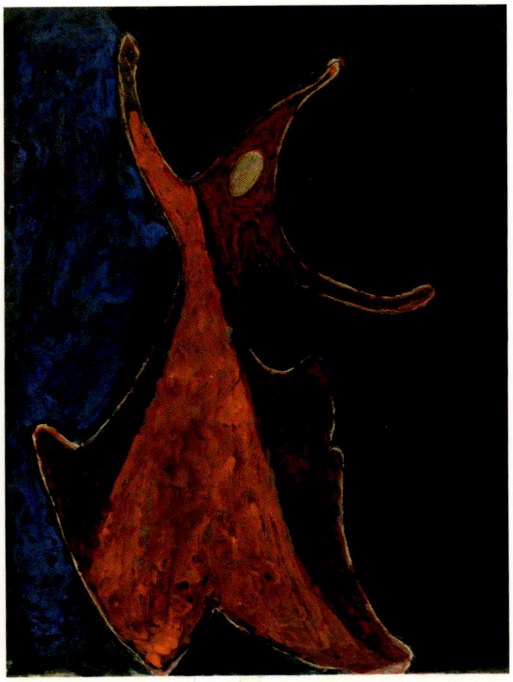

7.

8.

9.

10.

11.

12.

13.

14.

15.

16.

■ 00.2680.16 Dancing Girl

This figure is quite geometric, with a strong resemblance to folk elements, with triangular head-gear.

■ 00.2093.16 Dancing Female Figure

The figure has a decidedly Southeastern face, wearing a Bali or Javanese crown.

■ 00.3120.16 Standing Woman

The figure is of a dancing girl with a raised head, wearing a veil (touch of mystery?).

■ 00.3355.16 Two Figures

The figures belong to a clown-piper in the company of a dancing girl. They evince a strong folk element.

■ 00.3358.16 Dancing Female Figure

The figure holds a piece of cloth in her left hand and has two clothes-ends. It seems Indian.

■ 00.3359.16 Dancing Female Figure

The figure is similar to the above, with a head cover.

■ 00.3360.16 Dancing Figure

The figure has a very clear face with a hand raised. The posture seems quite balletic.

■ 00.3373.16 Dancing Girl with a Veil

The figure has a distinctive Manipuri veil. The lower skirt is quite gorgeous.

■ 00.3385.16 Bending Female Figure in Profile

Drawn on 8-11-1935, it is the figure of a dancing girl, with sinuous curves like 'S' and has interesting resemblance with a winged bird.

■ 00.3386.16 Figure in Design

It is a dancing girl ensconced in a couch. The design has thin lines, suggestive of decorative elements.

Motion and Emotion of Dancing Figures

Preliminary comments as above on the twenty-five dancing figures, identified out of twenty-five hundred of Tagore's paintings, perhaps raise more questions than they provide answers for. Some of these questions are formulated in a nutshell, aimed at the fine-arts cognoscenti, for examination with a toothcomb:

■ There are many figurines with distinctly Western gestures of the balletic kind. How clear is the resemblance and where did the inspiration come from?

■ There are some with typical costumes and crowns of the Asia-Pacific kind. What were the influences of Java and Balinese dances that Tagore witnessed in 1926–27 on his paintings?

17.

18.

19.

20.

21.

22.

23.

24.

25.

■ Some folk elements are clearly reflected. Could these be from the folk dances of Bengal and, if so, which forms?

■ Central Asian dance idiom of Iran (Tehran, as signed there) also occurs, with veils and with the Sufi-like raising of the skirt-ends. What were the inspirations?

■ Among the several elements of Indian choreography reflected, which *mudras, charis, gatis, bhramaris* and *utplabanas* were most dominant?

■ The dancing figures here vary from the surreal to the expressionistic. What abstractions, symbolisms and stylisations were evident? What were their very sources of inspiration?

■ In these paintings, Tagore's fancy navigated between imagination unbound and reined-in imagination. Were there any boundaries?

■ Is there any possibility of a digital analysis of the core elements?

■ Tagore highlighted motion as being fundamental to dance (as voice is basic to music) and was a votary of Herbert Spencer's theory of feelings. How much did he extrapolate these theories in his dance portraiture?

■ In particular, Tagore himself, while he was teaching, would lift the end of his cloak in a very Sufi-like fashion. Did the image continue?

■ Finally, Ruth St. Denis danced to Tagore's poetry and interacted with him in New York in 1930. Did Ruth influence Tagore?

Conclusion

One can visualise the 1928–40 scene at Santiniketan when Tagore was creating his music dramas and dance-dramas on one hand and showcasing them on the proscenium stage on the other hand. Simultaneously, he was painting his dancing figures with often a mystic vision. While the former genres have been analysed many times, the latter genre of his capturing dance on canvas—literally in many hues— remains ignored and unexplored. The dozen issues raised above are an effort to call attention to this really neglected area.

Catalogue of Tagore's Dance-related Paintings

1. 00.1981.16 Dancing figure

A figure in dancing movement. Waterproof ink and pen: orange, black, red, blue, green blue used with brush and pen on paper. Unsigned, n.d. [c.1929–30]. 38 x 39 cm.

2. 00.2327.16 Dancing figure

Black-and-white line drawing. Pen ink: black used with thin pen on paper. Signed 'Rabindra' in Bengali script, bottom right. 19 August 1935. 23 x 29 cm.

3. 00.2387.16 Two figures

Pen ink: red, black used with pen and brush on cardboard. Signed 'Rabindra' in Bengali script, bottom left. n.d. [c.1929–30]. 21.5 x 33 cm.

4. 00.2550.16 Dancing figure

Standing female figure with a veil. Pen ink. Waterproof ink and poster colour: blue, red, white, brown. Black used with pen and brush on paper. Unsigned. n.d. [c.1933–34]. 22 x 28 cm.

5. 00.2568.16 Two dancing figures

Pen ink. Waterproof ink and watercolour: red, black, orange, blue, yellow used with pen and brush on paper. Signed 'Sri Rabindra' in Bengali script, bottom right. n.d. [c.1929–30]. 24 x 32 cm.

6. 00.2598.16 Dancing figure

Poster colour, pen ink and waterproof ink: red, blue, brown used with pen and brush over pen ink drawing on paper. Unsigned. 'Darjeeling. 8 June 1933'. 21.5 x 28 cm.

7. 00.2599.16 Dancing figure

Pastel red, pen ink. Waterproof ink and watercolour: violet, yellow, blue, red used with pen and brush over pencil drawing on paper. Unsigned. 'Teheran. May 1932'. 21.6 x 28 cm.

8. 00.2600.16 Dancing woman

Textured with crayon pencil. Crayon pencil: yellow, red, blue, brown used on paper. Unsigned. n.d. [c.1932–33]. 20.3 x 31.5 cm.

9. 00.2601.16 Dancing girl with red skirt

Textured with pen and brush. Pen ink and waterproof ink: blue, red, green, orange used with pen and brush over pencil drawing on paper. Unsigned. n.d. 'Jodhpur'. 18 x 25.5 cm.

10. 00.2602.16 Dancing figure

Dancing female with raised hands. Black-and-white, textured with thin pen. Pen ink: black used with thin pen on paper. Unsigned. '08.11.37'. 21.5 x 33.3 cm.

11. 00.2603.16 Composition with three dancing figures

Black-and-white, textured with pen. Pen ink: black used with thin pen on paper. Signed 'Rabindranath' in Bengali script, bottom middle. 'Bombay. 02.12.33'. 21 x 26 cm.

12. 00.2605.16 Dancing female figure

Pastel, pen ink, waterproof ink: blue, pink, yellow, brown, black used with brush and pen on paper. Signed 'Sri Rabindra' in Bengali script, bottom right. 'March 1932'. 21 x 29.5 cm.

13. 00.2631.16 Two figures

Two figures in rocky landscape. Waterproof ink. Pen ink and poster colour: yellow, blue, red, black, white used with pen and brush over pencil drawing on paper. Unsigned. n.d. [c. 1931–32]. 21.5 x 32.5 cm.

14. 00.2632.16 Two figures

Male figure with a turban and female figure with a crown in dramatic gesture. Textured with pen. Pastel and pen ink: blue, yellow, black, red used with pen and brush or back side of brush on paper. Signed 'Rabindra' in Bengali script bottom left. '18.12.33'. 25 x 24 cm.

15. 00.2645.16 Two figures like puppets

Pen ink and waterproof ink: green, brown, red, orange, black used with brush and pen over crayon pencil drawing on paper. Signed 'Rabindranath' in Bengali script, bottom right. '10.10.34'. 25.5 x 35.8 cm.

16. 00.2680.16 Dancing girl

Black-and-white angular drawing. Pen ink: black used with thin pen, reed pen and brush over pencil drawing on paper. Signed 'Rabindra' in Bengali script, bottom middle. n.d. [c.1929–30]. 22 x 29 cm.

17. 00.2093.16 Dancing female figure

Water colour, pen ink: blue, green, orange, brown, yellow used with brush and pen on paper. Unsigned. n.d. [c. 1932–33]. 17 x 23 cm.

18. 00.3120.16 Standing woman

Waterproof ink and pen ink: brown, black, blue used with brush and pen on paper. Signed 'Sri Rabindra' in Bengali script, bottom middle. n.d. [c.1930–31]. 18 x 25.4 cm.

19. 00.3355.16 Two figures

Dancing female and a male figure with flute in a garden. Pen ink, poster colour: blue, pink, brown, green, yellow used with thin brush on paper. Unsigned. n.d. [c. 1934–35]. 17.5 x 25.5 cm.

20. 00.3358.16 Dancing female figure

Black-and-white sketch with pen. Pen ink, black used with thin pen on card. Unsigned. n.d. [c. 1929–30]. 8.5 x 13.5 cm.

21. 00.3359.16 Dancing female figure

Black-and-white sketch with pen. Pen ink: black used with thin pen on card. Unsigned. n.d. [c. 1929-30]. 8.5 x 13.6 cm.

22. 00.3360.16 Dancing figure

Textured with pen. Pen ink: violet, black used with thin pen on card. Unsigned. n.d. [c. 1930–31]. 8.8 x 13.6 cm.

23. 00.3373.16 Dancing girl with a veil

Crayon pencil or pastel and pen ink: yellow, black used over pencil drawing on blue silk, pasted with board. Unsigned. n.d. [c. 1934–35]. 21.7 x 26.5 cm.

24. 00.3385.16 Bending female figure in profile

Textured with thin pen. Pen ink: blackish green used with thin pen over pencil drawing on paper. Signed 'Rabindra' in Bengali script, bottom left. '8.11.35'. 8.9 x 25.5 cm.

25. 00.3386.16 Figure in design

Black-and-white. Pen ink: black used with thin pen over pencil drawing on paper. Unsigned. n.d. 16.2 x 24.3 cm.

Vyjayantimala Bali portraying Chandalika.

Part Four

Afterwards

Tagore once averred that his music would remain as a lasting heritage in his land and the people would be singing his songs everywhere in time to come

Tagore's Dance Legacy

Tagore once averred that his music would remain as a lasting heritage in his land and the people would be singing his songs everywhere in time to come. This has come to pass today. What is more, dance has also become an integral part of this legacy and the terpsichorean mood prevails in treating his wealth of *sahitya* (literature), as available, to be re-mapped and re-interpreted through dance all over the land almost every day. The upsurge continued very much after his death and reached a new momentum during the Poet's birth centenary in 1961 when there was a countrywide spurt of visualising Tagore through dance using the media of poetry recitation, theatre, mime, opera, musical, tableau, ballet, music drama and dance-drama.

In order to ascertain the mood of Tagore's dance after Tagore and in the spirit of creating documentary record for posterity, a large sample survey was undertaken among nearly fifty pioneers as well as young choreographers of Indian dance to ascertain:

- In their illustrious career, which major themes of Tagore have they presented on stage?

- What has been the really distinctive choreography they have adopted to interpret Tagore?

- What is their personal take on the legacy of Tagore's dance?

Almost all of them have magnanimously responded, furnished information and even supplied pictures. They were divided in two parts:

- Pioneers (who emerged before or during the Poet's birth centenary of 1961 or could present their Tagore-based choreography soon after);

■ Young choreographers (who appeared on the scene 1970 onwards and have continued in the last four decades).

While almost all responded, a few mentioned about not having performed Tagore. What follows is an edited summary of the replies received to the three questions posed, with the names of the choreographers alphabetically arranged.

Amala Shankar: Legendary companion of Uday Shankar.

Pioneers

Amala Shankar

Based in Kolkata, she is the foremost living exponent of creative dance, after Uday Shankar and runs the Uday Shankar Cultural Centre.

■ In 1961, on the occasion of Tagore's centenary, an ambivalent Shankar was persuaded to produce the ballet *Samanya Kshati* at the behest of Jawaharlal Nehru. Amala was the queen in the ballet and Ravi Shankar did the music. The ballet became an overnight success and Shankar took it to the USA in 1962. Next he did *Prakriti O Ananda* based on Tagore's *Chandalika*. Amala choreographed *Chitrangada* and *Kal Mrigaya* with the students of Uday Shankar Cultural Centre in later years.

■ She personally does not think that any particular dance form can be categorised as Tagore's Dance or Tagore would have himself done it. When she first witnessed Tagore's dance, it was completely based on Manipuri. To put it in a nutshell, classical dance forms of that time, and the styles of the places he had visited, influenced Tagore's dance to a great extent.

■ Tagore once wrote a letter to Uday Shankar in which the Poet showed great conviction in Uday Shankar's style of dance, which could free the dances of India from the conservativeness and reservations and give a fresh flow to it. Dance, for its own sake, is soulless. One must feel bliss, a divine touch, through one's dance.

Asit Chatterjee and Gayatri Chatterjee

Originally students of Uday Shankar, they both taught in Rabindra Bharati and danced in Kolkata for long, evolving their own style.

■ They produced *Shyama, Mayar Khela, Valmiki Pratibha* and a special Tagore theme *Viraha Milan*. In 1961, they also performed *Chitrangada*.

■ Choreography was in Uday Shankar's style of dance. They also adopted Shambhu Bhattacharya's style with masculine virility. Later, Asit developed his own form, which combined *Madhura Rasa* and *Vira Rasa*.

■ Tagore had an upbringing in the environment of music, dance and acting around him. Both Uday Shankar and Tagore wanted imagination and innovation in dance to have an open door. Tagore wanted a chemical synthesis of Manipuri, Kathakali and Bharatanatyam in as creative a fashion as possible.

Bipin Singha and Kalavati Devi

Outstanding Manipuri duo who opened their pioneering school in Kolkata and taught generations of Manipuri dancers.

Kalavati Devi: Expounding on Tagore's dance.

■ They produced *Bhanusingher Padavali, Chitrangada, Kal Mrigaya, Tasher Desh* and *Ogo Shono Ke Bajaye* (inspired by some of his songs on flute).

■ Tagore wanted to give a visual expression to his songs through a body of language that would not threaten the flow of his melodies and was spellbound by the sinuosity of Manipuri dance. They used both *tandava* and *lasya* aspects. In particular, choreographing *Tasher Desh* was a challenging one, as they had to modify the free-flowing, wave-like movements of Manipuri into rigid ones and break the torso movement of the dance form that resembles figure '8' into small fractions in order to match the stiffness of the Cards: representing age-old social bondages and a crumbling frame of mind.

■ While choreographing his dance-dramas and telling his story, Tagore often borrowed facial expressions, dramatic poses and hand gestures from various Indian dance styles such as Manipuri and Kathakali; the movements of Kandyan dance of Sri Lanka; and dances of Southeast Asia. Thus he developed one of India's modern dance styles, namely, Tagore's Dance. Since Tagore did not strictly codify his movements, as he did with his songs, various experimentations are taking place with his dances and themes. Such changes are welcome, provided they do not tamper with the aesthetic value of his thoughts.

C.V. Chandrasekhar

Based in Chennai, he is an outstanding teacher as well as choreographer in Bharatanatyam over five decades.

■ Both he and his wife Jaya choreographed a number of Tagore's dance-dramas and composed dances on Tagore poems on *Varsha, Vasanta* and *Sharad*. Indeed, Tagore's poems and dramas brought out the painter, musician, dancer and actor in him. The dramas they choreographed were: *Mayar Khela, Shyama, Valmiki Pratibha* and more than thirty songs.

■ They used only the Bharatanatyam technique and took certain liberties in their choreography, such as increasing or decreasing the number of repetitions, interspersing the lyrics with mnemonics specific to Bharatanatyam, and so on. All this was some forty years ago since when Tagore's Dance, as practised now, has undergone many changes. Their daughter Manjari's solo work *Ahalya* was seminally influenced by Tagore's poem *Ahalyar Prati*.

■ What Tagore liked watching the most was the sway in body movements which merged with his music. Tagore had taken elements from classical dances and created movements to suit his music.

Chitra Vishwesharan

Chennai-based renowned Bharatanatyam dancer and choreographer, running her reputed dance school.

Left and facing page: Shyama: *Enacted in Bengali in Kalakshetra under Rukmini Devi Arundale.*

■ Growing up in Kolkata, she learnt Tagore's music and participated in several of his dance-dramas. She revived two songs from Tagore's *Gitanjali*. Chitra chose seven stages in a woman's life—as mentioned in ancient Tamil literature— and set them to Carnatic music.

To describe the seven stages, she retained Tagore's poems in Bengali. For childhood, for instance, she used a poem where Tagore described the blossoming of flowers and the flowers dancing in the breeze. She drew a parallel between a child and a flower: to reflect that joyous phase of life.

■ She used her forte of the Vazuvoor style of Bharatanatyam.

■ Every production on Tagore has to be the result of intense research, revisiting his thoughts and re-assessing them. Tagore has always so many dimensions. The challenge is to set the concept clear and condense the enormous material to come up with a concise production.

Darshana Jhaveri

Mumbai-based eminent Manipuri dancer, with sisters Naina and Ranjana, all trained by Bipin Singha in Kolkata.

■ She performed *Bhanusingher Padavali* and *Chitrangada*. In 1961, she produced *Rituranga* with Kalavati Devi. Later, the same collaboration continued for *Tasher Desh* and *Kal Mrigaya*.

■ She used *tandava* and *lasya* from the pure traditional elements of Manipuri. She thought Manipuri suited best Tagore's dance mood: in its beauty and variety. Darshana also used *Lai Haraooba, Cholam Tandav* from *Sankeertana* and *Thang-Ta* martial art. Regarding rhythms for Tagore's themes, she used those not used in Manipuri, namely, *Duitaal Macha, Triputa Saweari, Jhanptaal* and *Maitei Surfanktaal*.

■ Manipuri seems to suit Tagore's themes the best. These days, Bharatanatyam and *Kalari Payattu* are being added to Tagore's repertoire, but it is not necessary to go beyond the Manipuri tradition.

Govindan Kutty and Thankamani Kutty

A redoubtable pair of dance gurus of Kathakali and Bharatanatyam, they settled in Kolkata and trained many scores of dancers in those two disciplines.

■ They produced *Chitrangada, Shap Mochan, Mayar Khela* and 'Abhisar' (the poem on which *Natir Puja* was based).

■ Keeping the vision of Tagore intact, they adopted different South Indian dance styles to suitably depict different characters of the dance-dramas. From 1958 onwards, they saw several changes in depicting Tagore's themes. Initially, the dance would only support the song, with the dancer moving softly according to the song, without any strong beats and cross rhythms. Noticing a void in dance choreography, they felt the urge to use some prominent classical styles to portray characters more vividly. The main idea, however, was to use the *bhava* of the character. To depict the events and characters in the drama more strongly, the use of *ghungroos* became a necessity too.

■ Tagore did not set any rules to express his themes, but wanted one to feel his emotions and to interpret the events in one's own way. Since the classical dance styles in Bengal were not very strong when Tagore planned his dance-dramas, he might have wanted to use two Indian classical styles for his productions: Kathakali, more theatrical and appropriate for the male characters; and Manipuri for the soft female characters. Choreographers and performers use these forms according to their conviction, which they believe was Tagore's vision in depicting his themes through dance.

International Centre for Kathakali (ICK)

ICK is the premier Indian institution for conducting several teaching and training courses on the Kathakali style as well as for arranging productions.

■ Immediately following the Tagore birth centenary, ICK geared up to produce *Chandal Vikshuni*, based on *Chandalika,* directed by Sadanan Balakrishnan. The production ran successfully over 1965–68.

■ The dance drama was rendered in pure Kathakali style.

Kanak Rele

Based in Mumbai, she is the seniormost Mohiniyattam scholar, dancer as well as choreographer; founder of the Nalanda Research Centre.

■ She was brought up at Santiniketan from 1944–49 and steeped in Tagore's dance-culture, having seen all productions. Her production *Kalyani* (which is based on *Chandalika*) was performed in Delhi in 1996 and came for criticism from the Tamil Brahmin community for having called the untouchable girl 'Kalyani'.

■ Kanak Rele used all Kerala-based choreography styles, including *Teyyam, Kalamezhuttu* and ritual dances of Kerala. She used the concept of 'Shaman' based on *Veliccha-badu*. For this, she had gone to the South and recorded their chants, while wearing heavy *shilambu* (anklets) with a modern touch.

■ To her, Tagore is an icon, including his music, which she can sing.

Mrinalini Sarabhai

A direct student of Tagore at Santiniketan and the founder of the famous Darpana Academy of Performing Arts in Ahmedabad, she still performs as a nonagenarian, with scores of choreographies to her credit.

Chandalika: *Mother's pride and daughter's repentance.*

■ She participated in all the dance-dramas of Tagore. He admired her work and always appreciated the South Indian techniques which she used. In *Mayar Khela*, Tagore wanted her to do all the men's roles! Tagore always left the dancing to dancers like her. Most group scenes were done in Manipuri style, which was taught in Santiniketan. Later, when Kelu Nair was teaching, Mrinalini used Kathakali also.

■ In Darpana, Mrinalini choreographed *Chandalika* (Bharatanatyam); *Tasher Desh* (free style); *Chitrangada* (Kathakali as well as Manipuri); *Tagore the Poem* (Bharatanatyam and Kathakali), besides the plays *Visarjan* and *Karna-Kunti* in Gujarati. Incidentally, she led a forty-three-member Indian dance ensemble to China in October 1978. On the first night, they danced *Tasher Desh* and other items. Next morning the Ambassador requested Mrinalini to delete *Tasher Desh* from the programme. Of course, Mrinalini understood as it showed regimentation and the country was China! In her interpretation of *Tasher Desh* (1961), she expanded Tagore's anti-Brahmanism to envelope all 'isms', and their unrelenting and stifling rules. She created new movements to suit the theme and it was highly appreciated. As the overture of the recent Dalit's human rights hearing, her daughter Mallika used Mrinalini's five-minute piece from *Chandalika* and the song: *'Oke chhuyona chhuyona chhi...'* (Don't you touch her, that untouchable lass, fie on her...) and set the tone for the atrocities that were recounted by the Dalit victims throughout the day. In *Tagore the Poem*, she took the poem: 'Where the mind is without fear...' and showed how we as a nation have failed to get even close to his dreams. As a pointer, she translated the first line 'Where the mind is without fear...' once again using Prakriti's plight in *Chandalika*.

Mrinalini and Mallika Sarabhai in Chandalika.

Narendra Sharma (as told by Sangeeta Sharma)

Having recently passed away, Sharma was a direct disciple of Uday Shankar at Almora and has been a harbinger of creative modern dance at school level for thirty years and through his group Bhoomika in Delhi.

■ Most of Sharma's choreographic creations—with an open outlook towards the Indian contemporary scenario—were inspired by Tagore. Sharma's *Flying Cranes* (based on Tagore's poem 'Hamsa Balaka') depicted a flock of migratory cranes visiting their annual winter retreat, a lake in the warm South. Sharma's *Antim Adhyay*

(The Last Chapter) created visual images of the episodes and situations of life around, when man becomes victim of his end: The Death, based on one of Tagore's last poems. Sharma's *Prarthana* (The Prayer) was an attempt to give artistic form to Tagore's poem: 'Where the mind is without fear'. Like Tagore, Sharma considered it to be of the highest importance that people be able to live and reason in freedom. His attitude to politics and culture, nationalism and internationalism, tradition and modernity could all be seen in the light of this belief.

■ Tagore was one of the first to support and bring together different forms of Indian dance. He helped revive folk dances and introduce dance forms from the other parts of India.

Padma Subrahmaniam

Based in Chennai, she is the doyen of what she calls Bharatanritya. She is running Nrithyodaya for several decades.

■ During Tagore's hundred years' celebrations in 1962–63, Padma and Shyamala Balakrishna (an ace singer) sang together twenty songs of Tagore in a bilingual form: first in Tamil and repeated in Bengali. During the one hundred and twenty-fifth anniversary of Tagore's birth in 1986, she choregraphed hundred songs of *Gitanjali* (in Tamil). She also produced *Shyama* in Tamil.

■ She used mixed choreography in the Santiniketan style, taking the help of Kanai Kumar, an ex-Santiniketan student. She had *Shyama* interpreted spiritually, with one girl representing *Atma* (soul) when she calls for good sense to prevail, but the perception changes midstream once trouble starts and she is no longer sure if she has understood what *Atma* really is: an inner journey of Padma herself.

■ It was Tagore who first thought of the need to make Indians proud of the Indian culture and its performing arts. He knew that art and culture could be a unifying factor in India. He was such a *deergha darshi* (far-seer) that he combined Kathakali with Manipuri. He had Kathakali masters, Bharatanatyam masters, Manipuri masters and many such artistes from different parts of India at Santiniketan and created a Santiniketan style of dance. Tagore was not a dancer, but a great visionary who made it possible for many Indian arts to live and flourish together.

Rita Ganguly–Kothari

Based in Delhi, she was a child prodigy, having won many national scholarships including in Kathakali and Bharatanatyam.

■ Rita's father had a base in Santiniketan, from where she attended schooling and learnt Manipuri and Kathakali, besides classical music in the early 1950s. Santidev made Rita, at eleven, play Madan in *Chitrangada* when the girl for that role in a visiting team fell ill. Santidev also allotted her the role of Srimati in *Natir Puja* in 1955 and made her learn authentic Baul. She also essayed the roles of second

Chitrangada in *Chitrangada*; Shyama in *Shyama*; and Sudarshana in Raja. She was made a showpiece to VIPs, having topped in most subjects! Santidev did not like temple dancing of the *Dasi Attam* kind such as Bharatanatyam, Mohiniyattam and Odissi. He interpolated in Tagore's Dance elements of Kandyan dance. Having his land holdings in Orissa for a long time, Santidev wanted his pupils to imbibe its stimulating and sensuous movements. Manipuri dance was viewed as part of social expression. She also performed, under Santidev, with a large number of Tagore songs.

■ On the whole, Rita found in Tagore's Dance a subtle blend of Javanese, Manipuri, Kathakali and Kandyan but not Bharatanatyam. She produced *Tasher Desh* at NSD: based on Paul Klee's famous modern paintings. She also produced *Chandalika, Shyama, Valmiki Pratibha* and *Muktadhara*.

■ Tagore need not be used as a peg for tentative theories, he knew exactly what he wanted. He was a true Sufi savant, a sublime exponent sans spectacular extravagance. He was ahead of his times. If one explores his expressions and inner feelings, one can only delight in the understanding of what he wanted to convey.

Rukmini Devi Arundale (as told by Pushpa Shankar)

Doyen of Indian dance and founder of Kalakshetra in Chennai.

■ In 1961, she choreographed *Shyama*, with songs daringly rendered in Bengali even for a southern audience. For this, she commissioned Mani Krishnaswamy, the famous vocalist, to learn the original Bengali songs. Her dance-drama did exceedingly well and Kalakshetra toured Australia with *Shyama* in 1966.

■ In *Shyama*, she used Kathakali for the male dancers and Bharatanatyam for female dancers and improvised with the sit-down posture, including the honeymoon scene. There was no special stage-set.

Singhajit Singha and Charusija Mathur

Based in Delhi, they are among the foremost Manipuri choreographers, running Manipuri Nartanalaya with many Manipuri dance-dramas to their credit.

■ In 1961, they choreographed two of the most famous songs of Tagore for Max Mueller Bhavan.

■ Their choreography was entirely in Manipuri style, using it as a language to interpret the poetry and express the spirit. Tagore's poems, of course, appear to go much beyond the word meanings, with their own language and music.

■ It was no mere coincidence that Tagore adopted the Manipuri style for most of his dances, even by adopting Manipuri dance teachers from communities settled outside Manipur, probably for the facility of their knowing the Bengali language. Themes expressed by Tagore had their explicit identity, in keeping with the spirit of his meaning. Giving it a visible form and to keep it languid (not jarring or angular) was the purpose of his dance. His lyrics and poems already contained an aesthetic art form; dance was an outward projection, close to his visionary ideas.

Shanti Bose

Trained in Rabindra Bharati under Uday Shankar, he was the latter's ballet master in the late 1960s. He runs his own repertory company in Kolkata.

■ From 1969 onwards, Shanti produced *Chitrangada, Shyama, Tasher Desh, Chandalika, Shap Mochan, Valmiki Pratibha, Mayar Khela, Kal Mrigaya, Varsha Vasanta* and *Samanya Kshati* (as a blend of film, music and dance, with Panu Pal), the last one in 1972. In *Samanya Kshati*, which was revived in 1972 and ran many shows thereafter, he did the king's role and Anupama Das was the queen.

Shanti Bose as Arjun in Chitrangada.

■ With grounding in the Academy of Dance, Drama and Music (later, renamed as Rabindra Bharati), he blends dominantly Shankar's style with a mix of Kathakali and Manipuri.

■ Tagore's melody as well as the words constitute the total body that he has to interpret. The meaning of his words has the supreme importance and he makes himself responsible for visualising the mood and the spirit: using Kathakali for *vira rasa*, and Manipuri for *lasya* and *shringara*.

Sonal Mansingh

Based in Delhi, she is among the foremost exponents of Odissi and Bharatanatyam styles in India. She established the Indian Centre for Classical Dances and trained several dancers.

■ In 1961, she presented her first performance on Tagore at Bharatiya Vidya Bhavan in Mumbai. None other than Pankaj Mullick came from Kolkata to sing the four songs to which she danced. Since then, she has included Tagore's poetry in her repertoires of Bharatanatyam and Odissi. In recent years, she worked with Reba Som on creating a composite repertoire: *Sure Sure Taale Taale* (In Melody and in Rhythm) which became popular among a cosmopolitan audience. In this programme, they included poems like 'Jonaki' (the Firefly), 'Hey Nataraj' (O Nataraj...) and many others.

■ Dancing to Tagore's poetry is always a spiritual experience, because there are sweet and simple phrases through which he invoked the Infinite and the Formless. The melodies and easily comprehensible rhythmic structures of his compositions give an opportunity to a dancer to interpret the poem. There is also enough space to be filled with one's creative imagination and interpretation which is the hallmark for a great work of poetry.

Uday Shankar (as told by Shanti Bose)

The harbinger of modern dance in India.

■ In 1961, he produced the Tagore poem 'Samanya Kshati' (The Negligible Loss) with elaborate sets as a full-fledged ballet, with Ravi Shankar composing music and lending his voice, along with Ali Akbar's accompaniment and Lakshmi Shankar's voice. Shankar was the resplendent king in the music-based ballet and Amala Shankar the queen in 1961–62. As another innovation, Shankar took up a four-line poem of Tagore: 'Udaar Charitanam' (Of the Open-minded One) and clubbed it with 'Samanya Kshati' during his presentation. In 1966, he presented *Prakiti-Ananda* based on *Chandalika* and used Kamalesh Nandy's instrumental music.

■ Choreography for 'Samanya Kshati' by Shankar was entirely in the balletic form by using the storyline with instrumental music and without any spoken text. It was repeated in 1961-62. Tagore's short poem 'Udaar Charitanam' had the sketchiest outline with Shankar making it a fifteen-minute choreographic work with six girls, dancing around the little flower placed around the stage-corner. It was a piece of great charm, without any of Shankar's characteristic showmanship that had been evidenced in 'Samanya Kshati'.

Valmiki Banerjee

Based in Delhi and considered among the foremost choreographers in the capital, this octogenarian has dedicated his entire life to Tagore's dance through his Delhi Ballet Centre running over six decades.

■ He has, in his long career, produced all the dance-dramas and all the operas of Tagore. In addition, he has presented the plays *Visarjan, Kaler Jatra* and the long poem 'Karna-Kunti Samvad' through mime, tableau and dance.

■ He calls his dance form Rabindranatyam, as he sincerely believes that Tagore's dance can be viewed as yet another classical style: with its rich repertoire that already exists and with enormous potential of adding *sattvik, angik* and *aharya abhinaya* on the lines already indicated by Tagore. He has formulated the complete syllabus and step-by-step curriculum for teaching Rabindranatyam to his pupils and demonstrated the same in many places in India and abroad.

■ Tagore's educational concepts permeate his dance thoughts, as primarily they were formulated to create holistic education. His mind was catholic, progressive and open to qualitative virtues wherever he could find them. Above all, Tagore imbibed folk culture and incorporated it into his dance form: to give the latter an organic entity.

V.P. Dhananjayan

Based in Chennai and a product of Kalakshetra, he (with his wife Shanta) has been an ace dancer and choreographer in Bharatanatyam. His school, Bharata Kalanjali, produced many good dancers over years.

Shanta and V.P. Dhananjayan in Chandalika.

■ While at Kalakshetra, Rukmini Devi produced *Shyama* in 1961, where he played the role of Uttiyo and Shanta was one of the village belles. Shanta also assisted in singing the whole dance-drama throughout their Australia tour in 1966. Their institution Bharata Kalanjali produced *Chandalika* in 1984.

■ He used the idiom of Bharatanatyam and folk movements to suit the lilting music and rural characters in *Chandalika*.

■ Tagore's dance is 'music of the body', and it has a judicious amalgam of Kathakali, Manipuri and Bengal's folk traditions. His dance style suited his music very well; in fact, it always looked as though his music was expressed in movements of the human body. His was spontaneous music with characteristic expression (*bhava geet*), which communicated easily the contents of his beautiful lyrics.

Vyjayantimala Bali

Based in Chennai, she is among the foremost exponents of the orthodox Pandanallur style of Bharatanatyam and runs her own school, besides being a highly refined and popular actress on celluloid.

■ In the early 1960s, she produced *Chandalika,* which infused in the minds of the people the concept of equality of all human beings.

Vyjayantimala Bali in Chandalika.

■ She took pains to present *Chandalika* with simplified gestures in order that it could then be easily understood by any type of audience. It was executed in the Bharatanatyam tradition. Costumes, designed to preserve the simplicity and purity of the dance-drama, brought in a judicious blend of the classical and folk styles. It was a difficult subject to conceive and to choreograph, and quite challenging to her, because of its different moods and emotions. *Chandalika* gained stature with the rich and inspiring music composed by the maestro Ravi Shankar. They presented *Chandalika* with only dance, mime and music, minus Tagore's songs. Tapas Sen, the wizard of stage lighting, greatly contributed to the success of *Chandalika*.

Yamini Krishnamurthy

She is a legendary figure in the dance world. Based in Delhi, she is running her own Bharatanatyam dance school for many years.

■ In 1961, Yamini danced to three of Tagore songs.

■ Tagore's songs are very subtle for dance, because they are rooted in *ragas* and have set moods. They may appear short, but make profound and subtle statements, which transcend specific themes of nature and beauty. To a dancer like her, different images come surging in, that have to be aptly visualised and expressed in a mellowed fashion!

Yog Sunder Desai

Based in Delhi, and as a disciple of Uday Shankar, he has spent a lifetime in choreography in Kathakali, Odissi and several folk forms enriching his India Revival Group.

■ In 1951, when the noted danseuse Sadhana Bose performed *Tyag Abhisar*—based on Tagore's Buddhist theme—that she included in her dance-drama *Ajanta*, Yog Sunder partnered her and performed as Upagupta in Mumbai. He directed *Chandalika* in his Kolkata days, playing the role of Ananda. In 1961, he produced *Shyama*, translated in Hindi with music by Gyan Ghosh, retaining the original tunes. This was broadcast by the AIR. He also directed Tagore's abstract poem *Shishu Tirtha*, calling it *The Man Divine* during Gandhi's birth centenary in 1967. It was a landmark event, with the poem's theme depicting Gandhi's philosophy very well. He produced *Shyama* in Hindi on stage in 1975 and 1977, and toured England, Scotland, Ireland and Wales for a month in 1986 during Tagore's one hundred and twenty-fifth birth anniversary.

■ He utilised all three versions of *Shyama*—prose, poetry and music drama—to make the production more dramatic. He used Odissi for *Shyama*, Kathakali for *Vajrasen* and Yakshagana form and costume for *Kotal*. *Shyama* was written in the Greek opera style, introducing the chorus in between the scenes. He depicted the end of Shyama's tragic story in a different way: by bringing a net curtain between their hands to show the barriers that still persisted.

■ Tagore was the first person in the country to introduce the subjects of art, dance and music in regular courses for his institution at Santiniketan. Tagore invited gurus from Manipur and Kerala to teach Manipuri and Kathakali to students and adopted these styles to present songs and dance in dramas like *Shap Mochan, Chitrangada, Chandalika* and *Shyama*.

Young Choreographers

Alakananda Roy

She is a renowned dancer in Odissi style.

■ From 1970 onwards, she performed *Bhanusingher Padavali, Shyama, Chandalika, Mayar Khela, Varsha Mangal, Rituranga*, the poems 'Samanya Kshati', 'Kach O Debjani', 'Vijayini' and 'Sagarika' (on a floating deck on the Ganga). Her *Valmiki Pratibha* has been spectacularly performed by inmates of Presidency Jail and Midnapur Jail, using Kerala's *Kalari Payattu*, Manipur's *Thang-Ta* and Purulia's *Chhau* for the play's bandits and classical Odissi for Saraswati.

■ Her choreography is generally structured around Odissi that blends well with musical expressions and body movements. With Tagore as her own flesh and blood, she breaks many traditional forms of dance to suit her presentation, which must be *bhava pradhan* or mood dominated. Dancing for Tagore is liberation of soul to her.

■ Tagore does not at all allow her to think detachedly; he comes spontaneously from within. He himself broke so many forms that one learns such unconventional approaches directly from him!

Alpana Roy

An erudite academic, she is choreographer for Saptak, Santiniketan.

■ From 1991 onwards, she produced *Teen Taranga Milita Chhanda* (Three Waves in Unified Rhythm), grafting music, dance and acting together; *Chandalinir Jhi* (The Untouchable Lass), combining the prose-play and the dance-drama; and *Devi Nahi, Nahi Samanya Ramani* (I am Neither a Divinity nor an Ordinary Woman) putting together the three protagonists from *Shap Mochan, Chitrangada* and *Shyama*.

■ Whatever was felt to be the technique needed for the production has been used, without confining it to any particular form.

■ Tagore's dance had no universal form, being an amalgam of classical and folk idioms. Indeed, there could be no Tagore's Dance minus his music as an identifiable form, as one can identify Manipuri, Kathakali, Kathak or Bharatanatyam anywhere sans songs. The only aim is to express the *bhava* inherent in his music.

Amita Dutta

Based in Kolkata, she is a well-known academic and Kathak exponent running her own school for many years.

■ She undertook her journey into the realms of Tagore, based on songs from *Bhanu Singher Padabali*. In 1986, during his one hundred and twenty-fifth birth anniversary, she chose songs and poems on certain themes that would gel well with each other as well as with Kathak. Then came a series of presentations: *Baansi, Varsha, Rituranga* and *Biswa Beena Rabe*. Besides these complete dance ensembles anchored on Tagore's lyrics, she choreographed with individual songs for solo and group presentations using an attractive Kathak form, through *nritya* and interspersed them with lively *nritta*.

■ In choosing Tagore's lyrics for interpretation through Kathak, she kept the following ideas in mind:

- The song should easily fit into the Kathak milieu.
- It should give enough scope for rendering *abhinaya* and *nritta* in the traditional Kathak style.
- The song should be enriched by the dance enactment. The rich rhythmic and interpretative content of Kathak should make the song more attractive and enjoyable for the audience.

- It should be a popular song. This point is desirable because people are more at home with items that they can relate to.

Songs from *Bhanu Singher Padabali* blended well with the Kathak scenario. Braja Bhasha and the Radha-Krishna context are a part of Kathak. Using traditional *nayika bheda*, that is, different states of mind of the heroine, not only could she add colour to the opening line, but the dance also seemed like an age-old Kathak presentation. *Bansi* featured songs about the flute and its player. The songs begin with the heroine's first reactions at hearing the sound of the alluring flute. Desire, anticipation, eagerness, imagination and solace finally give way to despondency. All these songs helped her to delineate *nayika bhedas* and from the point of view of their subject, with ambience, rhythm and melody blended very well with Kathak.

- Tagore was a great admirer of both *nritta* and *nritya*. According to him, it is through dance that the static weight of the body is transformed to dynamism. While watching dance we are touched by the kaleidoscope of movements when the solid mass of the body finds expression in dynamic energy. Kathak also uses *Gat, Gat Nikas* and *Gat Bhava*, in which gait and movements are used to depict various situations and ideas. These are often used as ornaments to add vigour and diversion to lyrics, when the context permits. Tagore, himself, admitted that his songs are not written for any particular dance style nor was he the champion of any special form of dance. Whoever through his or her own dance style brings out the inherent underlying meaning of his lyric is doing justice to his songs.

Anjana Banerji

Based in Kolkata, she is a well-known exponent of the Bharatanatyam style.

- Her research project was to take the lyrics of Tagore and interpret them in Bharatanatyam idiom. She found some of the Tagore songs in *ragas* identical to the Carnatic ones of Muthuswamy Dixitar and Thyagaraja and these inspired her to blend Tagore's compositions within the grammatical framework of Bharatanatyam.

Initially, she chose those Tagore songs which were identical in spirit with the Carnatic songs as used for the items of *Padam, Varnam, Shlokam* and *Tillana*: to make her dance enjoyable and understandable in Bengal. Since Tagore's expressions were based on philosophical concepts, she concentrated on formulating human feelings, such as love and passion, universally acceptable to all parts of the country, in the spirit of national integration. Hence, she researched through the traditional medium of Bharatanatyam, keeping Tagore's innumerable and rich compositions in view.

- Tagore did usher in a new era: by evolving a simple dance form in the

Santiniketan style of graceful movements based on a combination of Manipuri, Kathakali and other folk elements of India. But that style could not boast of any stylised grammar or footwork based on rhythmic intricacies. Tagore indeed personally did not think it was necessary, since his idea appeared to be that everyone should be able to dance in joyous ecstasy!

Astad Deboo

Based in Mumbai, he is a noted contemporary dancer, offering special sessions to disabled children.

■ It was a dance festival that was held in Kolkata that commissioned dancers to create works being inspired by Tagore's themes. They were three translated songs from *Rabindra Sangeet*.

■ His approach to his works was his interpretation, titling it *Interpreting Tagore* through creative style.

Bharati Shivaji

Based in Delhi, she is a noted exponent of the Mohiniyattam style.

■ She spent a rainy season in Bangladesh, having choreographed two Tagore songs.

■ While no special choreography was used, the lyrical quality of the songs went well with Mohiniyattam through which she could communicate their spirit. As a dancer, she has experimented with unusual themes through Mohiniyattam, but here music blended with choreography.

■ Tagore's music is wonderful and suits well with the Santiniketan milieu, but she confined herself to Mohiniyattam, which was her forte.

Lubna Mariam, Bangladesh

Ex-Santiniketan, she is a leading exponent of creative dance in Dhaka.

■ In 1972, beginning with the co-choreography of *Shyama* with Laila Hasan for Bulbul Academy of Fine Arts (BAFA), she had a fruitful choreographic career, producing *Tasher Desh* (1974); *Shyama* (1984) and *Mayar Khela* (1985) the last two for Chhayanat; *Chandalika* (1997) and *Nahi Devi, Nahi Samanya Nari* (I am neither a Goddess nor a Common Woman, 1985, 2002) based on *Chitrangada*, both for Sadhona, with choreography by Sharmila Banerjee; *Bhanusingher Padavali* (2007) choreographed by Samina Hosain Prema; and *Hey Ananta Punya* based on *Natir Puja*, choreographed by Warda Rihab. Between the years 1972 and 1997, she choreographed innumerable dances on Tagore's lyrics, both individually and arranged thematically. They were *Rituranga: Six Seasons, Barsha Mangal, Vasanta Utsav, Nataraj, Pujarini, Ogo Shono Ke Bajaye* (based on lyrics on flute), and so on. Besides, she performed in almost all the dance-dramas for the Asramik Sangha of Visva-Bharati, under the guidance of Purnima Ghosh and as Radha in *Bhanusigher Padavali* under Nilima Sen. She also received guidance from Shailajaranjan Majumdar and performed choreographies of Kelu Nair and Muralidharan Nair at Santiniketan.

■ In the early tradition of dance at Santiniketan, all dances choreographed, performed and produced by Lubna were a fusion of styles, with Manipuri as the main weave. Though Kathakali and Manipuri were mainly used in Tagore's time, they gradually incorporated movements from the various styles such as Bharatanatyam, Odissi, Kathak, Kuchipudi, Mohiniyattam and modern creative dance styles. Lubna believes that several movements used in the choreography of Purnima Ghosh—which was later also used by Lubna—were from Balinese dancing.

■ Tagore's Dance, as the style of dance promulgated at Santiniketan, was the most dynamic legacy of the Poet. It is both contemporary and innovative, which leaves much room for creativity. However, high standard of proficiency and knowledge of all the forms being used is absolutely essential to avoid inept creations. There is also a need to be sensitive to Tagore's own aesthetics in order to be really true to his oeuvre.

Mahua Mukherjee

Based in Kolkata, she is an academic and principal exponent of the emerging *Gaudiya Nritya*.

■ She produced *Chitrangada, Chandalika, Nataraj* (based on creation-preservation-dissolution), *Sakal Raser Dhara* (nine emotions based on Tagore's poetry), *Amrita Rasa* (based on three protagonists of *Shyama, Chandalika and Chitrangada*) and *Ora Kaj Karey* (based on the work of building the village society).

■ Her choreography is based on *Gaudiya Nritya*, which Mahua has re-constructed from Bengal's own sources of art, terracotta and other artifacts. In addition, she has used Bengal's folk forms. In *Chitrangada*, she used tribal dance for the forest guards. In *Chandalika*, while using Sanchi Stupa as the Buddhist motif, she used tribal dance for the witchcraft companions and the *karma* folk dance.

■ When Tagore was looking at different forms of dance, he took the help of native kings for a dance like Manipuri as the major staple for Santiniketan or the Travancore king's help in bringing Mohiniyattam. For Tagore's dance, she feels that *Gaudiya Nritya*, from Bengal, is the best suited form to be associated with his rich *sahitya*.

Mamata Shankar

As Shankar's daughter, she had miles of advantage to propagate modern creative dance, basing her popular dance centre in Kolkata.

■ In 1979, she started working on Tagore's pieces and *Chandalika* was her first choreographic work. Later, she worked on *Horikhela, Shyama, Kal Mrigaya, Vasantotsav* and the orchestration on various Tagore's songs called *Tagore in Symphony*. *Horikhela* is devoid of any lyrics, being a musical drama based on the original poem, and *Tagore in Symphony* has the beautiful orchestration of various songs of Tagore composed on the six seasons.

■ She does not believe in such misnomers as Tagore's Dance. She thinks the classical dance forms of India as well as dances from Java and Bali and Sri Lanka's Kandyan dance found their way into the dances of Tagore's time and were hence termed as Tagore's Dance. She genuinely feels that the lyrics that Tagore penned are so powerful that these should be conveyed to the audience with all their emotions intact. While choreographing *Chandalika*, she wanted people to understand those powerful words of the songs and decided to employ more expression and body language, and less dance movement. She has tried to maintain the inner message and the storyline of Tagore's works while choreographing them in Uday Shankar's style of dance, which gives ample scope to bring out the essential theme through rich body movements and realistic expressions.

■ Reaching out to the audience while working on Tagore is a very important and difficult job, especially when she wanted to propagate Tagore's work through Uday Shankar's dance form. Crisp and tight scripts, proper movements and apt expressions do the trick when people do not want unduly long performances. If she wants to express themes that she has in mind through any classical style and if she ends up doing something that is not permitted in that form, it detracts from the classical authenticity. Uday Shankar's style of dance helps her to express herself with all the freedom she needs; it also allows her to portray Indian culture, heritage and roots through the universal language of dance.

Manjushri and Ranjavati Chaki-Sarkar (as told by Aishika Chakrabarty)

The mother-daughter duo, whom the land has tragically lost, were pioneers of *Nava Nritya*, an innovative synthesis of existing dance forms propagated by Dancers Guild in Kolkata.

A scene from Tomari Matir Kanya.

■ Manjushri innovated with *'Tomari matir kanya'* (I'm the daughter of your soil) from *Chandalika; 'Kon nutaneri dak'* (Beckoning of the New) from *Tasher Desh*; and *'Chitrangada'* from the original poem. She followed them up with allusions from *Natir Puja* and the poem 'Pujarini'.

■ *Nava Nritya*, first used by Manjushri and expanded by her daughter Ranjabati, is a fully-formed body language and is really a chemical synthesis of traditional dance forms. Structurally evolved from Bharatanatyam, Odissi, Kathakali, Manipuri, *Chhau, Kalari Payattu* and *Thang Ta*, it evolved in the 1980s as a transition from classical to modern dance.

■ Tagore's dance could be taken out of its narrow context and looked at *de novo* where there were no anklets, and costume was anything but ornate. Tagore was a new icon who provided socially new women beyond the stereotypes. A character like Bimala in his novel *Ghare Baire* (Home and the World) provided a new prototype that was in sync with Prakriti of *Chandalika* or the princess in Chitrangada. The dialogue of mother and daughter in *Chandalika*—through metaphors—was the first public political-social statement, providing a new framework of feminist thought outside the patriarchical orbit!

Preeti Patel

Based in Kolkata, she is a well-known exponent of the Manipuri style, running her group Anjika.

■ She choreographed the poem 'Chitra' with the 'ugly' and 'beautiful' princess, but omitting Madana, retaining the mystic and cosmic aspect of Love as worship of the spirit. All characters were male except the princess. She also did the poem 'Parishodh', with Shyama's action deserving harsh retribution.

■ In her productions, she used pure Manipuri style, complete with the musical instrument *pena*. She also used the martial arts of *Thang Ta*.

■ She appears somewhat disappointed at the current scene, where Tagore's intention of Kathakali for the male and Manipuri for the female does not appear to maintain its distinctiveness.

Sadhan Guha and Polly Guha

Based in Kolkata, they were a redoubtable dancer-duo in the creative style, with Sadhan Guha no more alive.

■ From 1976 onwards, they produced dance-dramas and music dramas such as *Shyama, Chitrangada, Chandalika, Mayar Khela, Kal Mrigaya, Valmiki Pratibha, Shap Mochan*, and then choreographed for the poems: 'Sagarika' and 'Viday Abhishap'. They also did the plays *Tapati* and *Arup Ratan* in dance.

■ Theirs was the gentle creative choreography of the traditional style, wearing sari on stage and avoiding strong, virile movements. For emoting, *bhava* remained important throughout. While Polly used Odissi for *Shyama*, Sadhan employed Kathakali. Since they were both with Uday Shankar during 1965–77, Shankar's creative style was their staple form.

■ According to Polly, the traditional form of Tagore should continue and changes should be minimal. Tagore's dance has all the potential for survival in today's world.

Saswati Sen

Based in Delhi, she is the doyen of Kathak dance, running Kalashram with guru Birju Maharaj and conducting workshops all over the globe.

■ She produced the poem 'Devatar Gras' as a solo; 'Pujarini' as group choreography; select songs from *Bhanusingher Padavali; Abhisar* in group again; and *Chandalika*, apart from the hugely successful poem 'Shuvakshan' which she took many times abroad.

■ Kathak dance has been her style and *abhinaya* her forte, which she always used for Tagore's oeuvre.

Saswati Sen: Noted Kathak exponent.

■ She feels a little confused in looking up to Tagore's Dance as a distinct entity. While all classical dances have their clear forms and as even Uday Shankar's creative style is distinctly recognisable, no form, as such, can be identified by her as Tagore's dance.

Sharmila Biswas

Based in Kolkata, she is a celebrated exponent of the Odissi style, conducting her group work mainly in an innovative Odissi idiom.

■ She experimented with Tagore's rhythm cycles used as parallel to the Odissi rhythm cycles and supported by Hindustani classical *theka* and Carnatic classical *theka*. Her other innovations were Tagore's songs in the seven-beat *Triputa Taal*; six-beat *Khemta Taal* and sixteen-beat *Akuti Taal*, with young teachers and interns playing around a central pillar, not to be counted out!

■ Playfulness, in fact, has been the hallmark of Sharmila within the ambit of Odissi. Taking Tagore songs that hint at meanings, she tried to create moods and visual pictures through her participants. In contrast, her choreography also expressed pensive and meditative moods, through subdued pangs of separation.

■ Tagore's songs in his music dramas and dance-dramas place the characters of the male above traditional myths and the female above all stereotypes. They deal with *bhava* as an external stimulation conducive to *rasa* in the spectator's mind. Above all, these songs are marked by three defined qualities—intelligence, restraint and solemnity.

Shovana Narayan

Based in Delhi, she is a highly erudite Kathak exponent, with her school producing a strong and talented team of competent disciples.

■ The songs and poems that she has performed to are *Gitanjali* and *'Jadi tor dak shune keu na ase'*. While doing *Abhinaya* in *Raja*, it seemed to her that it was exhorting one to pursue one's journey, despite abandonment or lack of support from others. We all are lonely even in a crowd. Her *abhinaya* from *Raja* depicted somewhere the hollowness and attraction of the 'obvious' so visible to life that eschews the real inside.

■ All the pieces were intense in mood, sombre in movement, and music and lighting were used to highlight the solemnity of the lyrical play.

■ Regarding Tagore's relevance today, what he gave and stood for were really beyond time. His thoughts, feelings and expressions were for all times pregnant with meanings and nuances. Each time we see his work, it throws open another door for us to saunter through, unearthing yet another vista of interpretations. These also colour our moods and vice versa, through their meanings. Tagore is for all times; he cannot be bound by finite terms!

Sruti Bandyopadhyay

Based in Kolkata, she is an established academic and a senior exponent of the Manipuri style, running her own group.

■ She produced *Bajao Re Mohana Banshi* (Play Your Entrancing Flute): based on four elements: awakening; romance; inspiration; and submission. *Offerings* was a bilingual theatre-dance production based on *Gitanjali*, with the English, *Song Offerings*, and the corresponding Bengali songs strung together, placed in the following order: Offering to self; offering to nature; and offering to the country. Indigenous theatre techniques were used with dialogues and songs blended with music and rhythm. *Alo* was a multi-dimensional concept of light, with innovative music composition by Dipak Choudhury. *Tagore and International Humanism* was a multi-media choreographic presentation on Tagore against war and on humanism. *Tin Kanya* was based on the three protagonists of *Chandalika, Chitrangada* and *Shyama*: to delve deep into their characters. She also worked on *Chitrangada, Bhanusingher Padavali, Shyama* and *Shap Mochan*.

■ Her training in Manipuri helped her immensely to choreograph on Tagore's lyrics and themes, and added to her exposure in 'Children's Little Theatre' in all dance forms emphasising the *abhinaya* aspect. The technique of expression is drawn from Indian and South Asian expressional vocabulary.

■ There have been two streams of presentation of Tagore themes in dance: either through the traditional approach or with experiments in all facets of choreography: from technique to space-usage, from costume to music. In the second stream, Uday Shankar choreographed *Samanya Kshati* as a ballet, while Manjushri Chaki-Sarkar looked into his dance-dramas from a very contemporary viewpoint. Tagore's dance always gives one scope to flower one's distinctive urges through his philosophy, through the idiom of dance.

Sudarshan Chakravorty

Based in Kolkata, he is a noted contemporary dancer who is running his highly successful Sapphire group.

■ Sapphire produced *Stream of Life* in 1997, based on the *Gitanjali* verses and tracing human life from birth to death, in all the hues of pleasure and pain, longing and failure, surprise and fear, denial and hope. The prayer-like quality of the verses were interpreted in experimental and abstract choreography in terms of patterns, visuals, images and influences of martial art design. Music was aided by Ian Richardson with South American rhythms and experimental strains by Vanraj Bhatia. Then came *Rituranga: A Symphony of Seasons*, in which Sapphire explored Tagore's sense of aesthetics and beauty of the Indian seasons and their essential harmony through a new-found contemporary dance form. Sapphire attempted 'block', 'break', 'contact' and 'support' of modern dance techniques, and added the ideas of the fragrance of flowers, the softness of green leaves, the rush of the wind and the sun's harshness. This marked an attempt to understand the classic and evergreen touch of Tagore through dynamic movements of modern dance within a grim mechanical world which still finds solace in the softness and caress of Mother Nature. *Rituranga* was essentially a pure dance creation, celebrating the six seasons with a bouquet of eighteen songs. On balance, Sapphire tried to capture the abstract quality of Tagore's compositions through an open-ended contemporary dance form.

■ Tagore's Santiniketan was distinct and identifiable: be it in the *gayaki* of his songs, the stylisation of his dance or the

Sapphire group: Contemporary symphony on dance.

innovation in the drape of its costumes. His dance language was clear and beautiful. It absorbed influences without aping them. Indeed, Tagore's style was a vision for the future of an Indian contemporary style of art and expression.

Swapna Sundari

Based in Delhi as well as Hyderabad, she is among the seniormost Kuchipudi exponents and is promoting Vilasini Natyam, Andhra's *devdasi* dance.

■ At the age of five, she sang in the Telugu rendering of *Chandalika* in Vizag. The lilting music was appealing to all age groups. As a professional Kuchipudi dancer in Delhi, she essayed the role of Mother at the age of fifteen in *Chandalika*, in the 1970s, when Prakriti was portrayed by a dancer in her thirties. She did so with relish...! She performed with live recitation of the poem: 'When the mind is without fear...' She fulfilled her dream of doing Prakriti in *Chandalika Kalapam* in the Kuchipudi format, in Hyderabad. Recently, she choreographed for a Tagore poem on autumn for her multi-media production.

■ She thinks both her idioms of Kuchipudi and Vilasini Natyam are so well suited to interpret Tagore that very little adjustment is necessary so far as technique is concerned. *Abhinaya*, too, flows easily in the case of Tagore's poetry. By and large, she has remained within traditional styles, identifying appropriate movements and making small extensions wherever necessary.

■ For its times, the form known as Tagore's Dance, had a lot of relevance. One can easily discern elements of Manipuri, Kathakali and so on, in its construct. There are so many other movements that must have arisen from the confluence of classical and folk traditions that have gone into the creation of the Tagore style of dance—the result of which is graceful and pleasing to the eye.

Highlights of Survey

It is indeed remarkable from the above compendium of responses from nearly fifty major choreographers of all hues that Tagore has pervaded the dancing psyche of the country in multifarious ways and forms and contents of his dance continue to be a living force. For instance, three major points are illustrated by the observations of Mrinalini Sarabhai, the only one close to Tagore who is still around. First, she executed Vajrasen in *Shyama* in the then emerging classical form of Bharatanatyam, and later, Mother in *Chandalika*, under Tagore's adoring eyes. This reveals the Poet's catholicity to forms. Second, Tagore asked her to do the male roles in *Mayar Khela* that shows the same openness abided till the very end. Third, for her cultural troupe visiting China in 1978, the performance of *Tasher Desh* was debarred, after the opening night, as it seemed to protest too strongly against regimentation by the prevailing establishment. This revealed the iconoclastic power that Tagore wielded even after some half-a-century after the play was written!

The nationwide celebration of Tagore's birth centenary in 1961 was, no doubt, a trigger for widespread choreographic efforts. This created a collective corpus of rich repertoire on Tagore. This was further boosted by the spate of cultural complexes that came up soon after, in Tagore's name, in the state and many district capitals, and gave another generation opportunity to 'taste Tagore', such as young Padma Subrahmanyam to sing some twenty songs and a five-year-old Swapna Sundari to join a university choral group in remote Vizag.

While it is futile to attempt any summary of the pan-Indian endeavour going on to re-create and re-capitulate Tagore's Dance ever since, three aspects stand out on their own, as follows:

- One, form-wise, nearly all choreographers have honed their own techniques to re-interpret Tagore using the eight classical styles, excluding though the recently emerged Sattriya dance, which is yet to come out of Shankara Deva's and Madhava Deva's oeuvre. Among the creative and modern forms, there is an excellent corpus: some following the footsteps of Uday Shankar; some coming out of his aura a little; and some trying to create a new contemporary idiom with features like 'block', 'break' 'support' and 'contact'. *Gaudiya Nritya* is a resuscitated Bengal-based traditional dance that is showcasing Tagore's themes.

- Two, form-wise again, there is a moot point whether Tagore's Dance has a stand-alone identity that can be recognised by itself—outside the patio of Tagore's performed literature—just as the eight Indian classical styles can be, or Uday Shankar style of modern dance is. One view, voiced by Lubna Mariam, is that the Santiniketan tradition is a dynamic legacy of Tagore and it has to keep room for creativity and innovation: with a high degree of proficiency and knowledge of all the forms, with sensitivity to Tagore's aesthetics and remaining true to his nuances. A contrary view is that of Valmiki Banerjee who looks at the corpus of Tagore's dances as an already classical *Rabindranrityam*: with enough elements of *nritya, nritta* and *abhinaya* of *sattvik, vachik, angik* and *aharya* kinds: simply waiting to be consolidated.

- Three, content-wise, the sailboat for the choreographic journey with Tagore's Dance has an exemplar argot of literature to fall back upon. Among dance-dramas, the choreographers, as above, showed a marked presence for *Chandalika* where the indomitable spirit of Prakriti rises like a Phoenix out of the ashes of a caste-ridden society and is attracted to Buddhism. *Chitrangada* comes next with her statement of femininity, followed by the other dance-dramas, music dramas and early operas. Long poems have found their choreographic preference. Theme-based poems have been a favourite. Among abstract poems, 'Where the Mind is Free of Fear' is an outright winner. His songs are very widely danced, with a preference for *Gitanjali* in the all-India scene. Interestingly, the choreographic scenario in Bengal and in the country has seen few takers for music dramas like *Vasant, Shesh Varshan, Naveen, Shravan Gatha* and *Sundar*—understandably for their highly lyrical and non-storyline nature. Also, with many a fragmented production of *Nataraj*, Tagore's major ode to the Lord of Dance, *Nataraj-Riturangashala*, has seldom come through in its entirety.

Vyjayantimala Bali: Proud moments in Chandalika.

Conclusion

From the largely national documentation attempted above on Tagore's Dance legacy, it is clear that the sincere choreographic interest exists and has been abiding. It is a pointer to a much larger need for documentation in the overall choreographic scene. The context of Tagore's Dance is relevant because Tagore himself was an ardent votary of documentation and, given a little longer lifespan, he would have been the one to initiate notation for his fast-flourishing dance oeuvre, as he did, most elaborately, for his music legacy: far, far earlier. 'Laban Notation', is being worked painstakingly abroad. Decidedly, there is very little similarity between the Western dance and the Indian tradition, but there are also surprisingly quite a bit of the basics that appears common between what the master codifier Bharata documented in *Natya Shastra* and what Laban and his progenitors are inventing for themselves in the West. Perhaps, in the forthcoming one hundred and fiftieth birth anniversary of Tagore in 2011, it could be the best tribute to the Poet, namely, taking some initial steps towards evolving notations for Indian dance—at least in training and teaching modules—that could eventually immensely benefit all dance forms, not excluding Tagore's Dance.

'Laban Notation' with Reference Points for Indian Dance

Laban Notation (also abbreviated to Labanotation) is a system of analysing and recording human movement. The original inventor was the Austrian-Hungarian, Rudolf von Laban (1879–1958), an important figure in European modern dance. In Labanotation, it is possible to record every kind of human motion. Labanotation is not connected to a singular, specific style of dance, but is based on natural human motion, and every change from this natural human motion (say, turned-out leg): to be specifically written down in the notation. Labanotation uses abstract symbols to define: direction of the movement; part of the body doing the movement; level of the movement; and length of time it takes to do the movement. The shapes of the symbols indicate nine different directions of space and the shading of the symbol specifies the level of the movement.

Labanotation is a record of how one moves so that one can do the same thing again and again—very instructive for any form of dance. The symbols are placed on a vertical staff, with the horizontal dimension of the staff representing the symmetry of the body and the vertical dimension representing time. The locating of the symbol on the staff defines the body part it represents. The central line of the staff represents the central line of the body. Symbols on the right represent the right side of the body and symbols on the left, the left side.

The staff is read from bottom to top and the length of a symbol defines the dimension of the movement. Drawing on Western music notation, Labanotation uses bar lines to mark time-measures and double bar lines are at the start and end of the movement score. The starting position of the dancer can be given before the double bar lines at the start of the score. Spatial distance, spatial relationships, transference of weight, centre of weight, jumps, turns, body parts, paths and floor plans can all be notated by specific symbols. Although the abstract symbols represent Laban's work on shape, Laban's theories of effort can be represented in Labanotation with the following four effort categories:

- Space: Direct/Indirect
- Weight: Strong/Sustained
- Time: Sudden/Sustained
- Flow: Bound/Free

As a development of Laban's theories, Laban Movement Analysis (LMA) includes studies in four interrelated categories: Body; Effort; Shape; and Space.

Body

Developed by Laban and his collaborator Irmgard Bartenieff, this category describes structural and physical characteristics of the human body while moving. This category is responsible for describing which body parts are moving, which parts are connected, which parts are influenced by others, and general statements about body organisation (akin to *anga, upanga* and so on; *mudras* and *shira bheda*; *greeba bheda, drishti bheda*, and so on in the Indian classical context). The Body category, along with the other categories, are applied to ever-extending fields, such as fitness, somatic therapies, rehabilitation, dance technique and more. Several sub-categories of body are: initiation of movement starting from specified body parts; connection of different body parts to each other; sequencing of movement between parts of the body; and patterns of body organisation and connectivity.

Effort

Effort, or what Laban describes as dynamics, is a system for understanding the more subtle characteristics about the way a movement is done with respect to inner intentions. For instance, the difference between punching someone in anger (or, killing a demon, in Indian classical context) and reaching out for a glass of water (or, extending hand in benediction, in Indian classical context) is slight in terms of body organisation, namely, both relying on extension of the arm. But the attention to the strength of the movement, the control of the movement and the firming of the movement are very different.

Efforts are of four categories, as indicated above, where the eight categories are descriptively named: float, punch (thrust), glide, slash, dab, wring, flick and press. These are collectively named 'Action Efforts' and have been used extensively to train the ability to change quickly between physical manifestations of emotion. Flow, on the other hand, is responsible for the continuity of motions. Without any Flow Effort, movement must be contained as a single initiation and action which is why there are specific names for the Flow-less Action configurations of Effort. In general, it is difficult to remove Flow from such movement and therefore, a full analysis of Effort typically needs to go beyond the Effort Actions.

Shape

While the Body category primarily develops connections within the body and the body-space intent, the way the body changes shape during movement is further experimented and analysed through the Shape category. It is important to remember that all categories are related and Shape is often an integrating factor for combining the other categories into meaningful movement (more detailed in Indian classical context as *adavu, karana* and *angahara*). Sub-categories of Shape are:

- 'Shape Forms', describing static shapes that the body takes, such as Wall-like, Ball-like and Pin-like;
- 'Shape Change', describing the way the body is interacting and forming relationship with the environment. There are three 'Modes of Shape Change';
- 'Shape Flow', representing a relationship of the body to itself, for example, amoebic movement or mundane habitual actions like shrugging, shivering, rubbing an injured shoulder and so on;
- 'Directional Flow', representing a relationship where the body is directed toward some part of the environment, such as Spoke-like (punching, painting and so on) and Arc-like (swinging a tennis racket, painting a fence and so on);
- 'Carving Flow', representing a relationship where the body actively and three-dimensionally interacts with the volume of the environment (kneading bread dough, wringing a towel, miming the shape of an imaginary object and so on);
- 'Shape Qualities', describing the way the body is changing actively towards some point in space, such as Opening (for example, growing large with extension) or Closing (for example, growing smaller with more flexion), besides Rising, Sinking, Spreading, Enclosing, Advancing, Entreating and so on;
- 'Shape Flow Support', describing change in shape to support movements in the rest of the body—present or absent.

Space

This category involves motions in connection with the environment, work with spatial patterns, pathways and lines of spatial motion (c.f., in Indian classical context, *chari, bhramari* and *utplabana*). There are ways of organising and moving in space that is specifically harmonious, in the same sense as music can be harmonious. Some combinations and organisations are more thematically and aesthetically pleasing, as for music. Space Harmony sometimes takes the set 'scales' of movement and reveals individual movement preferences. This category also describes and notates choices which refer specifically to space as follows:

- Kin Sphere—the area that the body is moving within and how the mover is paying attention to it;
- Spatial Intention—the directions or points in space that the mover is identifying or using;
- Geometrical Observation—where the movement is being done, in terms of emphasis of directions, places in space, planar movement and so on.

Major *Ragas* Used by Tagore

Adana: It belongs to Kanada *ang* and is played in middle and high octave. Lyric: *'Baanee taba dhaay dike dike…'*

Ashavari: It uses Sa Ri Ma Pa Dha (c D F G Ab) in the ascent and Sa ni dha Pa Ma ga Ri in the descent. In some schools, ri (Db) is used instead of Ri (D). There is also a Carnatic *raga* of this name. It is played in the morning—six to nine. The mood is of renunciation—grave and dignified. Lyric: *'Ashrubharaa bedanaa dike dike jage…'*

Bageshri: It uses Sa ga Ma Dha ni (C Eb F A Bb) in ascent and Sa ni Dha Pa Ma ga Ri (C' Bb A G F Eb D) in descent; Pa (G) is not used in a straight movement. It is played in the second quarter of the night. Its mood is calm and profound, deep and moving. Lyric: *'Je raate mor duyarguli bhaanglo jharhe... '*

Bahar: It uses Sa ga Ma Dha ni Dha Ni (C Eb F A Bb A B) in ascent and Sa ni Dha ni Pa Ma ga Ma Ri (C' Bb A Bb G F Eb F D) in descent. It is played in the second quarter of the night. Its mood is lively and charming, used in love songs. *Lyric: 'Aaji basanta jaagrata dwaare…'*

Basant: It uses Sa Ga ma dha Ni (C E F # Ab B) in ascent and Sa' Ni dha Pa ma Ga ri (C' B Ab G F # E Db) in descent. Ma (F) is used in some phrases. It is played during springtime. It expresses the feminine aspect of spring. Lyric: *'Aaji ei gandha bidhura sameerane…'*

Bhairav: It uses Sa ri Ga Ma Pa dha Ni (C Db E F G Ab B). Its time of play is the first quarter of the day. It is also used in morning invocation. Its mood is soft, tender and melancholy. Lyric: *'Tumi naba naba rupe eso prane…'*

Bhairavi: It uses Sa ri ga Ma Pa dha ni (C Db Ed F G Ab Bb). It is played in the day from nine to twelve. Its mood is very tender, loving and melancholy. Lyric: *'Saarthak janama amaar janmechhi ei deshe…'*

Bhim Palasi/Bhim Palashri: It is pentatonic in ascent, heptatonic in descent. It is played in the second part of the afternoon. Its mood is peaceful, tender and pleasing. Lyric: *'Amar sakal dukher pradip jwele karbo nibedan …'*

Bhupali: It uses Sa Ri Ga Pa Dha (C D E G A). It is played in the second quarter of the night. Its mood is of the joy of saintly detachment. Lyric: *'Prachanda garjane asilo eki durdina ghanaghataa…'*

Bibhas: It is pentatonic and played at sunrise. Its mood captures liveliness, and expression is energetic and challenging. Lyric: *'Aaji dhaner kshete roudra chhayay lukochurir khela…'*

Behag: It uses *raga* with Sa Ga Ma Pa Ni (C E F G B) in the ascent; Sa Ni Dha Pa Ma Ga Ri (C' B A G F E D) in the descent; F# is also used in some phrases. It is played at midnight. Its mood is melancholy in the calm of the night, with a thirst for enjoyment. Lyric: *'Aaj shraabaner purnimaate kee enechhis bal…'*

Bilaval: It uses Sa Ri Ga Ma Pa Dha Ni (C D E F G A B); commonly sung as Alaiya Bilaval. It is played during the day from nine to twelve. Its mood is active and tender, inquisitive, mixing joy and affection. Lyric: *'Jagate aananda jajne amaar nimantrana…'*

Brindavani Sarang: It uses Sa Ri Ma Pa Ni (C D F G B) in the ascent in Sá ni Pa Ma Ri (C' Bb G F D) in the descent. It is played at midday. Lyric: *'Taahaare aarati kare chandra tapan…'*

Chhayanat: It is a *sampurna* (all seven notes in both ascent and descent) *raga*, played in the first quarter of the night. Its mood is of prayer and joy with tenderness. Lyric: *'Doordeshee sei rakhalchhele amaar baater bater chhayay…'*

Des: It uses Sa Ri Ga Pa Dha (C D E G A). Lyric: *'Eso shyaamala sundara…'*

Gaur Sarang: Here Ri Ma and Pa (D F G) are predominant. It is played at midday. Its mood is of contentment, faith, tender and loving prayer. Lyric: *'Dukhero timire jadi jwale…'*

Hamir: It is hexatonic in ascent, heptatonic in descent. It is played in the first quarter of the night. Its mood is charming and lively. Lyric: *'Kata ajaanaare jaanaaile tumi kato ghare dile thnai…'*

Jhinjhit: It is a *sampurna raga* and was used much in the nineteenth century, it is no longer in vogue. It is heptatonic in both ascent and descent. Lyric: *'Ekasutre baandhiyachhi sahasrati man…'*

Kafi: It uses Sa Rig a Ma Pa Dha ni (C D Eb E G A Bb). It is played in the second quarter of the night. Its mood is light, happy and contented, very gentle and harmonious. Lyric: *'Aaji naahi naahi nidra aankhipaate…'*

Kalingada/Kalengra: It is hexatonic in ascent and heptatonic in descent; played in the early morning, before dawn. It has a clear satisfied expression. Lyric: *'Gharete bhramar elo gunguniye…'*

Kannada: It uses ga Ma Ri (Eb F D). It is played in the second quarter of the night. Its mood is of deep emotion and satisfaction with some happiness and passion. Lyric: *'Tumi kon bhanganer pathe ele suptarathe…'*

Kedar: It is *sampurna raga*. It is played in the first quarter of night. Its mood is pleasing and tender. Lyric: *'Aamaar mukti aaloy aaloy ei aakaashe…'*

Khamaj/Khambaj: It uses Sa Ga Ma Pa Dha Ni (C E F G A B) in the ascent and Sá ni Dha Pa Ma Ga Ri (C' Bb A G F E D) in the descent. It s played in the first quarter of the night. Its mood is of tender remembrance—joy, contentment with hope and desire. Lyric: *'Aaji jata taaraa taba aakaashe…'*

Malhar: It uses Sa Ri Ma Pa ni (C D F G Bb B) in the ascent and Sá ni Dha ni Pa ga Ma Ri (C' Bb A Bb G Eb F D) in the descent.

Miyan-Malhar: It is pentatonic in ascent and heptatonic in descent. It is played in the rainy season. Express monsoon rains, passionate and happy. Lyric: *'Kothaa je udhaao holo mor praan udasee…'*

Malkaush: It uses Sa ga Ma dha ni (C Eb F Ab Bb). It is played at midnight. Lyric: *'Aanandadhaaraa bahichhe bhubane…'*

Megh: It is of Kanada *ang* and evokes the rains. Lyric: *'Neel anjana ghana punja chhaayaay sambita ambar… '*

Megh Malhar: It is pentatonic in ascent and hexatonic in descent. It is played at night at all times during the rainy season. Its mood expresses happiness. Lyric: *'Ashharhh kothaa hate aaj peli chhaarhaa…'*

Multani: It is pentatonic in ascent and heptatonic in descent. It is played in the afternoon. Its mood is tender and melancholy, but also pleasing and lively. Lyric: *'Din jadi holo abasaan…'*

Paraj: It is hexatonic in ascent and heptatonic in descent. It is played after midnight. Its mood expresses satisfaction, contentment and appeal. Lyric: *'Aaji dakshina pabane dolaa laagilo bane…'*

Pilu: It uses Sa Ga Ma Pa Ni (C E F G B) in the ascent and Sá ni Dha Pa dha Pa ga Ri (C' Bb A G Ab G Eb D) in the descent. It is played in the fourth quarter of the day. Lyric: *'O chand chokher jale laglo joyar…'*

Puravi: It is *sampurna raga* and played in the last quarter of day at sunset. Its mood expresses prayer and request. Lyric: *'Dina sheshher raangaamukul…'*

Ramkeli: It is under Bhairava group. No Ri (D) and no Ni (B) in ascending. It is played in the first quarter of the day. Its mood is joyful, active and without the anguish of desire. Lyric: *'Bhor holo bibhaabaree…'*

Sahana: It is pentatonic in ascent and heptatonic in descent. It is played after midnight. Its mood is charming and graceful. Lyric: *'Ki gaba aami ki shonaabo aaji aanandadhaame…'*

Tilak Kamod: It is pentatonic in ascent and heptatonic in descent. It is played in the first quarter of the night. Its mood is graceful and lively. Lyric: *'Tomaar nayan aamaay baare baare balechhe gaan gaahibaare…'*

Todi: It uses Sa ri ga ma Pa dha Ni (C Db Eb F # G Ab B), Karnatak *raga* with Sa ri ga Ma Pa dha ni (C Db Eb F G Ab Bb). It is played in the first quarter of the day. Its mood is very tender and loving in appeal. Lyric: *'Kata je tumi manaharan man taahaai jaane…'*

Yaman: It is *sampurna raga*. It is played in the first quarter of the night. Its mood is joyful and contented. Lyric: *'Aamaar maathaa nata kore dao he tomaar charana dhulaar pare…'*

Yaman Kalyan: It uses Sa Ri Ga ma Pa Dha Ni (C D E F # G A B). It is played in the first quarter of the night. It is softer than Yaman, with a mood of peaceful joy and with veiled melancholy. Lyric: *'Mahaabishwe mahaakaashe mahaakaala maajhe…'*

Note: The above are all Hindustani ragas. A few Carnatic ragas, some Western melodies, and Keertan *and Baul traditions used by Tagore are not covered here.*

Bibliography

Anony. 1992. *The Natya Shastra by Bharata Muni*, Delhi: Sri Satguru Publications.

Chaki-Sarkar, Manjushree. 2000. *Nrityarase Chitta Mamo* (Bengali). Kolkata: Miranda.

Chakraborty, Rama. 2001. *Bhara Thak Smritisudhay* (Bengali). Kolkata: Tagore Research Institute.

—. 2004. *Pathey Chole Jetey Jetay* (Bengali). Kolkata: Ananda Publications.

Chakraborty, Sukriti. 1991. *Bahilo Anondadhara* (Bengali). Kolkata: Desh Publishing.

Chattopadhyay, Gayatri. 1964. *Nrityakala* (Bengali). Kolkata: Nabapatra Prakasani.

Chattopadhyay, Suniti Kumar. 2002. *Rabindra-Sangame Dwipamay Bharat O Shyam Desh* (Bengali). Kolkata: Prakash Bhavan.

Danielou, Alain. 1980. *The Ragas of Northern Indian Music*. New Delhi: Munshiram Manoharlal Publishers Pvt. Ltd.

Devi-Choudhurani, Indira. 1989. *Rabindra Smriti* (Bengali). Kolkata: Visva-Bharati.

Devi, Pratima. 1993. *Nritya* (Bengali). Kolkata: Visva-Bharati.

Dewa B.C. 1974. *Indian Music*. New Delhi: ICCR.

Dyson, Ketaki Kushari and Sushovan Adhikary. 1997. *Ranger Rabindranath* (Bengali). Kolkata: Ananda Publishers.

Ghosh, Santidev. 1982. *Gurudev Rabindranath O Adhunik Bharatiya Nritya* (Bengali). Kolkata: Ananda Publishers.

—. 1987. *Rabindranather Purnango Shikshadarshe Sangeet O Nritya* (Bengali). Kolkata: Ananda Publishers.

—. 1992. *Rabindra Sangeet* (Bengali). Kolkata: Visva-Bharati.

—. 1999. *Nrityakala O Rabindranath* (Bengali). Kolkata: Ananda Publishers.

—. 1996. *Jeevaner Dhruvatara* (Bengali) Kolkata: Ananda Publishers.

—. 2003. *Java O Bali Nrityageet* (Bengali). Kolkata: Vishva Bharati.

Ghosh, Shambhunath and Anindita Ghosh. 1999. *Rabindra Nrityer Ruprekha* (Bengali). Kolkata: Sangit Prakashan.

Javeri, Darshana and Kalavati Devi. 1990. *Manipuri Tala Prakasha* (English). Banaras: Chaukhambha Oriental.

Mukhopadhyay, Mahua. 2000. *Bharotiya Nritye Trayee: Jaydeva, Chaitanyadeva, Rabindranath* (Bengali). Kolkata: N.E. Publishers.

Nair, D. Appukutan and K. Ayyappa Paniker (eds.). 1993. *Kathakali: The Art of the Non-Worldly*. Mumbai: Marg Publication.

Parimoo, Ratan. 1972. *Paintings of the Three Tagores*. Baroda: MS University.

Roy, Arun Kumar. 1986. *Rabindranath O' Chalachitra* (Bengali). Kolkata: Chitralekha.

Sen, Amita, 1977. *Santiniketaner Ashram Kanya* (Bengali). Kolkata: Tagore Research Institute.

—. 1983. *Ananda Sarbokajey* (Bengali). Kolkata: Tagore Research Institute.

Singh, Guru Bipin. 1995. *Bhangee Pareng (Bhangavali)* (English and Bengali). Mumbai: Manipuri Nartanalaya.

Spencer, Herbert. 1888. 'Origin and function of music'. In *Essays: Scientific, Political and Spiritual* (English). London: William and Norgate (Used by Tagore (1992) in 'Sangeeter utpatti o upajogita', in his *Sangeet Chinta*, Kolkata: Visva-Bharati.)

Tagore, Rabindranath. 1973. *Geeta Bitan* (Bengali). Parts 1, 2 and 3. Kolkata: Visva-Bharati.

—. *Chirantan Rabindra Rachanabali*. CD—Indian Edition. Kolkata: Celsius Technologies Pvt. Ltd.

Glossary

abhedya: limbs pierced and worn

abhinaya: dance expressions, especially of face

adavus: total body postures in Bharatanatyam

advuta: mysterious

aharya: costumes and decorations

aharya abhinaya: adornment and costumes

akar-matric: form-centric

akhada: place of practice

alankara: embellishments

alpana: folk figuration with votive and decorative motifs

anga rachana: decoration of body and limbs

angas: limbs

angik/angika: gestures through limbs

antara: the second stanza of Dhrupad lyric

araimandi: standard standing posture in Bharatanatyam

aropya: put around limbs

asamayukta: single hand with twenty-eight gestures

Ashram: hermitage

atibhanga: bent in four segments like Nataraj

Atma: soul

baaya: small drum

Bai-jis: courtesans

bandhaniya: tied up on limbs

batik: appliqué work of Indonesia, now prevalent in India

baul: mendicant

Bhandari: treasurer

bhangi parengs: body movement series

bhata: low tide

bhava: mood

Bhavnritya: mood dance

bhaya: terror

bhayanaka: terrible

Bhikshus: monks

bhramari: whirling, seven types

bhuma: cosmos

bibhatsa: odious

bol: mnemonics

chalan: gait

champak: a fragrant flower

Chandali: low-caste girl

chaste: limb movements

chegila: bell-metal gong

chenda: musical drum from Kerala

damru: small drum, attributed to Shiva

deergha darshi: far-seer

desi: regionally prevalent

devadasis: god's maids in temples; singers and dancers to the gods

doms: attendants at crematoria

drishtibhed: eye-movements

edekka: musical drum from Kerala, capable of note-playing

ekaharya abhinaya: single dancer donning multiple roles

ektara: the single-stringed drone instrument

esraj: bowed-string instrument

gamakas: staccato form of musical embellishment

garbhadeep: lamp in sanctum sanctorum

gayaki: subtle singing style

gharana: a specific style of singing, strictly following the guru

ghumur: a string of bells

ghungroos: anklets

gitkiris: deep-throated form of musical embellishment

gopis: milkmaids

gribabhed: neck movements

guru–shishya parampara: master–disciple relationship

guru–shishya talim: teacher-disciple exercise

hasa: merriment

hasya: humorous

Hemanta: the Indian season between winter and spring

jaatis: rhythm variations

jati: self-identity

jugupsa: disgust

kaash: a form of grass with long, white flowers

kajari: a form of folk music, sung during the rains

karana: composite poses in Bharatanatyam dnace

kartal: cymbals

karuna: compassion

kathakar: story-teller

keertan: collective devotional singing

khali: blank

khatkas: a form of musical embellishment

khoai: rugged banks

khol: an East Indian drum, played at both ends

komal: semi-tone

kotal: the police-chief

kritis: set compositions by South Indian musicians

krodha: fury

lasya: subtle grace

lokadharmi: dance explicit to the public

maddalam: a form of musical drum

madhya laya: medium tempo

Maghi: full moon in mid-January

mandala: circular positions

manjuri: approval

mantras: Sanskrit hymns and chantings

margam: set sequence of a classical dance-style

margi: classical forms

maya kumaris: illusive maidens

meend: glissando

mehfil: musical soiree

mohini: enchantress

mridanga: drum

mudras: hand-gestures

mukhaja: facial

murli: flute

nagara: a form of musical drum

nattuvanars: conductors

natyadharmi: stylised dance, opposed to *lokadharmi*

Nava Ratri: nine days of fasting in April–May

niyam: rule

nritta: pure body-lines

nritya: interpretative dance

padachari: feet movement

padams: lurical songs, interpreted in dance

padavali: narratives on Radha–Krishna

pakad: combinations of musical notes in *raga*

pancha bhuta: five primal elements

pancha nadai: five rhythmic sound variables

pavo: a form of dance

phank: gap

pindi bandha: female group dance

prakshepya: worn over limbs

pratibandha: closely-knit dance

pung: Manipuri drum

pusta: material objects

Ramprasadi: special *keertan* attributed to the famous Kali-worshipper Ramprasad

Ras Lila: Krishna's love-play with *gopis*

rasas: flavours, evoked in spectators of dance

rati: love

raudra: impetuous, angry

ravenhatta: a bowed-string instrument from Rajasthan

sahitya: literature

sam: completion of time cycle in music

samabhanga: equipoise like the Buddha

samayukta: both hands together with twenty-four gestures

sanchari: (music) third stanza in Dhrupad, (dance embellishments)

sanchari bhava: transitory embellishments

sandhima: joined objects made out of cloth, hide, mat

sankhya-matric: number-centric

sattras: monasteries of Assam

sattvika: aesthetic expressions of face in dance

sattvika abhinaya: facial aesthetics

shanta: peaceful

shanti: serenity

Sharad Purnima: full-moon in autumn

sharira: body

shefali: a form of fragrant, autumnal flower

shehnai: musical instrument of the clarinet family

shilambu: anklets

shoka: sorrow

shringara: erotic

shringara rasa: mood of love

sthayee: predominant stance in dance

sthayee bhava: predominant sentiment

stupa: large, circular votive structure

sutradhar: story-teller

taan: sallies

taan kartabya: vocal display of sallies

tala: rhythm cycle

tali: simple clapping

tandava: the vigorous

tappa: a form of classical music with dominant staccatos

tehai: three-fold rhythm-cycle

thumri: popular style of light classical music

tribhanga: bent in three segments like Parvati

tulsi: votive plant worshipped in households

upangas: semi-limbs

urumandi: standing posture in Bharatanatyam

uttariya: body cover

utplabana: jumping, five types

utsaha: enthusiasm

vachika: text/song interpreted in dance

Vanadevis: forest deities

varnams: elaborate item of Bharatanatyam, with *nritta* and *nritya*

Varsha: rain/monsoon

Vasant: spring

Vasant Purnima: full-moon in spring

ves: costume

vestima: objects produced by wrapping

vihara: residence of Buddhist monks in a monastery

vilambit laya: slow tempo

vira: heroic

vismaya: astonishment

vyajima: objects made out of mechanical devices

zari: filigreed textile-decoration with silvery threads

Acknowledgements

The author is indebted to many institutions which include:

- Sangeet Natak Akademi (SNA)—for an initial research grant;
- Indian Council for Cultural Relations (ICCR)—for international travel support to Brisbane, Australia;
- World Dance Alliance: Global Summit—for accommodation and major part of the hospitality in Brisbane, Australia;
- Doordarshan Archives—for mooting the idea of DVDs on 'Tagore's Dance' and initiating the process with Visva-Bharati authorities;
- Rabindra Bhavan Archives and Library, Visva-Bharati—for dialogue and major audio-visual and textual material;
- Kala Bhavan Archives and Library, Visva-Bharati—for dialogue as well as part visual material;
- Sangeet Bhavan, Visva-Bharati—for dialogue;
- Paatha Bhavan, Visva-Bharati—for dialogue and part textual material.

Individually, the author owes immense gratitude to Mrinalini Sarabhai, Amala Shankar, Vyjayantimala Bali, Yamini Krishnamoorthy, Shanti Bose, International Centre for Kathakali, Singhajit Singha, Padma Subrahmaniam, Thankamani Kutti, Darshana Jhaveri, Gayatri Chatterjee, Polly Guha, Kalavati Devi, Rita Ganguly-Kothari, Sonal Mansingh, Kanak Rele, Lubna Mariam, Aishika Chakrabarty, Alpana Roy, Mahua Mukherjee, Sharmila Biswas, Sudarshan Chakravorty, Pushpa Shankar, Bharati Shivaji, Shovana Narain, Yog Sunder Desai, Sangeeta Sharma, C.V. Chandrasekhar, Swapna Sundari, Anjana Banerjee, V.P. Dhananjayan, Sruti Bandyopadhyay, for sharing their own (and for a few, their gurus') choreographic experience on Tagore's Dance.

The author also owes heartfelt thanks to Swapan Majumder, Sushovan Adhikary, Alpana Roy, Dilip Hazra, Swati Ghosh, Guru Valmiki Banerjee, Sudhir Chanda, Ramen Dutta, Santanu Chakravarty, Guru Singhajit Singha, Sanjeev Bhattacharjee, Geeta Chandran, Guru Unnikrishnan, Deepti Omcheri Bhalla, Maitreyee Pahari and, above all, to Moushri Singha and Sampa Ghosh for personal help and unstinted support. Responsibility for all faults and shortcomings remains, however, with the author.

Index

Note: Page numbers with *p* indicate photographs.

NIYOGI BOOKS on *Rabindranath Tagore*

- Rabindranath Tagore: A Pictorial Biography
  by Nityapriya Ghosh

- Architecture of Santiniketan
  & Tagore's Concept of Space
  by Samit Das

- Tagore's Paintings: Versification in Line
  by Sovon Som

- Selected Essays, Speeches, Letters of
  Rabindranath Tagore
  Compiled, Translated and Edited by Subhrangshu Maitra

- Symbols and Songs:
  A Study of Leitmotif in Tagore Songs
  by Kishore Chatterjee

- The Four Quartets
  Translation of Chaturanga by Nirmal Kanti Bhattacharjee

- The Inverted Mirror:
  Cartoons on Rabindranath Tagore
  by Sushovon Adhikari

- King of the Dark Chamber
  Translation of Raja by Rabindranath Tagore

- Rabindranath Tagore: His World of Art
  by Supriya Roy and Sushovan Adhikari